Making a Living

Making a Living

PLACE, FOOD, AND ECONOMY
IN AN INUIT COMMUNITY

— – —

Nicole Gombay

PURICH
PUBLISHING
LIMITED
SASKATOON, SK. CANADA

Purich Publishing,
Box 23032, Market Mall Post Office, Saskatoon, SK, Canada, S7J 5H3
Phone: (306) 373-5311 Fax: (306) 373-5315 Email: purich@sasktel.net
www.purichpublishing.com

Library and Archives Canada Cataloguing in Publication

Gombay, Nicole, 1965-
    Making a living : place, food, and economy in an Inuit
community / Nicole Gombay.

Includes bibliographical references and index.
ISBN 978-1-895830-59-0

1. Inuit – Food – Québec (Province) – Puvirnituq. 2. Inuit – Food – Economic aspects – Québec (Province) – Puvirnituq. 3. Inuit – Québec (Province) – Puvirnituq – Economic conditions. 4. Inuit – Québec (Province) – Puvirnituq – Social conditions. 5. Inuit – Government policy – Canada. I. Title.

E99.E7G64 2010   305.897'10714111   C2010-906934-X

Edited, designed, and typeset by Donald Ward, who also created the maps.
Cover design by Jamie Olson.
Index by Ursula Acton.
Printed and bound in Canada at Houghton Boston Printers and Lithographers.

Purich Publishing gratefully acknowledges the assistance of the Government of Canada through the Canada Book Fund (CBF), and the Creative Industry Growth and Sustainability Program made possible through funding provided to the Saskatchewan Arts Board by the Government of Saskatchewan through the Ministry of Tourism, Parks, Culture and Sport for its publishing program.

This book has been published with the help of a grant from the Canadian Federation for the Humanities and Social Sciences, through the Aid to Scholarly Publications Program, using funds provided by the Social Sciences and Humanities Research Council of Canada.

Printed on 100 per cent post-consumer, recycled, ancient-forest-friendly paper.

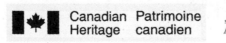

Contents

Acknowledgements

I have endeavoured to provide a fair reflection of my experiences in Puvirnituq. I am indebted to the members of the community who accepted my presence there.

Many, many people have helped me along the way. Some tolerated my questions, others read and commented on drafts of the manuscript, and still others gave me moral support when I needed it. I am grateful to all of them. I want particularly to thank Brydon, André, Lucassie, Marie, Adam, and Paulusi.

I have tried to ensure that there are no factual errors in this manuscript and hope that you will forgive any that might appear.

All photographs are by the author, except for the shots of the opening of the Co-op on pages 104 and 107, which are courtesy of Janice Callahan, and the truck parked outside the Co-op on page 132, which is courtesy of Diane Ruru.

NOTE: When the research for this book was originally undertaken, the dictates of the ethics review committee at the university I was working at were such that I was required to ensure that all the people to whom I spoke remained anonymous. For this reason, all names in this book are pseudonyms.

Regional map of Nunavik

Baffin
Island

HUDSON STRAIT

Ivujivik

Mansel
Island

Salluit

Kangiqsujuaq

Akulivik

Quaqtaq

UNGAVA PENINSULA

Killiniq

Puvirnituq

Kangirsuk

UNGAVA
BAY

Aupaluk

Inukjuaq

Tasiujaq

Kangiqsualujjuaq

HUDSON
BAY

Kuujjuaq

Belcher
Islands

NUNAVIK

Umiujaq

Kuujjuarapik

I

— – —

Placing Economies

TELLING STORIES ABOUT FOOD AND MAKING A LIVING

Introduction

FOOD IS SUCH AN IMPORTANT PART OF LIFE, yet many of us think little about it. I have just finished a bowl of soup. The main ingredients — beets and cabbage — I bought at a local market. I went on a sunny Saturday morning and was drawn to a stall of autumn vegetables. I handed over my cash, took the vegetables home, and eventually made the soup. As I ate it, I thought how, despite the fact that I had made it, I had only a vague understanding of its ingredients. Where did the seeds come from, and who had planted them? Who tended them as they sprouted and grew? What had the weather been like while they were growing? What bugs had attacked the plants and how had they been held at bay? Who harvested the cabbage and dug up the beets and cleaned them off? Had the farmer's hands grown blistered and calloused in the process of bringing the vegetables to market? Who had laboured to make sure I had something to eat? Perhaps the two women who ran the stall were the people behind all this work, but I did not know. I simply drove to the market with money I had earned from my job, and handed it over. Now here I was, eating soup.

That I should be so far removed from the food I was eating is not unusual in my society; I am inclined to think it is not unusual in many societies. For most of us, invisible hands aided by unseen forces are behind the things we consume. Two things, among others, enable us to consume with such ignorance: markets and money. I go to the market, I hand over my money, and I get the food I want. All the other invisible processes that brought my soup to the table fell into place without my having to know much about them. But in going to that market and in handing over my money, I am at once participating in and ignoring a whole set of histories, a whole set of social relations, a whole set of ways of thinking about, and behaving in, the world. Part of what I wish to do in this book is step back and make visible some of these invisible processes, for behind something as simple yet vitally important as food lie a host of issues related to how we order and make our way in the world. I propose to consider the meaning of food, and what is entailed when we remove ourselves from its production by means of the market economy.

I propose to do so in a particular context: among the Inuit of the eastern Canadian Arctic. The provision of food is fundamental to how their economy is constructed. It has determined their survival. They do not take it for granted, for it is critical to how they conceive of and construct their place in the world.

The Inuit economy, until relatively recently, has operated according to altogether other means than the market economy that enabled me to eat my soup. In most instances, Inuit are well aware of the means by which their food was produced. Because of people's participation not only in the eating of food, but also in the getting and distributing of it, they are generally aware both of its importance to them and of their wish to preserve their capacities to continue participating in these processes. For many Inuit, these processes are tied to their way of life. The production, distribution, exchange, and consumption of food is inexorably linked to how they conceive of and construct the world around them. These conceptions reflect not simply the mechanical processes involved in procuring food, but are linked to larger cosmological notions about the nature of existence and the place of humans in the world. These, in turn, are linked to a host of other processes: ideas about the role of the individual in relation to society, the experience of being in the elements rather than removed from them, notions of temporality, and understandings of history grounded in place. An important component of these elements is that they developed and operated outside the market economy. Since time immemorial, without markets and without money, Inuit have managed to make a living and supply themselves with the necessities of life.

Try to imagine how you would have to live were you to be involved in producing everything you ate. Try to imagine how that would affect how you interacted with the world around you and how you spent your time.

How would you relate to others and to the environment that provided you with food? How would you make your living? What would your day be filled with from morning to night, from season to season, from year to year? Then think about what happens when the market economy comes into the equation. How would all these things be affected when you no longer had to produce everything you ate but could buy your food? Where would you get the money? How would you spend your time? How would this change in your circumstances affect your concerns about the world around you? These questions are inherently economic, and are intimately tied to the quality of our lives. They are the questions I explore in this book. They are the questions Inuit society is confronting, at a fundamental level.

For Inuit, the economy operates in two fundamental realms, neither of which is isolated from the other, but each of which is informed by markedly different means of operating. First, there is the local economic system that sprang from, and is a reflection of, Inuit beliefs and ways of working. Such an economy has been called variously an "indigenous" economy,[1] a "community" economy,[2] or an "informal" economy.[3] All are, to varying degrees, used to describe economies that are related to systems that are particular to a place and its people. Such economies have often fallen under the umbrella of the term "subsistence," which is commonly used in relation to Inuit. The term, linked to the idea that people are eking out a bare existence, carries negative connotations that do not reflect reality.[4] The notion also has the effect of freezing Inuit in time, preventing them from commercial development.[5] For these reasons, I have chosen to use the term "vernacular" economy[6] to identify the economy associated with the ideas, processes, social relations, values, and institutions that Inuit link to the produce of hunting, fishing, and gathering. The term allows room for the idea that people are constantly changing, while at the same time implying that such change has a local flavour. It is appropriate in this context because it is devoid of many of the value judgements associated with the term "subsistence," and suggests important links between economy and place.

The second economic realm in which Inuit now function is the market system that came with the arrival of non-Inuit to their region. It is an economy in which transactions rely on money as a medium of exchange. Under a market economy, prices are self-regulating, which means that markets must be allowed to function without interference. In the process, nature becomes interwoven with processes of commoditization as its products become fodder for the market. Each market exchange is discrete; there is no expectation that it will entail an ongoing social relationship. As a result, social relations become embedded in the economy rather than the economy being embedded in social relations.[7]

These two economies, the market and the vernacular, have been operating in tandem — sometimes in apparent isolation, but in fact increasingly overlapping and mixing together, with the distinction between them becoming blurred. Inuit are not living in isolation from the market, but must come to terms with the fact that their economy exists within the market. The term that is commonly used to denote this is a "mixed economy," wherein neither of the two economic systems exists in a pristine state, but each must be understood as connected to the other. At issue for Inuit is what this means for them and how they are making sense of the mixing. What I argue is that, in comprehending this process, we need to recognize that the Inuit economy is intimately linked to people's understandings of place, which, in turn, relates to such things as their experiences of time and history, their understandings of natural forces, their basic notions of value, and their conceptions of community and the social institutions that sustain it.

My interest in this topic is the result of conversations with a friend involved in the northern business world. As an Inuk,[8] he was drawn to this world because he saw it as a way of ensuring that Inuit take some control over their destinies. If money makes the world go around, he at least wanted to make sure that Inuit might be able to influence its direction. Over the years I have seen how Inuit *are* participating in, and dependent upon, a monetary economy, and I have seen how this has provoked some confusion. As money has moved into the region, people have had to learn what kinds of trade-offs are involved in getting it.

On the one hand, Inuit have expressed a desire to hold on to their traditions of hunting, fishing, and trapping. This has been at the root of all Inuit land claims negotiated in Canada.[9] On the other hand, they are aware that their economies cannot rely solely on the traditions of the past. Like the non-Inuit who have moved in and occupied their lands, Inuit live in houses that have central heating. They watch television, and use skidoos, motorboats, and rifles to hunt. None of these things springs from the local environment, but rely on an inflow of goods and cash that can be got only through participation in the market economy. They know they need money even to pursue the traditional elements of their economy. Bullets, rifles, gas, skidoos, and canvas for tents, among other things, all cost money, and as far as money is concerned, one thing is clear: for many Inuit it is in short supply.

By southern standards, northern economies are based on a limited set of activities, so the options for gaining access to cash are few. Since the period of contact with Europeans, Inuit have earned cash through such occupations as the fur trade, whaling, the sale of arts and crafts, social transfer payments, and employment in an assortment of public and private ventures. These forms of income have generally either proved unsustainable or of limited impact, and are open only to a few. Moreover, such cash as does come into northern settlements does not stay there for long; rather, it circulates briefly, benefiting few, with a small percentage staying in the North before it heads for richer economic centres in southern Canada and elsewhere.[10] So while money, which is now necessary to maintain Inuit ways of living in the Canadian Arctic, does come into northern communities, very little of it actually contributes to a sustainable economy based on northern resources and expertise.

One potential way to expand the sources of cash income available to Inuit has been to sell the produce from people's hunting, fishing, and gathering commonly referred to as "country foods." This has led to a meeting of the two economic systems, the market and the vernacular. In the past, these economies generally operated separately, and under quite different rules. The vernacular economy of Inuit is predicated on sharing, and relies on a whole set of institutions and moral principles that are particular to Inuit. Through the process of commoditization, the local economy has become incorporated into a market economy that is predicated on monetary exchange. The principles that inform each system can be at odds. Marx argues that, when markets gain control of vernacular economies, land and labour become commodities; people sell their labour and products from the land in exchange for money. Yet, as Karl Polanyi argues, "Labour is only another name for human activity that goes with life itself, which is not produced for sale, but for entirely different reasons, nor can that activity be detached from the rest of life, be stored or mobilised: land is only another name for nature."[11] Thus, in selling their labour and the produce of the land, people must separate themselves as workers from the larger context of their lives as human beings with social and emotional connections and needs, and must start to see the produce of their land as independent from the larger natural context of which it is a part. This means that, in order to participate in the logic of the market economy, we must develop blinkers. Tensions between local and "global"[12] economic systems point to a key question about how the capitalist logic of accumulation (i.e., the pursuit of surplus capital amassed through excess production) has transformed local economic logics. How does a local economic system adjust itself to a global economic system when each is predicated on different concepts of value, different ideas of the role of the individual in relation to society, and different concepts of access to and control over resources? In selling country foods, Inuit are obliged to confront these questions and learn how to accommodate the influx of new ideas and ways of living to pre-existing concepts about how the world operates. They are not alone: in their encounters with the forces of globalization, vernacular economies the world over have had to make similar adjustments.

The commoditization of country foods provides an ideal forum in which to look at how local and global economic systems are meeting. At first glance, the commoditization of country foods would seem a suitable way of making sure that Inuit are able to earn much-needed money while promoting some of the very activities for which they need that money; it appears to provide an appropriate meeting between local and global economies. The sale of country foods would not only seem to strengthen the local economic system, but it also looks like a reasonable way of ensuring that economic development takes advantage of the conditions specific to place. Such development might overcome many of the problems of money coming into and circulating within communities, thereby promoting more sustainable economies that will, in the long run, be less prone to outside influence.

Theoretically, then, it appears that the selling of country foods has much to be said for it. The idea was picked up in the 1990s by the Makivik Corporation,[13] which embarked on an economic development scheme to commercialize caribou in Nunavik.[14] A settlement in which I happened to be working at the time was debating whether its members wanted to participate in the project. Some were concerned about the implications of selling caribou meat. I was not part of the discussions and was not privy to the nature of these concerns, but some time later I read that the project had, in fact, ceased operations within the community.[15]

The more I learned about the selling of country foods, the less clear the issue became, and the more contradictions started to appear. Obviously, some people had reservations. Among other things, they were concerned that the selling of country foods would affect the tradition of sharing that has been central to the vernacular economy of Inuit. It appeared, above all, that it was the selling of country foods — as opposed to other goods — that disturbed people, so it was with interest that I read one day the following letter from an Inuk to the editor of a northern newspaper:

Country food shouldn't be sold

I have been noticing some things changing in Inuit culture over these last couple of years.

I keep hearing on the radio that there is country food for sale. It doesn't happen much here in my home community — there is the occasional sale of fish to the co-op, but I rarely see the sale of a seal from one person to another person.

People in my home community still share their country food, and it is part of Inuit culture. I think the sale of country food should not be allowed and should be stopped.

Sharing is part of Inuit culture, and it should remain that way.

Pilitsi Kingwatsiaq
Cape Dorset[16]

If country foods are a fundamental component of the Inuit vernacular economy, and sharing is the mechanism that has regulated how it functions, we need to develop an understanding that these processes are inextricably linked to how Inuit perceive and operate in the world around them, and, moreover, that how Inuit are reacting to the commoditization of those foods reflects generations of experience. We cannot gain a well-informed appreciation for the meaning of food in Inuit society if we do not also have some understanding of how it relates to the place whence it comes, to the ways people understand that place, and to the ways those understandings influence socio-economic processes. Food, place, economy, and society are all bound together.

This book uses the commoditization of country food as a means of exploring how Inuit are experiencing a number of interlinking issues. Some Inuit, interested in developing a means of injecting money into the northern economy, have been commoditizing country foods in various ways, but this practice has been a point of contention for others in the Eastern Arctic.

As a starting point for understanding the issues, we need to focus at the level of the community, for it is within communities that the contradictions involved in this question are most evident; it is within communities that people truly confront them. Joe needs money and sees the selling of country foods as a way of getting it, yet Peter, his neighbour, sees this as an objectionable act that goes against the moral imperative to share food. Thus, any understanding of people's perceptions of the processes of commoditization must be gained from within their communities. So we need to move to one such settlement to start to understand this.

Welcome to Puvirnituq

Flying into Puvirnituq after several stops up the Hudson Bay coast — first Kuujjuaraapik, followed by Umiujaq, and then Inukjuaq — the settlement looks much like its predecessors. There are the fuel tanks for the electrical generators and the various vehicles that maintain life in the North. There is the old Hudson's Bay Company post with its ubiquitous white walls and red roof, kept perhaps as a talisman for colonial history in the North. There are the school and the hospital, and the roads leading to the garbage dump, the pump house, and the sewage lagoon. There is the Co-op and the Northern Store, the Anglican church and the government offices. There are the houses, each looking like the others, varying according to colour and the year they were built. There are the dogs, and, depending on the season, the skidoos or four-wheelers.

Standing in town, you hear the buzz of skidoos along the main drag, their drivers stopping in front of the Co-op for a quick shop and a chat. There are people strolling by, on their way to visit friends or relatives. People look at you and smile and say, "Hello." Going into someone's house you might hear a television, or the radio playing in another room.

Perhaps there will be children fiddling with this or that, and waiting on the stove is a kettle filled with endless cups of tea. Here is where people live. Here is where they spend the vast majority of their time — inside these houses and within the confines of the settlement.

When you are standing in town, with the schools to your back, the courthouse and Co-op to one side, and the government offices in front, you might be forgiven for thinking that what you see is what you get: this is all there is to life in the North.

But beyond the buildings, stretching as far as the eye can see, are the water and the land, and a world in which Inuit have exclusively lived until very recently. And when you are out there, Puvirnituq is no more than a speck on the horizon, insignificant in the vastness of it all.

The settlement is no more than a thin veneer on a place that is full of history and memory and experience. In people's minds, and in their understandings, out there the land is as inhabited as the settlement. Spread out along the coast, in the bays, on the islands, at the tops of hills or nestled beside lakes and rivers are campsites, caches, travel ways, a birthplace or a death place, areas where one will find geese and caribou, fish and berries — all the things that have enabled Inuit to make this place their home for generations. Out there is a world and way of life that rotated around the seasons and the animals. Survival depended on knowing these things and knowing how to use them appropriately. As Jamisie told me:

> Traditionally, we were wanderers of the land. We never lived in one place. One place couldn't sustain the people. If you stayed in one spot, then you would decimate the wildlife population, and also the vegetation. So naturally, we moved to one spot seasonally, like in Puvirnituq, for instance, the Puvirnituq river system. For caribou, they used to go inland. And then that was at the time when the skin and the fur was at its best. The hair is not too long and the skin is at its prime. That's in August, September. Then in July, they were out in the bay where the char were plentiful. And then, as the fish were moving closer to the river, they would move with the fish, to be near. And also in springtime, when it's time to get skins for the *qajait* and the boats, naturally, they would go out to the sea ice and harvest the sealskin they needed, and the fat would be stored for *misiraq*, for the summer, and even to next winter. So that's how we used to live.

I ARRIVED IN PUVIRNITUQ at the beginning of October 2001. The world was still reeling from the events of September 11 when people watched as hijacked planes flew out of the sky into the economic and military heart of the United States. This was a globalizing world, and I was part of it. I arrived in Puvirnituq fresh off a plane from Montreal, fresh off a plane from Amsterdam, fresh off a plane from Stockholm, fresh off a plane from Moscow. I arrived in Puvirnituq under autumn skies, ready to plunge into my research with the buzz of travel in my head. I arrived in Puvirnituq to study how the foods that people got from the water and the sky and the land fit into the lives of the people of the community. More importantly, I wanted to understand how these foods fit into the systems of meaning that people participated in and carried around in their heads.

I arrived in a town on the shores of Hudson Bay, with a suitcase full of Mediterranean almonds, Ontario honey, and Swedish cup-a-soups. I arrived in the house that was to be my home for the next few months, a house with white walls, and windows overlooking the water and the treeless horizon. I arrived and met the woman who was to be my host.

I unpacked my bags and we sat sipping tea, trying to get a sense of one another. Though it was the end of the season and the leaves of the plants hugging the ground had turned brown, she asked whether I liked berry picking. The last of the season could still be found. She had been out recently, and we were eating the fruit of her labour. "Oh yes," I assured her, I liked berry picking. "Oh yes," I said, full of the hum of planes and cities and movement. "Oh yes," I said, while inside I wondered when I had last done this, when I had last been out in the elements to look for food, when I had last dressed warmly with the sky overhead and the wind at my back searching for something to eat.

Soon after coming to Puvirnituq, and faced with the intricacies of modern life in the North, I wondered how looking at the selling of country food might in any way do justice to that complexity, let alone be of service to the community that had agreed to have me in its midst. I said as much one day to the community council. One councillor, someone I had met before and who later invited me to spend time with him and his family, said that they *wanted* me to do this work. It might help to explain something of who Inuit are to the government people who made decisions affecting them, but who often seemed to lack an understanding of the larger context in which such decisions were applied. Essentially, he wanted me to produce a reflection of Inuit life, one in which the multiple realities of what it meant to live as Inuit might become more evident to outsiders.[17] Repeatedly, he would point out the ways in which non-Inuit had imposed systems of operating — wildlife regulations, training standards, ideas of right and wrong — that were reflections of their own systems of belief, but did not always sit well with the people to whom they were applied.

On a flat, grey day in November, we went out fishing and trapping with his sons. The sky and the land were cloaked in haze, so that it was difficult to see where one ended and the other began. They had checked the fox traps — nothing so far — and set new ones, spreading the jaws open and placing them carefully in a bed of moss and snow, peeing and laying other enticing smells and titbits in the centre and around the traps to draw the animals in. My friend remarked that his wife hoped to use what furs they might get this season for the hoods of the parkas she intended to make.

It was a good day. I enjoyed being outside. My spirits expanded with the horizon, and I had been warmed by the freshly brewed tea and boiled Arctic char that we had consumed huddled behind the *qamutik* to keep out of the wind. Thinking about the joys of this life, I turned to my friend and said that he should keep what he had a secret, otherwise many people would come and over-run this place. Thinking of other things, no doubt, he responded that, on the contrary, he wanted me to let outsiders know what was there — to

The Anglican church in Puvirnituq

help them understand something of what the lives of Inuit entailed and of the logic that governed their lives — so that non-Inuit would stay away and not interfere.

This, then, is an important goal of this book. Although its focus is the impacts of processes of commoditization on Inuit, this needs to be contextualized within the larger perspective of what it means to be an Inuk living in Nunavik. If one considers the economy in terms of the institutions that sustain it, then one must necessarily talk about the role of sedentarization, education, social relations, and systems of knowledge, for they all shape how people experience and participate in economic processes.

Many of the people I have met in the North have strained against the ignorance of outsiders whose influence they increasingly feel. It has sometimes caused Inuit to be reluctant to talk to me; at other times, it has been the very reason for their willingness to talk to me. Aware of this contradiction, I have tried to reflect something of the larger realities of Inuit ways of perceiving the world.

Narrative

Trying to understand people's understandings of a given set of circumstances, no matter what their culture, is not a straightforward exercise. People are not automata, they are not static, they are not uniform, and they all have their own stories. As individuals, we attach different meanings to the experiences we have, based on our abilities, backgrounds, and circumstances. We can be fickle. The significance we give different phenomena can change from one moment to the next, or from one setting to the next. This presents a challenge to anyone who is trying to understand human experience in all its complexity, but by developing a sense of what various people may experience in a given set of circumstances, we may come to understand the meanings they give to their experiences.

Although lists of country foods consumed by Inuit, their mass and monetary value, may provide some understanding of what is involved in the commoditization of country foods, this is only a beginning, a partial understanding. There are missing layers to this story. What about history? What about the senses involved in getting and eating that food — the feel of the air as you hunt for animals, the squirming of the fish in your hands, the smell of seal meat cooking in a tent as the rain falls, the reassuring sound of a distant engine coming back in the night across stormy waters? What about the memories people carry around with them related to food — the bay where you took part in a beluga hunt as a child, the island up the coast where you waited out a squall and drank tea while people played cards and told stories of past exploits? These experiences are cumulative, and, whether consciously or not, are intimately linked to the meanings people give to their food. Human actions are determined first by the meanings we give to our experiences.[18] I am not in search of numbers here. It is the quality of one's experience that counts, and by looking more deeply at it we are able to fill out the picture, to add some other dimensions that might not be apparent in a list of numbers.

Life is complex. Try as we might, we do not live with clear-cut narratives and conclusions. Life is open-ended and meandering. Lived experience is not as ordered as researchers might like to believe, and there is no single, unchanging, legitimate way people experience the world that will fit inside a tidy theoretical package. There are as many ways of experiencing the world as there are people to experience, and, as we know from our own lives, this experience can change. The whole story can never be told. What is revealed is only partial, a snippet of an ever-changing reality. People say one thing and do another. They say one thing for "outside" consumption, knowing that there are hidden complexities. In telling their stories — "we always share food" — they are also fashioning themselves in their world as they would wish it to be.

People in Puvirnituq would tell me things they wanted me to hear (as do we all, much of the time), and in talking to me they might have chosen to reinforce certain ideological notions of what it means to be Inuit in a non-Inuit country. This is part and parcel of what is involved in trying to communicate across differences, and in talking to me they were, indeed, trying to explain who Inuit are. This "messy text"[19] tries to reflect the multi-faceted, multi-vocal, and perhaps contradictory understandings that people have, and, like narrative in Inuit society, at times these voices are designed to communicate messages without necessarily telling the reader what they are.[20] We are all involved in constructing meaning.

For this reason, various voices are embedded in this text. Each of these voices reflects a particular time and place, a particular message given and received, a particular creation of identity and ethnicity that communicates what people want others to consume and how they wish to be perceived, a particular construction of a world that is not static. In talking, in writing, and in reading, we are constantly defining and redefining our experiences. We are constantly sending out and receiving messages. Such messages are often simplistic and contradictory, but they are the stuff of life; they are the narratives that help to place us in our worlds and construct our realities.

Grounded in phenomenology, my aim here is to communicate something of the everyday, lived world of human experience. Such experience is not just intellectual, but sensorial and emotional. The traditional academic language of the dispassionate observer contradicts this notion of communication. So I move from the disembodied voice of an observer to that of an emotionally involved and sensorially experiencing participant, in order that the reader may start to sense this place on the ground. The experience of life — its full import — comes out in the details. The sights and sounds and smells of a place, the rhythms of life, the comings and goings of people and things, the chance remarks, the sideways glances, the momentous and the inane, have an often unrecognized impact on how we think about and live our lives. They add colour to life, and are important components of the places we inhabit.

Place

People's ways of being in the world rest partially on the notion of place and our experience of it. While the literature on place is vast,[21] the main issue here is how one might think about place phenomenologically. How might we conceptualize place, in the abstract, in order to analyze how it is experienced? As discussed in chapter two, such experience is in many ways central to how Inuit perceive and give meaning to country foods. By extension, it is also built into the development of the economy that arose among Inuit as it relates to those foods. Food and economy cannot be understood without first understanding the character of the place whence they come and the experience of being in that place. Thus, chapter two provides an in-depth analysis of the myriad means by which Inuit construct and experience place in relation to food. But what exactly is meant by "place"?

In simplistic terms, one might say that place is space with feeling. Space is the context for place, but we all live in place. It is through human perception and experience that we transform abstract space into concrete place, and *vice versa*. Experience of place can be understood as the product of an interaction among three realms: nature, meaning, and social relations.[22] The physical structure of a place, the social systems that exist there, and the meanings we give to these things all determine how we experience place.

These realms do not operate in isolation; rather, each is linked to and influences the other at particular times and in particular settings, and each sphere develops through time. Place is not static, but in constant flux.

The experience of place has an impact on many things. It can affect our individual and collective identities. It can shape and be shaped by our emotions and memories. A church is not a forest, which is not a subway station, which is not a mountaintop, a classroom, or the tundra. The feelings we have in each of these places, the associations we have with them, the kinds of societal structures that develop in each, are very much linked to those places. Place is a fundamentally important context for human experiences and activities.

In part, people come to understand themselves and the world through what they do in a place. If we think about country foods in the context of place, for example, we must think about how country foods are connected to people's understandings of natural systems and social systems, and to the meanings with which they are imbued by people in the interactions of these systems. Thus, in the getting, sharing, and eating of country foods, many Inuit are constantly constructing and reconstructing perceptions of, and experiences in, place. Through country foods, nature, social relations, and meaning are all bound together. Thus, in hunting, fishing, and trapping, in moving over the land, sea, and ice, Inuit forge and reforge their collective and personal histories. Food — the getting and consuming of it — can serve as a means of forming and reforming identity, constituting and sustaining community, accentuating socio-cultural and political boundaries, and defining and confirming one's knowledge of the environment.

At the same time, although experience of place is linked to country foods, place, by extension, is also deeply bound up in the economic system that has developed in relation to those foods. In this book, I have tried to comprehend how experience of place is tied to economic systems and how economic systems can form experience of place. When one thinks of economics, what come to mind most often are such things as banks, equations, or fiscal policy, all of which seem far removed from place and country foods. But there are other ways of understanding economic systems.

OCTOBER 12, 2001: I went for a walk tonight . . . to the point and saw the garbage burning in the darkness — an eerie and comforting sight. On the way there I passed lots of people on four-wheelers who had been to the dump to garbage pick. The sealift [supply boat] just came in, so there's lots to be had. One man passed me with a chair in front and sheets of plywood behind — along with a kid.

As I walked I thought about how meaningless my work was — how I was imposing something — searching for an order, but what about the context? Why focus on hunting and money when there are so many other things that are going on in people's lives? How does this matter in a context where there's so much more hidden behind the smiles and the politeness? And here I am searching for something that seems to ignore these larger issues. . . .

As I walked back to town I heard dogs barking in the darkness. Someone was coming to feed his dog team. And I heard a motorboat heading back to town. Then, true to what I'd been told, the northern lights guided me in an arc, back to where I wanted to go. And I followed them. No one in town was tempting fate, whistling to call down the lights to come and knock off their heads. I waved at a guy who was standing outside his door smoking and watching me go by. And he waved at me. And then I walked in the door to the noise of the TV and slowly my wonder dissipated.

Issues of Economics

When I asked someone in Puvirnituq how Inuit translate the word "economy" into Inuktitut, she was hesitant. After consulting others and looking it up in a book provided by the local school board, she concluded that the term used to communicate the idea was *kiinaujatigut makittarasuarniq*, which translates as, "by money try to stand by itself." This event, as much as the definition itself, is revealing. First, my informant's confusion was typical of many people's experience of things economic. The way non-Inuit economic systems function can be obscure. At best, many of the basic assumptions and workings of economics can be worked around; at worst, they are a complete mystery. This is the case for many people, Inuit and non-Inuit alike. What puts Inuit at a disadvantage, however, is that some of the building blocks of Western economic systems can be nonsensical. It is not just that their rationales seem ludicrous, but the very concepts simply make no sense from an Inuit perspective.[23] Generally, Inuit cannot conceive of how one can own land.

The second way this Inuktitut definition is revealing is that it assumes that economics has, at its root, to do with money. This is certainly the case in Western systems, where money is synonymous with all things economic, particularly in the context of economics as practised by banks and governments. But this is neither fundamentally nor necessarily the case. Economic systems associated with money overlie more essential processes that determine the form and functioning of economic structures. These processes are based on social and cultural systems and on the institutions that people develop that reflect and promote those systems.[24]

If we set aside the assumption that economics is based on money, and start with its essential building blocks, any number of other definitions emerge. At its most basic, economics consists of "the social relations people establish to control the production, consumption, and circulation of food, clothing, and shelter."[25] These are the bare essentials of survival, and each is tied to, and affected by, the other. Such an understanding of economic systems relies on Polanyi's idea that they should be understood in terms of social relations and the institutions people develop that reflect and promote the values held by a given society.[26] It is important, then, to consider the nature of these values.

Economic systems create and sustain certain values. These are associated with larger moral and existential concerns which, in turn, determine appropriate forms of behaviour. If we want to understand economic systems, then, we must learn something not only about how people get things, but why we want them.[27] Such reasons can exist at many levels, great and small, both conscious and unconscious. They can be based on individual or group interest, on moral imperatives, on ideas of personhood, or on explanations about the nature of existence. The construction and maintenance of social relations, the designation of value, the formation of identity, and the assignment of morality occur not only in the context of production and consumption, but also in distribution and circulation.[28] This means that, in trying to understand economic systems, each of these steps in the process should be considered, for if one limits analysis to only part of the equation, some of the nuances might be overlooked.

So, to understand the vernacular economy associated with country foods, one must consider them not only as part of an economic system that provides the necessities of life, but also as a set of values that affect ways of understanding and operating in the world that extend beyond humans to include larger physical and metaphysical issues.

For many Inuit, the economy associated with country foods is linked ideally to their minds, bodies, and spirits. It rests on the need for respect for, and living in balance with, all elements of creation. In looking at their economy, one must consider not simply the harvesting, distribution, exchange, and consumption of country foods, nor the social practices associated with these procedures, but a whole range of processes, values, and understandings that are essentially cosmological. Such cosmological considerations are manifest in our economic behaviours. Whether we see God in every blade of grass, believe we will be reincarnated, or consider ourselves to be living in a godless universe, these essentially cosmological beliefs affect the way we conceive of and use resources. Let us return to the ground for a moment and consider how this discussion of economics and the previous discussion about place fit together.

The Place of Economy and the Economy of Place

Nature, people and their social relations, and the various culturally determined meanings we ascribe to them, are bound together through place. One facet of the social institutions that people have created is economic. Here, too, place plays a role in determining the shape of the institution.

The links between economics and place are dialectical. On the one hand, the particularities of place produce distinct economic systems; on the other, particular economic systems produce distinct experiences of place. Systems of production, circulation, consumption, and reproduction are based in, reflect, and construct the values inherent in place. Such an economic system is both created by, and creates, specific social relations; it is embedded in, and embeds, particular systems of meaning; it is reflected in, and reflects, particular links to the natural world. Thus, an economics of place is not only about the natural systems in which it functions, but also about the particular cultural, social, historical, and political systems in which it is embedded.

How people perceive their place, what meaning it holds for them, has formed the often unrecognized foundation of the economy in the North. The natural systems, the social relations that have developed, and the meanings that people have given to these things are all intimately linked to the economic system that underlies the production, distribution, exchange, and consumption of country foods. The economic system associated with hunting and gathering is formed in, and forms, experience of place. So this book is not only about the economy of place, but about the place of economy.

Having set the foundation for analysis, let us consider how these issues appear in an Inuit context. Chapter two expands on the notion of place to delve into its more metaphysical qualities. In it I discuss the recursive links between place and food — exploring something of the place *of* country foods and place *in* country foods. The chapter provides a framework for understanding the meanings that these foods have for many Inuit and the ways in which place is both experienced and constructed by Inuit in the process of getting, distributing, and consuming country foods. It is only once we are equipped with such an understanding that we start to comprehend the significance of what might be entailed when these foods become commoditized.

In chapter three I examine, in a general way, many of the regulatory and political approaches taken by non-Inuit to economic development in the Canadian Arctic. These serve as a backdrop for discussing larger issues of the political economy of Nunavik. This will enable the reader to appreciate some of the economic circumstances in which the idea of commoditizing country foods have come into being.

In chapter four we move from the general to the specific as the reader is introduced to more particulars about Puvirnituq, the settlement in which this book is grounded. I explore the various means by which country foods are commoditized in Puvirnituq and consider some of the reasons why it is done as it is.

Finally, in chapter five I look at how all these matters have come together in the reactions of people to the commoditization of country foods.

As each chapter builds on its predecessor, what will became apparent is that how Inuit live reflects, and is a reflection of, their experiences, and so is a construction, sometimes conscious and sometimes unconscious. We are all constantly in the process of building our lives, of negotiating with forces that lie within and beyond our control. We are literally making our livings. For people like the Inuit, whose lives have been drastically changed by Euro-Canadian systems and processes, sometimes quite small matters can be touchstones for much larger issues. By looking at country foods, by thinking about what they mean to people and what is involved in their commoditization, I came to understand that these foods reflected something of the constancy and inconstancy of life for Inuit, and were linked to the vast changes that all people, but particularly those who have been colonized from outside, have had to confront and adjust to in order to survive.

2

_— – –_

The Place of Country Foods /
Country Foods in Place

DURING THE AUTUMN AND EARLY WINTER OF 2001, war, violence, and destruction set the backdrop for my time in Puvirnituq. One Sunday early in October I came in from a walk to visit a friend and his wife. We sat together on their sofa and watched on their big-screen TV as George W. Bush announced that he was planning to attack Afghanistan. Some days later, there was talk on the radio of possible terrorist attacks on nuclear power plants.

I looked around me at our houses with their electric lights and oil-fired furnaces. I looked at the daily flights from Montreal delivering lettuce and frozen pizza to the shelves of the Co-op. I watched the four-wheelers that zoomed around town or carried people further afield to hunt, fish, or pick berries. I felt the cold setting in on the land, and I thought, _This life we are living all comes from somewhere else. What happens if everything falls apart, and our lifelines to the South are shattered?_

The more I thought about it, the more I realized that, if the southern world were crumbling, I was in one of the best places I could possibly be. There were people here who knew how to run dog teams, how to build igloos, how to find and kill animals, how to use animal fat to heat their homes, how to make clothes from animal skins, how to store food for times of need. Then I thought, _But what can I contribute to all this? I'll just be dead weight._

I said as much a few days later when visiting my friend Jamisie and his family. He laughed and replied, "Don't worry, we'd look after you. We wouldn't let you die."

ONE OF THE MOST STRIKING THINGS about living in the North is that there is no way of separating the food I eat from an awareness of the place it comes from. Whether it is knowing that I saw the fish I am eating being pulled from the net, or the fact that the peaches on my plate are thousands of kilometres from any tree that could have borne them, I cannot help but be conscious of the juxtapositions of food, in and out of place.

For most of us, food simply appears on the shelves of the local market. It is predictably there, and usually tastes as expected — which is to say, it has met standards and regulations. Whatever the season, we can expect to find it. It is food out of time and out of place. A rare few have a more profound understanding of where their food comes from and what has been involved in its production. This is certainly the case for most Inuit, for whom the getting of food entails understandings about themselves and their position in the world that are quite different from most Canadians'. As people hunt, fish, or gather food, the material and immaterial worlds blend in complex ways, with layer upon layer of meaning and understanding. The getting of country foods is about understanding the land in which one lives. It is about building up an awareness and knowledge of one's place in the natural world. It is about making sense of oneself in time and place. It is, as people have told me, about *real* life. Ultimately, the getting of country foods is built on and helps maintain a set of moral principles about the world and how to live in it. In getting country foods, people contribute to the construction of place and reflect constructions of place.

According to Finn Lynge, four values are essential to the Inuit way of life:

nunamut ataqqinninneq: a sense of pride in knowing the land; "feeling it in our bones, knowing its whales and caribou, its endless plains and mountains, its light and dark . . . its hardness and its beauty — pride and respect for the land!" (n.p.);

akisussaassuseq: a sense of responsibility to the land and to everything that lives there; so people harvest only what they need and act as caretakers of the resources that surround them;

tukkussuseq: generosity and hospitality that stress the importance of ties to extended family;

inuk nammineq: personal independence and individual strength, which leads to a distrust of distant rulers, and encourages the development of the ability to judge for oneself and to act accordingly.[1]

All these values apply in both the getting and eating of country foods. In Marxist economic terms, one might speak of producing, distributing, and consuming country foods, and of reproducing these processes. Such terms, however, do not get at the deeper levels of understanding about the nature of being, the nature of understanding, the larger whole in which life is lived. It is only with an understanding of that larger whole that one may begin to grasp what the selling of country foods might represent to people.

Niqituinnaq

Generally, the term used in Inuktitut for country foods is *niqituinnaq*, which literally means "regular food."[2] The importance of this food is reflected in the fact that, although many people eat store-bought food, when it comes to having cravings for food or when people feel they need something truly nutritious or satisfying, they turn to country foods. People who are in the South for any period of time — attending school, for example, or for work, or in hospital — often travel with country foods, or have them sent to them by friends and relatives. Country foods are also commonly distributed by family and friends among the different settlements in Nunavik, either simply because they were thinking of them or as the result of a request for food. Often, on stop-overs, travellers will be greeted at the airport by people who either hand over or receive country food before continuing on their way.

People even mark a spatial distinction between country foods and southern foods. A friend once pointed out to me, "You guys say, 'Well, it puts food on the table,' but that's wrong. It's 'Well, it puts food on the floor.'" This seemingly insignificant distinction reveals something of the different universes inhabited by Inuit and Euro-Canadians, a difference that Inuit physically mark in the eating of the two foods. When they eat country foods, Inuit generally sit on the ground around the food, cutting it up, the men with their knives and the women with their half-moon shaped *ulus*. If the meal consists solely of *Qallunaat*,[3] or non-Inuit, food, or has another course that is essentially perceived to be food from the South, people will get up off the floor to eat it at a table.

The country foods that people eat reflect the places they are from, and so vary from community to community — depending on what is available in the region — from season to season, and from individual to individual. In Puvirnituq, people rely heavily on caribou, Canada geese, and fish, particularly Arctic char and whitefish. Someone told me that Nunavik women are plumper than those in Nunavut because they eat so much fatty Arctic char. Reliance on these foods is similar for Nunavik as a whole, although it has changed over time.[4] The consumption of caribou meat has increased in Nunavik as a result of a general increase in the caribou population. In other areas, where sea mammals are more abundant, they represent a large portion of the diet. What people eat, then, is subject to the conditions particular to their places (see Appendix 1).

Unlike many in southern Canada who have avoided seasonal limitations either by moving food production indoors or importing food from the four corners of the earth, Inuit eat particular species at particular times. When the geese arrive in the spring until their departure in the autumn, they are an important component of people's diet. The seasonal ripening of berries, the reproductive and developmental cycles of animals, the movement of animals based on the seasons, all determine what people eat and when.

Seasons, Weather, Time, and Country Foods

Weather and season affect the quality and behaviour of animals, and so dictate both the quantity and the accessibility of food. In Puvirnituq, people are able to fish primarily in the summer when the Arctic char are moving out of the inland lakes into the waters of Hudson Bay. Imalie, a woman in her 40s, commented that in the winter of 2000, caribou were hard to find, and since Arctic char cannot be found close to town during the winter, people relied mainly on seals. Animals are hunted at particular times of their reproductive cycles, or are easier to catch in particular seasons. Seals, for example, are more easily hunted when they are layered in fat and do not sink when they are shot. Canada geese are easiest to get when they are unable to fly during their summer moult. Animal furs, too, are thicker and healthier depending on the season.

People constantly monitor animal movements. This was why, in the past, Inuit moved from area to area. Today, people continue to study the movement of animals and react accordingly. In the spring and summer, when the anadromous fish such as Arctic char move out of freshwater lakes into the salt waters of Hudson Bay, people move their nets further and further along the rivers until they reach the bay, and follow the fish back again into the lakes at the end of the summer.

People also note nuances of taste, with certain animals tasting better at certain periods of the year. Many avoid male caribou when they are in rut, because the meat tastes less good. In contrast, they prize male ringed seals when they are in rut, because their meat has greater warming properties.[5] If a fish has been dead too long in the net, its flesh can taste watery, and the same species can taste different depending on what lake it comes from, or whether it has been caught in freshwater or in saltwater. The taste of food is affected even by its means of transportation: food transported by dog team tastes better than food transported by skidoo because it has not picked up the fumes from the gas. Processes of industrial production have not standardized country food, and people continue to note how environmental conditions affect its quality.

Signs of the changing seasons can also predict the availability of certain foods. In the Belcher Islands, for example, people know that the Canada Geese are moulting when the central stalk of a particular species of grass may be easily pulled out. In Puvirnituq, the first summer rainfall after their arrival marks the beginning of the time when Canada geese start to moult. The names of various lunar months reflect animal behaviours. In Puvirnituq the March/April moon is *Natsialuit* (seal pups), the April/May moon is *Nukpaluit* (caribou calf), the June/July moon is *Manniluit* (eggs). In regions where the climate is more severe, names for the lunar months may vary because the animals' reactions will be delayed. So, for instance, although the March/April moon is a time for seal pups in Puvirnituq, its name in Iglulik — *Avunnit* — denotes "female seals who have miscarried."[6]

If the seasons and the weather affect the behaviour and availability of animals and the taste of country foods, they also influence people's access to them. At the end of autumn and the beginning of the winter, it can be difficult to get out of communities to get the food because the ice is not yet stable and there may not be enough snow to travel by skidoo. This is also a time when the weather can be unsettled. In October 2001, country foods were scarce in Puvirnituq because bad weather prevented people from going out:

> Winter was often very hard. Sometimes all we had to eat was a type of porridge made out of seal's blood which we would share with our neighbours. When we had nothing else, we were forced to eat seal skin strings, the bottom of old kamiks and we even resorted to the fur-covered skins. We removed the fur before eating the skin.[7]

This quotation reveals more than might be apparent at first. In extremely difficult conditions, people were sometimes obliged to eat some of the very things that would have enabled them to continue to hunt, thereby jeopard-izing their survival. There are stories of people being forced to eat their dogs, their clothes, even their tents to stave off starvation. Today, although their children have experienced nothing of such a life, people in their 40s and 50s can still recall times in their childhood when they were, indeed, starving. Ad-amie told me that, as a child, his family was once reduced to eating ptarmigan droppings, which they collected and made into soup. He remembers being told that if they did not have a sense of appreciation while making it, the soup would not taste good, so they worked hard to feel appreciative.

In times of plenty, they would save food. The coastline around Puvirnituq is dotted with caches that were once used to store it. Like silent markers, they are testaments to a way of living that endured for thousands of years. It was partly in response to the seasonal and variable availability of food that Inuit developed the practice of sharing it. Thus, Asen Balikci describes the seasonal patterns of food sharing around Puvirnituq.[8] During winter, the whole camp formed an economic unit within which people shared country foods. This was not the case in spring, when these foods, especially seals, were easier to get. People spent the summer preparing dried meat and blubber to cache for winter use, and these were later shared with those in need. Yet sharing did not stop in the summer, either, for seals and belugas were divided equally, and blubber was stored for communal use as dog food in the winter. In the late spring and autumn people fished with nets, and they shared less because the weather had less effect on their ability to obtain food.

These days, people in the Canadian Arctic are not so tied to the whims of nature. Their access to food is more predictable than it was when they relied exclusively on what they could harvest locally. They have access to foods from the South, and they may fill their freezers with locally caught food when it becomes available. Yet, although no longer reliant on caches of stored food for their survival, people continue to prepare dried meat for the pleasure of eating it. It is part of their culinary tradition.

VISITING JINNIE'S HOUSE ONE EVENING, we sat at the kitchen table talking about this and that, while two women added highlights to their hair. Chil-dren raced around in and out of the house, the television was playing in the background, and we sat chatting and eating — tearing dried Arctic char with our teeth from strips of mottled skin. Its orangey-pink flesh tasted rich and full of oil. Jinnie's mother had prepared it earlier that week when she was out camping.

THIS FOCUS ON FOOD, the awareness that its availability varies from location to location, from season to season, from moment to moment, requires that people be alert to the state of the natural world. They must go out into it and endure its realities in order to get food. In doing so, they confront its constant transformations.

The physical realities of the natural world, the knowledge of its unpredictability, translate into deeper existential perceptions about the nature of reality in general, and time in particular. People in the Arctic must necessarily be aware that their environment is constantly changing, everything is in flux, and the future cannot be predicted. They cannot make firm plans, for the future is always contingent on uncontrollable forces; people must adapt to the unpredictability of life. This is an intrinsic part of the Inuit mindset.[9] In the face of an often hostile and uncertain environment, Inuit have learned to be adaptable. If the future cannot be predicted, life must be lived very much in the present.[10] "We live in the moment," people have told me. "Today is today, and tomorrow is tomorrow. Don't bring today into tomorrow, and don't bring yesterday into today." Such an approach to time affects what gets done and how it gets done:

Drying Arctic char and seal intestines

This is the way my grandfather was raised. Out on the land and back in the past, everyone had to learn to get ready quickly. You were always supposed to be aware of what is going on, never let the others wait. There was always an urgency to get somewhere, whether you were going home, going to a new campsite. It is because we used to have to follow the land's changes. It might not be good travel conditions later on. Things like climate, ice, and water conditions can change so quickly.[11]

In the Arctic, people do not assume they have authority over time; rather, they adjust to the instability and impermanence they see around them.[12] This means that people let go of the past and do not assume that the future is controllable. The world is a place of hidden forces that must be accepted and to which one must adapt. The assumption that matter is controllable and permanent has little place in Inuit epistemology. Time and space are always in flux.

One of the few things that is predictable is the land. This is not to say that its behaviour is predictable, but its very existence can always be relied upon:

The Land is the one thing that has always seemed "real" to Inuit in the rather chaotic existence that has engulfed them since the arrival of Europeans. Most of their language . . . hinges upon interaction with the features, flora, and fauna of the Land, and therefore it seemed like the one thing upon which Inuit can rely — the one thing that will not change, even though generations, technology, and traditions may. Even the word "Inuit," although mistakenly translated as "humans" or "people" actually means "the Ones Who Are Here," meaning the ones that dwell on the land itself. They take it for granted that Inuit and the Land were made for each other — that the two are inextricably linked.[13]

Given this existential reality, the concept of owning the land and all it contains becomes nonsensical. How can one own that within which one's being is contained? The possibility of humanity's transcendence of, and mastery over, nature is anathema to hunter-gatherers the world over.[14] Underlying Inuit notions of the land and sea are a whole set of beliefs about the environment and about their rights to its use.

Common Property and Country Foods

At a very basic level, the idea that any one individual may own the land and its resources goes against all that most Inuit believe about the natural order of things:

> In the past, I've never felt easy saying I'm from Nunavut, because it means "our land." I can say the same for the sea. I've always believed that what we get from the land and the sea are given to us from our Creator. And that we are simply babysitting the land and sea, which will be returned to Him. I've never felt easy saying that the land and the sea is for sale. I don't think it is ours to sell or buy.[15]

If one does not own the land or the sea, neither can one own the resources that come from them. In principle, all have a legitimate right to use them, and they all must be shared with others.

In places where ideas about common property have prevailed, people live on the land and perceive its resources in ways that affect many aspects of life. Ideas about common property define how people occupy space, how they interact with the environment, and how they relate to one another.

In contrast, peoples who have embraced the concept of private property generally assume that common property regimes mean that such areas are a kind of no-man's land where no one has responsibility for the resources, and, as a result, there is a free-for-all use of them. Nothing could be further from the truth. Common property is not the same as property that belongs to no one, and to which anybody may have access.[16] There is a distinction between land tenure, which assumes ownership of the land, and territoriality, which implies something to which one has certain rights of use, but that is shared with others.[17] Access to the common property resources of the land and water are, in fact, managed, but without any of the codified institutional structures required by private property systems. Common property systems rely, in part, on recognition of people's customary use and knowledge of an area. So, for the Inuit of Nunavik, although the land cannot be owned, there are use rights associated with the extended occupation of a particular area, or from the construction and maintenance of structures in a particular area, such as hunters' blinds, stone weirs, food caches, or cairns for caribou drives.[18] In Puvirnituq, certain areas are known to have been commonly occupied by certain families, with family names associated with camp sites, hunting areas, trap-lines, and trails. Each nuclear family had a set of camps within a general area where they moved, depending on the season, with perhaps two or more camps associated with each season.[19] Different people might use the same land at different times, or they might use them together. So, during the yearly cycle among these different sites, individual families were not necessarily the only people to occupy a particular site. Different groups came into regular contact with one another. For example, prior to settlement, Inuit from the Puvirnituq area would move inland up the Puvirnituq River to hunt caribou during the spring and early fall.[20] This brought them into contact with Inuit from other regions who were doing the same thing.

The fur trade had an impact on the way people used the land. Around Puvirnituq, when people were earning significant money from the fur trade, families were known to have their own trap-lines, which others avoided. There were also trails associated with these families; some of them were known to be for use by everyone, but others were generally reserved for that family so as to preserve the resources along that trail.[21]

Although there are areas where certain families fished or hunted or trapped — areas where they have done so for generations, and continue to do so — they do not feel they *own* those areas, nor that they own the animals or plants they find there. The land is "not owned by Inuit, but neither was it supposed to be subject to ownership by anyone else, for it is absurd in traditional Inuit thinking to mark off land or sea as personal property."[22] One might more properly understand them as having an affiliation or connection with a given area.[23] So, although in Nunavik, as in other parts of the Canadian Arctic, there are areas that particular groups of families have tended to use, this does not necessarily mean that others were, or are, prevented from using those areas.[24] Today, if people know ahead of time that they are going to a particular family's area, they will inform someone from that family; that person, in turn, might suggest they go where they are more likely to find food, or that they avoid certain areas because they have been recently hunted, or they are being rested to ensure that stocks recover. Such suggestions are merely that — suggestions; they are not attempts at exclusion. To say, "This is my area and you may only go to this particular location and harvest this much of that particular thing" would be considered rude and inappropriate. Communication about such matters is subtle. If someone appears in an area where they have not traditionally gone without having informed someone affiliated with the area, people from that area might feel put out by it, but they would likely not confront the newcomer, since the land does not belong to them. However if that same person has informed someone in the group of his or her intended use of the area, that would be acceptable. It is expected that people tell those who traditionally use an area if they have been, or will be, in that area, and they are expected to treat it with respect. There is a circularity in this exchange. Family affiliation with a particular area means that they look after the land, not only in terms of the resources it contains, but in terms of its larger state of being. They have knowledge about its condition, and others benefit from that knowledge by letting the custodians of the land know of their presence; in passing on this information, they also contribute to its ongoing maintenance. Inuit function on the assumption that property is held in common and social relations and responsibilities accrue from this fact.

Common property regimes regulate relations between society and resources and between the individual and society as a whole.[25] Generally, the primary obligation is to the community, with reciprocity playing a pivotal role in ensuring that the commons function properly. This, in turn, forms the basis for regulating the use of the commons. Customary use does not preclude the use of those territories by others.

Yet, access to common property is not open access to all. It operates only when those who use the resources have some influence over others who use them, which ensures that they are harvested wisely and respectfully. Where no such respect is shown, problems can arise. If people use resources without informing others of their presence or without engaging in the reciprocal relations that govern resource use, it can breed ill-will. As Tim Ingold points out, common property is a mode of communication, whereas private land tenure is a mode of appropriation.[26]

Ideas about the land, the lakes, the sea, and the resources contained in them function at many levels. In order for common property regimes to work, not only must appropriate relations between society and resources be respected, but appropriate social relations among individuals within society must be observed. These relations rely on an understanding that the individual has responsibly to the collective, and must not act in his or her own interests. The interests of the collectivity must generally be considered before those of the individual.[27] One of the ways this responsibility is maintained is by stressing that resources should be conserved; people must take only what they need. Should they take more, they must share it with others or face social censure.

Excessive individual gain from a communal resource threatens not only the resource but the society that depends on it. Someone who repudiates this obligation to the collective good may even be overcome by harmful forces that are beyond human control. There is the story of Lumaaq, a woman who did not provide properly for her blind son. Eventually, because of her ill treatment of her son, she was pulled into the sea and transformed into a fish-tailed being.[28] People still see her from time to time.

As this discussion suggests, common property is not only a physical thing, but also knowledge and a way of thinking about the world.[29] Societies that operate on the basis of common property systems see themselves as transient and the land as something more permanent; the individual recedes in importance. "Land appears as the rock upon which individual life, like the wave, rises and runs off. Therefore immovable property is disposed towards allowing the individual to move into the background, his relationship to the collectivity here being analogous to his relationship to objects."[30] This is why common property underpins and is underpinned by community. This is why, for hunter-gatherers, possession of the land is really a matter of looking after it, of tending the creative forces located within it. They are custodians of something that belongs to all, and thus, they have a responsibility to all.

Drying a sealskin in Puvirnituq

Animal Relations and Country Foods

How often have most Canadians spent time in a hunting environment — that is, a place where hunting is part of everyday life? Those who do not come from such a milieu might recognize only the outward physical manifestations of this way of life. They might see houses with skidoos, four-wheelers, a *qamutik*, and dogs outside them. Perhaps the only overt indication that hunting actually occurs might be a sealskin stretched on a frame and leaning against a house to dry. But behind these outward signs lies a world of ideas about what animals are, how they function, and how humans think about them and behave around them. It is a world that tends to be invisible to the person passing through. She may see people with guns or fishing rods. She may see people returning to town with bloody bundles of meat wrapped in caribou skins or fish lying in a tub, but she will not generally be privy to the world of ideas that links those animals to the people who have caught them.

For Inuit, awareness of the relationship between them and the animals starts as soon as they are born. In the past, in the Belcher Islands, immediately after a child's birth, the midwife would put a piece of meat in the newborn's mouth, welcoming it to life, and only afterward would it be given the mother's breast. Most children in Inuit communities still grow up in a world in which life and death are closely linked. They know that only a thin line separates the two. The connection between them is not hidden. From the time that they are babies in the *agu* (hood) of their mothers' *amautiit* (parkas), children see seals shot, caribou butchered, berries picked, and they eat fish straight from the hook. As soon as they are able, children are encouraged to take part in these activities.

Each point along the way in a child's development as a hunter is marked with pride. On the east coast of Hudson Bay, when children kill their first animals, they generally save them and bring them to their *sanajik*, who is the person who first put clothes on them after they were born.[31] A comparable relationship would be that of Euro-Canadians' godparents. Visiting my neighbour one evening, I found him kneeling on the floor plucking a Canada goose. He told me his seven-year-old *angusiaq*, whom he likened to a godson, had brought it to him. It was his *angusiaq's* first goose. Throughout their lives, a *sanajik* will receive a child's first fish, first goose, first ringed seal, first polar bear, and so on. Similar relationships exist from Alaska to Greenland.[32] Such first gifts, known in Puvirnituq as *pijurutik*, reflect larger cosmological issues related to the cycles of life. Part of the role of a *sanajik* is to ensure that his or her *angusiaq* or *arnaliaq* (goddaughter) follows the cycles of development appropriately — not simply physically, but also cognitively and morally.[33] So, for example, Davidialuk Alasuaq, a man from Purvirnituq, described how a child figuratively made its first kill by knocking down its *sanajik*, who fell to the ground as though he were a dead animal. This was designed to overcome the child's hesitation and encourage him to become a hunter. Similarly, when a child killed a small animal, the *sanajik* would behave in such a way as to encourage the child to think she or he had actually caught a large one.[34] When Davidialuk Alusuaq caught a cod, his *sanajik* behaved as though it were a beluga, and it was shared as one would share a large animal. The giving of first catches and the *sanajik*'s distribution of the catch reflects the fact that the *sanajik* is accorded the symbolic status of the acquirer of the meat, and may preside over its division and distribution.[35]

Since people are present at the moment of an animal's death, and celebrate a child's achievement in each successful hunt, Inuit are not shielded from the significance of death in the same way as Euro-Canadians, who are removed from these processes. They learn to accept death as an integral part of what it means to live. This involves a fine balancing act: people are encouraged in their success but discouraged from committing excess. On the evening I met my neighbour plucking a goose, I had been out with someone who killed a caribou. It was the first time I had seen such a large animal killed. Though I had become accustomed to witnessing the death of smaller animals, I felt the caribou's struggle deeply, and was embarrassed by my emotions. I asked my neighbour if he remembered how he felt when he first killed something. He paused and said, "Proud."

In order to live, people must kill, but my neighbour's pride on killing his first animal was not something that came from having a sense of power over the animal he killed. The foundation of relations between Inuit and the animals is respect. In Inuktitut there is no word for "respect"; this is simply the best translation they can find for *pitsiatuq*, the word they use for how animals should be treated. It connotes doing something nicely or well, with honour and awe.

This respect reflects an underlying understanding among Inuit that the world is ontologically unstable. It can change at any moment, from one thing to another, with the boundaries between the human and the non-human, the physical and spiritual, easily breached.[36] Inuit cosmology is full of stories of people who transform into animals, and vice versa.[37] Ann Fienup-Riordan argues that the fundamental instability of the nonhuman world, with its latent capacity to cross boundaries into the human, means that Inuit take care to ensure that these boundaries are kept in place by establishing rules that both create and maintain the difference between the human and nonhuman worlds.[38] At the same time, they are deeply aware of their connections with that world, with its potential passages — for good or ill — to the human world. They treat animals accordingly. In the Belcher Islands, for example, when people found a beached dead animal, they had first to hit it with a rock in order to bring it back to the realm of human existence. As the person who told the story said, it had to be "back on earth" to make it safe to eat.

This connection with the nonhuman world is a fundamental component of how Inuit understand their relations with animals. This is why Inuit hunters put themselves in the place of animals. Animals have personhood.[39] They talk about animals as behaving in the same way as humans: they have similar motivations, compulsions, and emotions. In relating themselves to the animals, in understanding them in the same way as they would understand themselves, hunters are careful to treat animals as they would wish to be treated themselves.

In a world in which survival is based on dependence on the environment, people are acutely aware that theirs is a vulnerable position. If the animals do not appear, or if the hunter is unable to kill them, then the humans will die. The hunter and the hunted are interconnected. Animals choose to give themselves to the hunter, but equally, the hunter relies on the willingness of the animal to do so. Respect for animals is paramount in Inuit belief.

"What you do to the wildlife during your life," Adamie told me, "there's going to be signs in your life, towards the end, at your death. The things that you do to the wildlife, it's going to have the same effect":

[A]ny creature that walks on the earth is for the earth. They do something on the earth as a worker. There's a use for it. Nothing is useless. As long as you can see something, it's not useless. It may be a little bug — may be good for a big bug. So anything that was put, that was created, you've got something useful for.[40]

The environment is literally alive. The various elements of the environment are infused with purpose. Since animals choose to give themselves to the hunter, they must be honoured in return. Such beliefs form the foundation of morality, are translated into practical knowledge, and are embodied in rules about how to hunt properly. The rules are many, and they vary from place to place. While they are fundamentally based on respect, there are other principles that govern how people must treat animals.

One should never talk ill of animals, for they can hear people talk. Nor should one kill profligately or disturb the animals needlessly. Any inappropriate treatment can have drastic consequences. Simigak talked about what befell some people on the coast south of Puvirnituq who hunted walrus inappropriately:

> A hunter has to be *humble*, otherwise, if he talks and says that he's a good hunter, the animal spirits will hear him and he can become a very poor hunter and will starve. That's what happened to the people of Quktaak, back in the forties. They had become too arrogant, since they owned more than one Peterhead boat. That was in between Puvirnituq and Inukjuaq. Yeah. The Quktaak people. Yeah, they would go out to Inukjuaq first and then go out to the Sleeper Islands. They got to the point that it was so easy to kill, they just killed for the tusks, cut the head off, save the tusks, and get back. But they were cursed after that, to the point that . . . they were unable to get *any* seals for a whole year, unable to get *any* caribou, *no* foxes. They had to resort to stealing other people's meat caches for one year. And . . . people knew that it was a curse over arrogance.

The mention of animal spirits is encapsulated in the notion of *inua* ("its person"), which animals and some inanimate objects possess.[41] An animal's *inua* has the capacity to appear as its spiritual double in human form. It is the *inua* that enables animals to be conscious, have awareness of themselves and others, and so be able to observe human behaviour and hear what they say. It is the potential power of these spirits to slip into human-like form or to know of humans' actions that means that the animals and the locations to which they belong must be treated appropriately. Otherwise, humans may face dire consequences.

The deep injunction against mistreating animals has meant that Inuit are profoundly troubled by the arrival of non-Inuit who attempt to tell them what to do, but appear to lack the moral basis for being trustworthy as far as the treatment of animals is concerned. Many Inuit mistrust the animal rights movement, and are resentful of what it has done to their lives: killing the fur trade, a component of their economy that allowed them to spend time on the land while also earning money from the by-products of that time. Given the ways they treat animals, Inuit ask how southerners can come north with the attitude that they know what is best for the animals. Jamisie once commented that in the South, animals are raised in cans, already prepared to be eaten. From his perspective, such treatment is the antithesis of how animals should be cared for. Inuit see the way animals are raised on southern farms and see both suffering and a denial of the respect that is required in humans' relationships with animals. At least in the North, people argue, the animals live good, free lives until they give themselves to the hunter.

Tied to the notion of respect is the idea that people must never feel they have power over an animal or brag about killing one.[42] Jamisie complained about *Qallunaat* hunters who come north and just shoot into a herd of caribou, injuring not one but many, and taking only the best parts of the meat while leaving the rest behind.

Since the exchange between the hunter and the hunted is based on respect tinged with awe, and on the idea that the animal has chosen to give itself to the hunter, many people say that you must look an animal in the eye before killing it. Kublu, a man in his 40s, told me that this was particularly important for polar bears, which are very powerful animals.[43] Adamie later explained the reason for this. As a hunter, he has a relationship with the animals he is hunting; there is a connection between them that makes them part of a larger whole. They are interconnected in ways that go beyond expression. The look that passes between a hunter and the hunted is an acknowledgment of what is being done; it is an acknowledgement of what is being given and what is being received. Adamie said one cannot really understand this feeling until one has experienced it, and added with regret that these days even some Inuit do not know it. The notion of connection between human and animal goes counter to Western ideas about nature as something "out there."[44] For many hunting and gathering peoples, nature is something within, and they are part and parcel of it. Adamie went on to say that, for many people, the power of nature, the power of human relations with animals, can be too great to talk about, so often they do not do so, and are discouraged by their elders from doing so. The animals can hear what is said about them, so it is best to remain silent.

The idea that the natural world is profoundly linked to the people who inhabit it appears at various levels in the language. Adamie once mused that Inuktitut — its sounds and form — must have come from the environment, from the land and the animals. At a conceptual level, certain words reflect this view. The word *sila* in Inuktitut means "weather," the "atmosphere," the "outdoors," or the "universe." *Sila* is at once a cosmic force and a component of all living things.[45] A related word, *silatujuq*, signifies "a wise person." Kublu explained that such a person held all the things from the sky, from the vast world, in his or her head.

If wisdom entails having an understanding of all that is outside, one component of such knowledge is an awareness that everything is interconnected; nothing happens in the world without affecting other things in foreseen and unforeseen ways. Such relational thinking reflects an understanding of the world in which "every organism is not so much a discrete entity as a node in a field of relationships."[46]

For many, there is a constant dialogue between humans and their surroundings. Things do not happen in discrete parcels. They are not bounded. Rather, actions can have numerous, often unforeseen, consequences. Given this, people must constantly watch their environment to make sure that they can understand how to react appropriately to the various manifestations of its interconnections:

If [a person] doesn't know what's going on in the surroundings, he's just going to concentrate on one thing. But [what] the hunter or trapper does is even though he may only be looking at one thing, he's also trying to observe his surroundings. He might do something, but a couple of months ago he saw something over there too. He might do something and constantly check it again without anybody really noticing. It's like that. Because as soon as he makes a move, or does something, he knows right away that something else will happen. That's how you deal with nature. "If I did this, if the ice conditions are like this, I know that it's going to be like that on the way. And if I do this, then it might be OK. But when I get to that area, then I'll go on this route." Like leads[47] and things like that, when you're travelling, then there's always one person that's leading. Because you're observing the things going on in surrounding areas.[48]

All these principles — respect, interconnection, absence of pride, absence of control, and interdependence — are central to the relations among Inuit, animals, and the larger environment, and they are translated into particular rules relating to particular animals. These rules vary from place to place, and are not necessarily unfailingly observed by all. At their core, however, they are an expression of the ideal. In southern Baffin Island, for example, people are required to leave the unused portions of the caribou that they kill — the offal or their skulls — on the land rather than on the ice. They are land mammals, and must not pollute the water. In the Belcher Islands, people must plant the tail feathers of a ptarmigan upright in the ground, and they must place the head of a bearded seal on the land. In a number of places in the southern Canadian Arctic people avoid killing walrus on the islands where the animals live or spend time.[49] If they do not do this, walrus will not return to that area. Similar rules abound across the Arctic.[50]

The ways animals must be treated, the ways they are perceived, find expression in the ways that people incorporate country foods into the social sphere. If the world is not under control, and cannot and should not be controlled, community and the sharing of food becomes one way that people have of alleviating the inconstancy of life. The sharing of country foods is both a symbolic and very real expression of underlying ontological and teleological explanations of the world. Not only do people use an image of social exchange in linking animals and their spirits with themselves, they also use the social exchange of the products of their hunting, trapping, fishing, and gathering to ensure that these things continue to be bestowed upon them. To ensure that these gifts continue to be offered, they must be shared with others. In this manner animal relations and social relations are deeply interwoven.

The Social Relations of Country Foods

Anyone who has spent time in Inuit communities cannot help but notice how food is continually circulating from one household to another, from one person to another, and sometimes across the community as a whole. In the production, distribution, and consumption of food, people are bound together in complex ways. People casually drop by for a meal without prior notice. When there is a successful hunting or fishing expedition, people come down to the shore to ask for some of the catch, or those with spare food call others to come and get meat, or they go on the local radio to say there is food available for those who would like it, or they simply drop food off at people's doorsteps. As one woman pointed out, money may not be easy to come by, but at least people are not going hungry. "It's the thing I like most about being Inuk — sharing food," she said.

Although the customs that guide the allocation of food vary across the Arctic, it is nevertheless an integral and pervasive component of life among Inuit.[51] All sharing must be understood in the context of societal connections and obligations rather than in economic terms.[52] Yet how these social relations are structured and regulated varies across the Arctic. According to a typology developed by Nobuhiro Kishigami, there are three types of sharing among hunter-gatherers: demand sharing (whereby food is given in response to a request that cannot be repudiated); sharing based on rules which establish who has rights of access to what; and voluntary sharing.[53] Voluntary sharing is the predominant form in Puvirnituq. This contrasts with the more formal, rule-based sharing practices among the Netsilik and Copper Inuit, where, historically, people had partnerships and gave one another names that designated a mutual obligation to share specific portions of an animal with a particular person.[54]

Hunting and food-sharing partnerships are a widespread and necessary form of social relations among Inuit. From kin-based whaling crews in Alaska to elective partnerships in the Eastern Canadian Arctic, hunting partnerships, with varying degrees of formality, continue to exist today among Inuit.[55] In Puvirnituq, such partnerships are voluntary, and although some of them are long-standing, others may be of a far more limited duration. With the more enduring hunting partnerships, people share the product of the hunt, both when they go hunting together and if they go hunting apart. In Puvirnituq a hunting partner, or *maqaiqatik,* is generally a friend, often from childhood, with whom one hunts for the rest of one's life. One man told me that, with his *maqaiqatik,* there is no need to talk. He knows what the other person has in mind; he knows whether and when he will shoot. If a hunter does not join his partner on a trip, he may get meat from him by asking for it either ahead of time or by meeting him at the shore on his arrival. In instances where a person has not had a particular type of meat in a while, his partner will invite his *maqaiqatik* to come and have some.

The sheer diversity of the vocabulary associated with sharing is indicative of its importance in Inuit society.[56] The words and their meanings vary from region to region and among dialects, but their variety reveals something of the complexity involved in ideas of sharing, and demonstrate the variety of social relations around food that exist in Inuit settlements.

In Puvirnituq, sharing food with people in other households — whether family members, neighbours, elders, namesakes, or anyone else — is called *pajuttuq* ("to bring something to someone"). The same word applies to giving food to people who come to meet a successful hunter on his or her return to the camp or settlement. Other forms of sharing include inviting kin or non-kin to a meal (*qaiqujijuq*), having a large community feast (*nirimatut*), giving food to one's hunting partner (*niujuattuq*), and the community-wide distribution of the catch of a large marine mammal such as a beluga (*niuju-qtissijuq*), while the person who distributes the food is called *niujuliuqti*.[57]

Sharing food within the extended family usually takes precedence, but once their needs have been met, sharing is then extended to non-kin. Generally food is given first to the elderly and the infirm, and thereafter it may be extended outward to the wider community. As one person told me, among Inuit the whole community is supposed to be treated as family. As if to confirm this view, another person told me, when I asked to whom he gave country foods, "Whoever needs it." This means not only relatives, the elderly, and the infirm, but also widows, single women, orphans, friends, those who ask for it and those who do not. Within limits, close relatives may generally take food without asking, while others can have it for the asking, though such requests are not made without due consideration to who is asking whom. One man commented that, depending on the size of his catch and how much he has to spare, he generally gives anywhere from half or more to others. This confirms the observations of researchers in Nunavik that the source of most food in the region comes from a limited number of people who are then responsible for dispersing country foods within their communities.[58] This suggests that reciprocity does not predominate in sharing relations, but that people give or redistribute food without any expectation of being reimbursed in kind.[59] Yet, as Barbara Bodenhorn points out, the notion of reciprocity is more complex than it appears at first sight. Networks of sharing come in two forms. In one, which generally involves close kin, sharing builds and sustains enduring relationships of mutual reciprocity in which there is a flow not only of food, but of goods, services, and company. The exchange is not *quid pro quo*; one person may receive food while the other returns the gift with child care or other services. The second form of sharing involves those who will never be in a position to repay the gift, such as elders or those in need.[60] Whatever form of relations such sharing instigates, the fact remains that a limited number of people supply country foods to many people and distribute it via networks of sharing. For this reason, hunters and fishers consistently try to take more than they need for personal consumption because they have also to get food for others outside their immediate families.[61] Again and again, food and society are seen to be woven together.

OCTOBER 18, 2001: The beluga hunters came back to town tonight after about a week away. Six boats arrived to cheers and whistles from the shore. The whole community seemed to be there to greet them. They had gathered on the beach long before the boats pulled in. There was something wonderful about seeing the lights come across the water. One boat was waving a flag. When they arrived people let off firecrackers and there were cheers for the hunters, and of course everyone was there with their bags to get a share of the meat. Old and young, everyone had gathered. They started the divvying up of the whales. I watched from a hill above the beach, with children for company, while the adults gathered in a light-filled circle to get their share. Pieces of *mattak* (beluga skin) were passed over people's heads to those behind. The excitement in the air was palpable.

As FOOD PASSES FROM PERSON TO PERSON, it helps create bonds within and among families, and within and among communities. When food can be spared, or when people need it, they call one another. Such sharing includes not only country foods but store-bought food as well. As one woman told me, "Giving away food makes you feel good."

Siblings give food to one another, children give food to parents and grandparents, namesakes give food to namesakes, a child's midwife or *sanajik* receives food, travelling friends and relatives may arrive with food from their

Arrival of the beluga hunters in Puvirnituq

home communities. The flexibility of Inuit social relations means that, ideally, no one is excluded from sharing networks: food must be available to all whenever it can be spared.

The first point of meat sharing comes with the hunt, when those who were part of the hunting group receive some of the game either at the site where the animal was killed or while it is being butchered.[62] Generally, when people are hunting together, no matter who kills the animal, it is shared equally, although the person who kills an animal generally gets the first choice of cut. Even those who have been out with the hunters and are involved in the most minor ways are included. This points to the distinction between a "share" and "sharing."[63] The former is granted in return for having contributed to a hunt, either monetarily or through participation, while the latter refers to the set of social relations that create and sustain relationships. The former does not necessarily forge ongoing relations of reciprocity, whereas the latter does. After a day out hunting with Jamisie, where I did nothing more than point at the heads of seals as they bobbed up in the water, he gave me a share of seal meat to take home. On another occasion, I received a piece of caribou. My receipt of such shares did not mean that I was expected to reciprocate in kind at some later date or that I had become incorporated into Jamisie's regular network of food sharing.

The second point at which meat is distributed comes once people have returned to the settlement. They then share with others, either distributing the meat among kin or, depending on the amount harvested, sharing it more widely. Once, for example, when we had got more geese than we needed, a general announcement was made on the local radio to let people know they could come to the beach for some meat.

The third point at which meat is distributed is through meals and the giving of meat through networks of sharing to people at some point after the hunt occurred.[64] When my landlady was away from town for any length of time, for example, her extended family would periodically check to make sure that I had enough meat and would tell me to come and get some.

Generosity in sharing food is the ideal, but there are subtleties involved in the process and the ideal is not always achieved. In the past, people were expected to share food unreservedly, except in times of famine. Lack of generosity was viewed as a shortcoming. However, some researchers contend that, with settlement, there has been increased individualization, and, as a result, sharing has decreased.[65] Although people are supposed to share if they are able, if they simply want to keep their food, or if they are asked for food by a particular individual about whom they have reservations, they might say that they have nothing to spare. People start to know who is likely to give them food and who is likely to say no. In other instances, although the request may be acceded to, the recipient may be aware by tone of voice or behaviour that the donor is reluctant to give it, and the recipient knows not to ask again. If the requester is known to be worthy, to contribute to the community, then the food will be given gladly by the same individual who will give reluctantly, if at all, to someone they hold in less regard. One person reported that, because his mother had been a midwife,[66] there were many people in the community who were willing to respond to his requests for food. But people sometimes resent sharing food, particularly when they feel that those who ask are contributing to their lack of it. For instance, a household in Puvirnituq went on community radio and asked for country food. To be reduced to making such a request on the public airwaves is considered embarrassing. A friend who heard the appeal said they were unlikely to get any meat because they were drug dealers and people objected to their influence on the community. Similarly, those who spend their money recklessly on gambling or bingo may be less likely to be the recipients of food when they ask for it.

There are certainly complexities in the process, but the expectation is that one ought to share. Those who do not give are considered misguided and will ultimately suffer for it. As one person said, people who do not give "will go through a very hard time getting food. It's *true*."

While I was in Puvirnituq, I remembered how, when my parents tried to teach me manners as a child, I would sometimes ask them why I should do a certain thing. Mentioning this, I asked some people in Puvirnituq what they had been told by their parents about the necessity of sharing. Each time I asked this question, the person would look at me in confusion, as if such a question were unthinkable, or perhaps simply dim-witted. Their response was generally that sharing was necessary because the precarious and unpredictable nature of life in a northern environment required it.

Today, when people are not so clearly reliant on the whims of nature for their survival, the moral imperative to share food, in good times and in bad, persists, for there is more involved than just food. In the past, environmental hardships required that food be shared, but this was strengthened by a whole set of beliefs about proper relations between humans and animals, concepts of common property, and ideas about identity, family, and community, all of which ultimately culminate in notions of appropriate social order.

Across the Arctic, many Inuit believe that sharing ensures success in hunting. People are successful when they share country foods, and share those foods in order to ensure success. Animals know how humans behave and bestow themselves on people accordingly. The animal does this because that hunter and his or her family act appropriately by following the rules of the hunt. One of the rules is that one should share what one receives from the animal. Those who behave appropriately will receive the animals' gifts again, while those who do not share will not be successful in the hunt, for the animals will withhold their bounty. "The more you give, the more you get" is a common expression in Puvirnituq and other Inuit communities I have visited. At one level, this may be a reflection of the fact that, when people share with others, others share with them in return. On another unspoken level, people are also acknowledging the links between humans and the animals they eat.

Sharing country foods is built into the individual's sense of identity. It is at the centre of a complex set of relationships that define and determine the nature of individual, societal, and community identities. Identity is neither simple nor fixed. People perceive themselves in different ways at different times and in different settings. One's identity is also formed in relation to a larger society, so that we understand who we are, in part, based on how we fit into society as a whole. When it comes to forming their identities, many Aboriginal peoples carry the added burden of tradition that forces them to try to balance some idealized version of aboriginality that may be an over-simplified historical remnant with the reality of lives lived in the 21st century. The balancing act has its good and bad points: on the one hand, it can offer stability; on the other, it can place unnecessary pressures on people to conform to something to which they do not relate or with which they no longer wish to associate themselves.

Since the 18th century, with the rise of liberal ideology in Europe, Western notions of identity have changed. Increasingly, people have tended to base their identity on the idea of an atomistic individual, with society then existing as a series of contracts between individuals.[67] It is the individual who rules in such a system, with individual rights and freedoms holding sway. The opposite is the case in Inuit societies, where individual identity is secondary to, and based on, larger social systems.[68]

In societies in which ideas about identity and morality emphasize the collective over the individual, a great deal of emphasis is placed on personal autonomy, but such autonomy relies on people recognizing that people are ultimately responsible to the collective and promote the well-being of the collective. In this context, people are judged on their state of being, and it is this state of being that is constantly reinforced by moral principles.[69] A person's state of being depends very much on his or her conduct within a set of relations with others in human society and with animals in the world beyond human society. In the case of Inuit, ethical codes related to country foods define how people should relate to one another and to animals. In both cases, these moral systems shape individual and collective identities. The supremacy of the collective over the individual is linked generally to ideas about common property, and specifically to ideas of sharing food.

Although at a very fundamental level the necessity to share food is bound up in the construction of an individual's identity in relation to the collective, Inuit have ways, particular to them, that express this set of relations. One of the ways Inuit establish individual identity is through names, and central to the system of naming are ideas of the *atiq* and the *sauniq*. In Inuit cosmology, people possess three souls: an individual soul (*tarniq*), a name soul (*atiq*), and a breath soul (*anirniq*).[70] The *tarniq* is specific to a person, lasts only his or her lifetime, and leaves the body on death. The *anirniq* is linked to larger creative forces attributed to God, and is a piece of those forces given to a person when she or he is born. Unlike the *tarniq*, it can sometimes linger after death. The *atiq* is the soul an individual possesses as a result of having a particular name.[71] When a person receives a name, she or he receives a list of qualities and relationships that are specific to it. The *atiq* implies a form of reincarnation. It is a major means by which a person's identity is established.

Linked to the idea of the *atiq* is the concept of the *sauniq*, which translates literally as "bone." A *sauniq* is a person who shares the same name as someone, but only if that name was given to signify the same person. Neither the *atiq* nor the *sauniq* is sex specific, although they can be gender specific. So, while certain qualities are passed on with a name, these are not necessarily linked to a person's sex. A female may receive a name that previously belonged to a male, and vice versa. But in receiving a name that was previously held by a male, a girl may be encouraged to practise what may commonly be considered male pursuits.[72] Bound up in all this is the tendency of Inuit to stress relational names and associate obligations with those relations. People often refer to one another not by their names but in kinship terms, calling someone "son," "older brother," "wife," "grandfather," or "cousin" rather than by their names.[73] As people establish their individual identities, their social relations, and their ideas of community, they draw upon concepts of the *atiq*, the *sauniq*, and the larger family relations.

When a child receives a name, she can also receive a set of qualities, abilities, relationships, and obligations that go along with it. I once asked a nine-year-old girl why she had grey hair; she responded that it was because her *sauniq* had had lots of grey hair. When I was working in the Belcher Islands, one of my colleagues adopted his wife's sister's child, whom he named after his father. My colleague then called that child "father," who in turn, called his adoptive father "son." Such relations radiate outward. Thus, my colleague's wife might call her adopted son "father-in-law," although, in fact, he was biologically her nephew, and he might call her "daughter-in-law." Such relationships repeat themselves throughout the generations, and again spread outward. People are constantly finding ways to establish links with one another, and creating such links where they might not obviously exist. A woman in Puvirnituq, for example, spoke of a man as her nephew because he was the son of her sister's *sauniq*. In this way, identity in Inuit communities is neither fixed nor stable, and everyone has the potential to become kin.

The getting, giving, receiving, and consumption of country foods can be closely linked with each of these forms of social relations and identity-setting processes. A man who was known in his lifetime to be a good walrus hunter may pass that ability on to his *sauniq* through their shared name. If someone has a *sauniq* relationship with another, either as a direct namesake or through the extended relations that get established through the name, that person may then have privileged relations in terms of sharing country foods. Kin is the basis of food-sharing relations, but the fact that kin relations are flexible and not based solely on biology, means that so, too, is the sharing of food.

Names can also help create a sense of memory and continuity in both the getting and sharing of country foods. In fact, they can be central to processes of meaning-making associated with those foods, whether in its production, distribution, or consumption. As names are recycled and the places associated with them continue to be used, there is a sense of continuity in place, and people understand themselves as deeply attached to place. As Hugh Brody writes, "To know the land . . . is to know oneself."[74]

Identity and country foods are linked in other ways. Although it was practised more in the past than it is today, and details vary from region to region, a common practice across the Arctic involves people receiving particular portions of animals based on their age and sex. In the Belcher Islands, when one is deemed an elder, one receives prime cuts such as the fifth and sixth vertebrae near a beluga's tail, or soft tissue from the top of its head. In

Puvirnituq, the portion along the spine and tail is for women while the skin on the head is for men. When the tail is being divided among the women, everybody knows because it is announced on the community radio. The same is true for other parts of animals. In Puvirnituq, parts of the head of a walrus (such as the eyes, tongue, and lips) were reserved for the women, but now such things are observed mostly by elders. For Canada geese, males get the breast and drumstick while females get the bony parts along the backbone. When Jamisie was telling me about this he stressed that each part had its own properties: the meat along the bone is particularly nutritious. To be given certain portions of meat is to be given an honour marking one's status in society. A friend once mentioned that he had asked for some prime cuts of beluga only to be told that he was not yet entitled to them since he had not reached the status of an elder.

It is not only what one eats, but how one eats it that is linked to identity. In Sanikiluaq, for example, men are discouraged from eating until their plates are clean or scraping all the meat from a bone, for if they do so, that is how the earth will be when they go hunting: bare, smooth, and devoid of game.

It is not only in its consumption that food is linked to identity, but also in its distribution. After a successful hunt, once the initial butchering has been done by the men on the land, the meat is further divvied up on return to the settlement. Once the meat is in the house, it is the woman who is in control; she is responsible for dividing up the meat and ensuring that it is shared with the appropriate people. When people call to ask for country food, it is the wife who decides what is to be given to whom. This means that part of a husband's success as a hunter is dependent on his wife. The animals are aware of her behaviour — whether or not she shares meat — and present themselves to her husband accordingly.[75]

Identity can be linked to country foods in intimate ways. "This is the way I think," said Peter Okpik. "A person is born with animals. He has to eat animals. That is why the animals and a person are just like one."[76]

Being "like one" with the animals can be extended to people's names. In Puvirnituq, in the days before there was a permanent settlement, when the members of a family with the name "raven" (*tulugaq*) were on the land and met members of the family carrying the name "rough-legged hawk" (*qinu-ajuaq*), they would greet one another by calling in their respective bird calls.

Country foods are increasingly used to distinguish an Inuk from a non-Inuk. Such distinctions function in two ways, internal and external to Inuit society. In Greenland, people use the eating of country foods politically, as a marker of true "Inuitness."[77] People are accused of not being real Inuit if they do not eat country foods. But the consumption of country foods is also used by people as a way of understanding who they are in relation to the larger, non-Inuit society. [78] In both cases, it becomes symbolic of stability and identity in the face of change wrought by the influence of non-Inuit on Inuit society.

Yet the creation and maintenance of identity is only one social function of country foods. At a fundamental level, in the getting, sharing, and eating of country foods, it is also profoundly linked to community construction and maintenance.

Before they moved to settlements, Inuit would congregate and disperse according to changing conditions and the seasonal cycle of harvesting food. In the winter, people in the region of Puvirnituq would congregate on the sea ice near islands in Hudson Bay where the ice is always broken and moving in winter. There, in larger groups, they would harvest and share food collectively. Once the warmer weather came, they would disperse into smaller groups, fishing at river mouths in the spring and camping along the shores of Hudson Bay. In August and September during a period called *uqutsaq* ("to get something warm"), those who were able would move inland up the rivers draining into Hudson Bay to harvest caribou meat and skins, for this was the

Learning to prepare nikuk *(dried caribou meat)*

time when the furs were best. During that move, those who had difficulty walking, such as elders and the young, were left at the mouth of the river to be picked up as people congregated again for the winter on the ice.[79] With sedentarization, such patterns of behaviour have changed, but the enduring relationships built up on the land over generations remain at the heart of Inuit food systems and continue to find expression in the getting and eating of food.

Harvesting in winter is generally the domain of men, who leave the settlement to hunt and fish either alone (if they are not going far) or in groups. Once the warmer weather and the longer days arrive, larger groups of families and friends go out. The spring is a time for ice fishing when many families together, young and old alike, spend a few days on the land. During the summer, people leave the settlement for longer periods to get fish, eider down, birds' eggs, geese, seal, and caribou. Once again, young and old, male and female, are part of the mix. Today, with the expense of camping, and given that people may have jobs that keep them bound to the settlement, people have less time and freedom to do these things, and trips may be restricted to weekends or certain age groups. One man complained that, since his older children had jobs, they were unable to come to their camp during the summer except for short periods. Only young children and those with enough seniority and cash to have longer holidays manage to spend an extended period of time at the family camp. Some communities, including Puvirnituq, are limited even in their weekend activities because, as Christians, they ought not to work on Sundays. Because fewer people can afford to take their families out, some people from Puvirnituq have started a summer camp where several couples spend two or three weeks on the land and bring groups of children from the settlement to live with them, each group spending a week at a time.

When people spend time on the land, they say it is a time when they live as they prefer, according to the rhythms of nature. Unlike life in settlements, where houses are separated into different rooms and people do not always know where others might be, people living in tents are many generations in one space, and are able to reaffirm time-honoured ways of interacting, each generation learning from, and looking after, the others.[80]

Marybelle Mitchell argues against the common view that the mode of production in indigenous societies was a form of "primitive communism." She maintains that the idea that food was shared selflessly and equally is a myth. Food-sharing practices, she contends, vary across the North and cannot be codified. Sharing was the result of co-operative labour forced upon Inuit by the quality of their weapons and hunting techniques. Thus, sharing was a form of insurance against times of future want.[81]

This is a question of perception. Mitchell may see sharing in this light, and her reasoning may make a certain amount of sense, but such a functionalist explanation can only be partial, at best. The fact remains that, on the whole, Inuit have seen food sharing as an unquestionable component of life in society. There may be times when sharing is unfeasible, but the ideal remains. Despite the fact that people are no longer so dependent on sharing food for their survival, food exchange continues, suggesting that technological limitations are not the only factor encouraging such behaviour.

The creation of community through the sharing of country foods was, in part, a necessity, built on an awareness of impermanence — of the environment, of the material world, of weather. People were, and are, patently aware that nature is something over which they have no control. The creation of strong societal bonds is a way of relieving that lack of control. Even today, when that lack of control seems not quite so overwhelming, when jobs, money, and the welfare state have moved in to ensure that people are no longer prone to the vagaries of fate, Inuit continue to share food. As Balikci put it, when discussing the persistence of sharing among Inuit despite the influx of cash and individualized work, the principles that food must be shared "seem a means for adjusting man not only to the environment but to society."[82]

For all the possible reasons that social systems are connected to the sharing of country foods, whether it is ideas about proper relations between humans and other animals, or ideas about identity construction, or the deterministic view that the environment requires that food be shared, the fact remains that for most Inuit the sharing of food is deeply embedded in their understandings of how to behave. In getting country foods, in sharing them with others, and in eating them, most Inuit, whether consciously or unconsciously, affirm a set of ideals about how they should function in the world as individuals, as communities, and as a people. To be Inuk is to share food, and to share food is to be Inuk.

Memory, Home, and Country Foods

We all have memories that come with the experience of life. They can be revived by a chance remark, a smell, a glimpse of something long-forgotten, a piece of music, a place. For most of us, these things are part of our everyday lives, but they help us to make sense of who we are, and they ground us in the places we inhabit. They help us feel at home.

Memory in place exists at many levels. In our individual lives there can be places that are meaningful only to us and help us to make sense of ourselves. They are the places that mark our personal moments of triumph or defeat, the places where we suddenly realized something, or where some remarkable event occurred. But there are also places that hold collective memories; they help us make sense of ourselves as a group, not only in the here and now, but through time. By spending time on the land, in travelling to look for food, Inuit pass landmarks that serve to remind themselves of who they are, both as individuals and as a collective. Such "memoryscapes"[83] contain hidden layers of meaning in the stories and events that are built into places.

This knowledge may not always be conscious. People may not pass caches or tent rings on or go to the same fishing area again and again and have an epiphany: "Ah, I know who I am!" But they do help to place people in their lives, and are part and parcel of their understanding of a way of life that is uniquely theirs.

The meanings of these places cannot often be gleaned simply from a name. It is the meaning behind the name that is built into people's understandings of those places. We camped for a couple of weeks in July at Qapirquktuuq, a site several hours' boat ride from Puvirnituq. I had never been to such a place. Above our white tents clustered by the shore were the stone foundations of buildings that had held many people, with massive stone benches. There were caches and graves and tent rings and *inuksuit*.[84] The place was full of the signs of the past. Although most of the people at the camp were Inuit who lived in Puvirnituq, among the visitors was a man from Montreal who was making a film. This was his second visit to the Arctic. The day he was to leave, I mentioned to him how amazed I had been at the vestiges of the past. He looked at me with a blank face. He had seen none of it, despite the fact that his tent was only metres from the stone houses. His response reminded me of a comment Kublu once made: "We have *lots* of history, only it's not written down."

As a visitor to the place, I could see the signs of its occupation by Inuit, but I could not understand them or relate to them as a person from that place. I did not grow up going there. I did not grow up knowing that here was where my parents and my grandparents and my great-grandparents went hunting and fishing and gathering. I did not grow up with the stories about this place that overlapped with my own life and way of living. I did not know that over that hill was a lake where the Arctic char are very tasty, or in that bay a whole camp of people once died due to illness, or by that river my great uncle and aunt would camp every spring. All these things serve to make the land a place of home and identity for many Inuit in a way that it could never be for me.

The researchers Zebedee Nungak and Eugene Arima provide many examples of how the landscape around Puvirnituq is littered with history.[85] At Kuuvik, 180 kilometres north of Puvirnituq, are many *inuksuit* that stand in a place where two brothers killed a number of people. At another place called Inikjuaq ("the big place"), across the river from Puvirnituq, is a site where there was a battle between two *Tuniit*, a people who preceded the Inuit. The marks of their skirmish are still visible on the land. The landscape is full of stories of hunger, of the supernatural, of the incredible feats of humans and animals, each of which gets told and retold so that it becomes a manifestation of memory and identity. Spending time on the land with Jamisie helped me to learn some of these stories.

Once, on a flat October day, we were out hunting by boat. We passed through a place called Upirngavik — "the spring place," because people would camp there in the spring — and Jamisie told me about a measles epidemic in 1963 when he was an eight-year-old child. It hit the whole community at once, and people were unable to go out and get food. Supplies were running low. Jamisie and his brother-in-law were the first to recover, so they went out hunting. In this place they had managed to kill enough geese to feed the community.

The following summer, I was out in a boat with Salamonie, zooming among the islands along the coast of Hudson Bay. We were a big group, in six boats, going from island to island looking for eggs and keeping an eye out for moulting Canada geese. The elder of our group, Miku, a man in his 70s, had recently got a new motor for his boat. According to his wife, he was so happy the wrinkles were falling off his face. As we travelled, Salamonie drew my attention to a marker high on an island out at sea, and said this was where Miku's father was buried. Pointing even further out, to some islands on the horizon, he said that as a child he had gone there with his parents to get seals because this was the place where the best sealskins could be found for making *qajait*.

For many of the people living in Puvirnituq, home is not simply the houses they live in, but a vast area. Even when they are not there, people know the shorelines and mountains, and lakes and hills, the seals and birds, the birth sites and death sites. Birth sites are particularly important: for many people, especially for those who have moved from life on the land to life in settlements, or for those who have moved to new places, the place of their birth is their real place, the place to which they belong rather than the other way around.[86]

Spending time on the land allows people to gain knowledge about the land, to learn that this is where good drinking water can be found, that is a safe harbour, this hillock marks the route to a camp site, up that river the blueberries are large and tasty. This helps people understand themselves in relation to the land. Such knowledge can be both practical and existential. As Rachel Attituq Qitsualik has written, "The land was the grocery and hardware store of Inuit, providing them with everything they required, including food and tools. Just as one knows one's neighbourhood or the town where one was raised, so Inuit regarded the entirety of the Land as their home."[87]

Among Inuit, this connection between land and home also links geography to identity. As a people who have had to rely on knowing the land where they are from in order to survive, this geographical identity is important. In fact, when people first meet one another they might ask where they are from — *Nani nunaqarpit?* — which translates as, "Where do you have land?" Such links to the land are profoundly important. Nunavik has several examples of settlements that have come into being because people from a given area could not feel at ease removed from the places they know and in which they feel at home. Akulivik was created by people who were moved to Puvirnituq when their trading post closed; however, since they did not want to be there, the settlement was built. Umiujaq was created by people who did not want to be in Kuujjuarapik; Tasiujaq was built for people who did not want to be in Kuujjuaq; and, although it later closed, Taqpangajuk was created by people originally from Killiniq who did not want to be in Kangiqsualujjuaq. In each case, although the people concerned were often related to people in the settlements they were leaving, the attachment they felt to the places they

Emptying a fishnet

came from and the knowledge they had about those places reveal how deep are the links between place, identity, and knowledge.

The world over, people have stories and events that link them to place, but this is particularly true in areas where people have lived over a long time, where their narratives make them of that place. According to archaeological records, Nunavik has been inhabited for more than 4,000 years. The area was home to the Dorset culture (a Paleo-Eskimo people known to the Inuit as *Tuniit*). The *Tuniit* were displaced approximately 1,000 years ago by the Thule culture, who are the ancestors of modern Inuit. They are of that place in a way no Euro-Canadian can be. Their culture and ways of knowing, their behaviours and understandings, reflect a people whose history is of that place. Such places are full of the past, full of an awareness that goes beyond life's daily workings. In spending time on the land, people reinforce their understandings of themselves through time and in time. "For people native to a place," writes John Moss, "landscape is an extension of being, as intimate and far-reaching as genealogy, an existential fact."[88]

Many of the stories that link Inuit to place came to be long ago. This is how land becomes linked to memory and home. In getting country foods, in spending time on the land, these links are continually being forged and reforged, so that past and present are part of an ongoing process of making meaning.

AUGUST 18, 2002: Yesterday we stopped for tea on an island. Near the shore were the usual papers, a can of cocktail sausages sitting in a puddle, toilet paper, chocolate bar wrappers, pop cans. But I went to some markers higher up on the hill. There was a stone circle — remnants from a tent long gone — nestled among some rocks on what had once been a beach. There was the usual cache. Then further on I came across some rocks lying in a depression. I *knew* they meant something, but I didn't know what. They didn't shout their presence; rather, I felt them. At the top of the hill, among the various *inuksuit*, was one that clearly said, *There is a grave here*. I could see the image of a person lying horizontally, straddled between two upright rocks. It was clear and loud in its silence. The whole place was loud with the presence of people. They were everywhere, leaving messages in rock. Then I went below to the others having tea by the shore, and I realized that there was information beyond the cans and the toilet paper. Somebody before us had caught a seal. The grease stains on the rock were there to see, I just didn't know how to see them at first — too busy looking at rocks.

Knowledge, Place, and Country Foods

Spending time on the land is a challenge, for one is vulnerable to the whims of unpredictable forces, at once seen and unseen. Knowledge plays a critical role in ensuring that people survive, that society reproduces itself, that life goes on. Knowledge about the weather and the behaviour of the environment in general is vitally important. The weather can change from one moment to the next. Animals may be found in the places that make sense to them: where there is food and drink, where there is shelter or fords, where there are breathing holes in the ice, where there are bays to keep out of strong currents or islands on which to rest. Animals with the capacity to kill may appear from around a corner. If misfortune should befall, help is not necessarily at hand. People must be knowledgeable about the workings of the world, for if they are not, the consequences can be drastic.

Early in December 2001 winter had finally settled in. The cold had arrived, the ice was strong enough to travel on, and there was enough snow to go out by skidoo. It had been grey, with wind blowing and snow falling. Together they flattened the world, making the landscape formless to my eyes. I had heard from Kublu that someone had gone out hunting "just for a short time," and not returned. A search and rescue team was sent out. On a dreary morning some days after his disappearance, I watched three skidoos cross the frozen river and head into town, and soon after, they headed out again, pulling *qamutiit* — sleds — behind them. They had found the man's body. His skidoo had broken down and he had frozen to death. He left behind a wife and small children.

Survival is not guaranteed. It depends on one's knowledge of the land, of how to behave and how to find one's way around. As various land use and occupancy studies attest,[89] people travel vast distances: in the past on foot, or by *qajaq* or *umiaq* (a large, skin-covered boat used by women) or dog team, and today using motorized vehicles. People carry immense maps in their heads. These maps are multi-dimensional and include time, space, and knowledge of the workings of nature. Although today such knowledge is less widespread, people still must know how to get from A to B, where safe anchorages and shoals are, places where the tides affect one's ability to get in and out, the locations of animal dens that must be avoided, areas where the ground is mucky and others where it is firm, locations where the animals go for food or where they generally travel during their cycles of migration. People must know the stars and the shapes of the mountains and valleys. They must know where to find drinking water and shelter from the wind. They must know when the ice is solid. They must know the areas to be avoided because bad things have happened there in the past: deaths, the appearance of creatures that are not human. As they travel, people must keep all these things in mind and travel through many dimensions of space, time, and existence.

While out camping with people in July, several hours from town by boat, I wanted to go for a walk. Asking Mosesie what was out there, he pointed to a hill in the distance and told me there was a spring there, but I should avoid it because there was also a wolf's den nearby. I was curious, but I heeded his warning and set out for another far-off hill. When I was near the summit, I heard a noise and looked to my left. In the distance, scores of Canada geese were running in low streams up and over a ridge, their necks spread forward, trying to be invisible in their vulnerable state: moulting, they could not fly, and having seen me, they knew that I posed a threat. Getting to the top of the hill, I faced into the wind of a clear, blue day.

On the way back, I stopped to rest among an outcropping of rocks. Not far away, I spotted a lone fox, jumping and prancing for what seemed to me nothing more than the sheer pleasure of being alive. I learned later that foxes often do this when they are hunting mice or lemmings and they are trying to make them curious and dislodge them from the moss or snow under which they are hiding. I watched it for some time. The fox seemed oblivious to my presence until I moved in too close, then she started an unholy screeching unlike anything I had ever heard. "Stay away from my cubs," she was saying.

I walked on, picking my way through bogs, jumping from tussock to tussock. I passed the skeleton of a caribou, recently torn apart, bits of meat still clinging to the bones. Then again, there came a noise. At my feet was a ptarmigan, standing with neck stretched up in warning. I stopped. It stopped. I made a step. It made a step. I let the bird lead me onwards. I looked for the young it was trying to protect, but could see nothing; I was a blind *Qallunaaq*.

As I reached low land it grew hard to tell where water ended and land began. The two were merging. But in between, I could see the countless webbed footprints and drifting feathers of nervously moulting Canada geese.

Eventually, coming back to dry land, I discovered a golf ball, then a candy wrapper, then the hole that the ball had never found. Then the caches appeared, and not far away, tent rings. I followed their lead back to the camp, and I never did meet the wolf that Mosesie knew waited on the distant horizon, beside the spring.

Among the things that people must know are how to read directions using the sounds of waves in the fog, or the shape of snowdrifts, or the stars. Adamie told me that the really knowledgeable can even recognize the four levels of waves that exist out on the waters, and they know how to navigate their way through them. They must know how to predict the weather, using the world around them. The clouds and the animals, the light and the winds, the ice and the plants, all have messages to tell the informed person.[90]

Edmund Carpenter describes how he has been out on the land with Inuit who are able to read signs that are invisible to him:

> By and large these are not actual objects or points, but relationships: relationships between, say, contour, type of snow, wind, salt air, ice crack. I can best explain this with an illustration: two hunters casually followed a trail which I simply could not see, even when I bent close to scrutinise it; they did not kneel to examine it, but stood back, examining it at a distance.[91]

Survival also depends on skill. I have been on an island in Hudson Bay and watched people fix broken propellers using their Coleman stove, rocks, and pliers. I have shuffled from side to side, stamping my feet and trying to keep warm on the sea ice as someone welded together a makeshift ski for a broken skidoo.

People must also know about the behaviour of animals, where they can be found, how to attract them. Once, when we were travelling by boat, I watched in amazement as Jamisie whistled to an eider duck flying away from us, high in the blue of an arctic sky. The duck, trapped by his call, did an about face and followed us until Jamisie stopped whistling and released it from its prison of sound. Another time, in the boat, we were looking for caribou. When eventually we spotted one, it stopped its grazing and looked up at us. Jamisie told us to raise our paddles over our heads to give the animal the impression that here were other caribou antlers so that it might not be alarmed. The hunt was successful. So people learn animals' habits and imitate them when hunting: honking to call down ducks and geese, or sliding on their stomachs over the spring ice in imitation of seals.

Sometimes, it is not knowledge about animals, but animals' knowledge, that ensures human survival. People know that if they watch animals closely, the animals will help them find food. During the summer, for example, when the Arctic char are out in the waters of Hudson Bay, people know that, when they see a flock of gulls or Arctic terns over the water, that is where they are likely to find char. Dogs are particularly shrewd; they know when there are polar bears about, and their barking warns people. Dogs also know how to find their way in a blizzard when humans are at a loss. They know routes they have taken in the past. Alurut, a man in his 50s, told me about sending a friend out to check his nets:

> I sent him out with my dog team telling him that, "Just follow; just follow them. You will get there." I used to have nets in the lake, and there was quite a few nets close together. I told him, "Just let them go there and they'll stop exactly where they are." He'd never gone there before. He didn't know. Only dogs know. So he got there. The dogs stopped there, exactly where my nets are, and when he finished, he went home with the fish. That's how the dogs are.

In observing the animals, in watching their behaviour, and in hunting and butchering them, Inuit learn a great deal about what they eat. In cutting up the animal, they learn whether it is healthy, what the animal has eaten, how old it is; they learn of its injuries and infestations, what to eat and what to leave aside.

I told an Inuk acquaintance about a misadventure of mine. It was lunch hour on a cold day in December, and I had gone alone to the spot where people get fresh drinking water. As in many Inuit settlements, although the houses in Puvirnituq have tanks that provide potable water, many people find that the water does not taste fresh, so they collect it from purer sources. The settlement and the roads around it were silent, held in the emptiness that takes over Arctic towns during lunchtime. I had many jugs to fill, and I was feeling quietly proud of myself for my initiative. Then I managed to get the Jeep stuck in a snowdrift. Knowing that no one would come to help me any time soon, I used all my ingenuity to devise a way out of it. When I finally arrived at the water spot, I found that snow had covered over the hole in the ice that people maintained to get the water. There was a small hummock of snow which suggested there was a hole underneath — hummocks of snow over open water are called *apputainaq* — but when I kicked at it, and my foot met solid ice. I kicked again, harder, but the ice did not give. I moved on to the next hummock and gave it a mighty wallop with my heel, and almost fell into the water. Some days later, mocking myself, I told this story to an acquaintance. He looked at me seriously and said, "You are learning. When you go out with people, you must always watch them closely."

This is how people get information and knowledge when they are out on the land. It is not taught in a linear, causal fashion. It is amassed slowly, over time, by observation, and by trial and error. Those who do not learn, go out at their peril.

One of the most subtle lessons I was taught by an Inuk friend involved something that took place far from the Arctic. Heading off for a working holiday, I complained about feeling frazzled. My friend told me that while I was there, I should go out and kill a goose; I should go out and find plants to eat. I responded that I had no need to, as the shop was just down the road. He replied, "No. Go out and *look* for it elsewhere." The process of getting food is as important as the product. It is not about having things under control, but about knowing and understanding what is there. From my perspective, it was the product that was of primary importance while the process fell into obscurity. Yet, as I have learned again and again in the North, process cannot be divorced from product. Much of what Inuit talk about when they discuss how to behave on the land reflects their recognition of this.

My friend went on to say that he had recently been out to pick springtime cranberries, the ones that appeared soft and full of taste after a winter buried under the snow. He said that he had found tent rings there, and there had been many of them. "It made sense that they were there," he said. I thought, *Here I am, living in a society that seems far removed from place. So many of the processes that govern the running of my society and the functioning of the economy — the "knowledge" economy — are beyond place.* The knowledge economy is an economy of exchange, not an economy of use. What is valued, in monetary terms, is predicated on activities that remove most of us from our place.

This sense of being removed from place, and the realization of the often unconscious knowledge that accompanies being in place, has periodically struck me while spending time in Inuit communities. Knowledge is not always something of which we are conscious, particularly if it is not formally taught, as is the case with much Inuit knowledge. The tradition of stepping back, identifying what one knows, identifying how to communicate it, and then doing so — which is at the heart of the Western system of education — is not generally part of Inuit tradition. Rather, people learn by observing and doing. This means that knowledge is not something outside oneself; rather, it becomes internalized and understood in innate ways. It is tacit knowledge.

This has important implications. First, people are not necessarily aware of what they know, particularly in the case of a people such as the Inuit who have been inundated with a whole new knowledge base, with new sets of skills and ideas about learning. Second, knowledge translates into action, both great and small, in ways we often do not even recognize. This came home to me most strongly while spending time on the land with people from Puvirnituq.

AUGUST 14, 2002: Just back from camping for a couple of weeks, and I find myself thinking about life out there under the skies of Hudson Bay. The only thing people seemed to worry about was the weather. Coming back to town was a real contrast. It has made me understand what Inuit have told me before: that they only feel truly themselves when they're on the land.

This difference between Inuit experience of life on the land and life in settlements seems most clearly discernible by differences in sleeping patterns. In town, many Inuit seem both to sleep a great deal and to approach paid employment very differently from their *Qallunaat* counterparts, who are far more driven. It really is a sign to me that life in town is lived according to the *Qallunaat* world, and people, being somewhat displaced in terms of how to operate in it, live accordingly.

In town, time and place are measured, controllable, and demarcated. The things Inuit know a lot about — the land, the animals — are not so valuable in a *Qallunaat* world. Imagine a whole society that is not *trained* for this life in town. People do not automatically fit into wholly different conditions. Knowledge about how to operate does not spring from nothing. Ways of being evolve, are taught and are learned, over time and in unconscious ways. When I was camping, I did not know what to do with the geese, caribou, and fish. I did not know how to move properly in a boat, how to remove fish from a net, how to prepare the food people had caught. I did not know how to skin an animal, eviscerate it, and cut through a joint. I did not know when to relax and when to take action. I did not know the rhythm of the day, and so could not focus or feel like a fully contributing and knowledgeable adult in comparison to the others who were with me. Somehow I imagine the inverse must be true for Inuit. What works in one environment, just did not in another.

THE KNOWLEDGE THAT PEOPLE HAVE DEVELOPED in order to survive on the land, the ways of being and operating that it engenders, are multifaceted and often unacknowledged. Yet for all that, many elements of this knowledge are discussed and compared among the Inuit. Whether it is over a cup of coffee, on the FM or short-wave radios, at the Co-op, or over the telephone, people exchange information about the things they have observed or done on the land. The location of animals, unusual behaviours, malformations in the animals people have caught, where they picked berries, the state of the ice, remarks about environmental conditions are all part of public discussion, and may be passed on from one person to the next. Such knowledge is ultimately common property and the sharing of it reflects a commitment to the well-being of society as a whole.

Health and Country Foods

Food is a requirement of human existence, but what we eat and how we eat are also very much related to how well we survive. For Inuit, at different levels, both physical and metaphysical, people's health was, and is, tied to country foods; they are a source of both spiritual and material well-being and nourishment.

Numerous studies have been done by non-Inuit about the health effects of eating country foods.[92] Although some research has focussed on the effects of contaminants in country foods and their concomitant impact on Inuit health,[93] on the whole, a great deal of the research has confirmed the fact that these foods are an important source of nutrition for Inuit. They have added health benefits, such as preventing heart disease.[94] But these studies simply confirm what many Inuit have always maintained: that theirs is the best food for them. Although these Western scientific studies are worthy, they take a perspective that is vastly different from Inuit understandings of the links between health and country foods.

Inuit have always been aware that their access to food was not guaranteed. Stories and personal experience of illness and starvation have not been forgotten. In fact, the name Puvirnituq may be linked to one such event. Its literal translation is, "Place where there is a Smell of Rotting Meat." There is some debate as to its meaning. Some say that the name comes from an accident in which many caribou were drowned and the smell came from their rotting corpses, while others claim that the smell was from a camp in which the families died of illness and there was no one left to bury the bodies.[95]

When food was scarce, people ate whatever they could find. This sometimes meant eating food that had washed up on shore, or that was left behind by animals.[96] I once met a man in Kangiqsualujjuaq whose family had vowed never to kill wolves. This was because in the past, they had been near starvation and come across some meat that wolves had left behind. That meat had saved their lives. In recognition of the gift, the family had sworn never to kill a wolf — an oath that was carried down through the generations.

Such stories are not restricted to pre-settlement times. As Jamisie's tale of near starvation during the measles epidemic in Puvirnituq suggests, even into the 1960s people were threatened with starvation if they could not find food. The first Catholic missionary in Puvirnituq recounts how, in the 1950s, he was pressed for time, trying to build a chapel and shelter for himself before winter set in. He had hired Inuit to help him in his task. At the first sign of passing animals, however, his employees dropped their tools and went hunting.[97] The money they were earning was of secondary importance to the immediate possibility of getting food.

Since that time, things have changed. Inuit rely more on imported foods, but at a fundamental level many people do not view it as wholly trustworthy. It is not truly healthy food, nor does it fill a person up properly or provide them with strength.[98] Many consider only country foods to be truly beneficial. Only country foods can really nourish people.

Particular foods have particular powers. In a place where the elements can kill, people remark that certain foods keep people warm. So ringed seal meat, particularly the blood and meat of a male in rut (*tiggaq*), keeps people warm, healthy, and strong.[99] Similarly, aged walrus meat (*igunak*) heats people so much that they start to sweat.

Some foods give the eater access to larger cosmic powers. Bernard Saladin d'Anglure recounts how a shaman was told that he might not eat lungs or heart until after he had developed his shamanic skills.[100] The heart animates the blood and is very powerful. Likewise lungs, which are involved in breathing, are full of *sila*. In consuming these foods only after gaining his shamanic powers, he was able to tap into the power of *sila* inherent in the foods. This may, in part, be the reason why Inuit talk about how their foods make them strong and lack of these foods makes them weak,[101] and why people remark of elders that it is only the meat from wild animals that truly satisfies their bodies, and store-bought food cannot be a replacement for them.

Certain foods and their by-products have been used to treat illness.[102] Lemming skins are used to treat boils. When I had a cough, people on the Belcher Islands told me I should eat raw blue mussels.

Although people are clear that country foods keep them healthy, there are times when these foods should not be eaten. There are restrictions on what pregnant women may eat. Although they are encouraged to eat country foods to ensure their own and the baby's health, they are also told to avoid certain foods. People on the Belcher Islands, for example, say that eating beluga flippers can cause malformations of the baby, and eating brains can cause the birth to be slow and arduous. Similarly, people on medication are judged to be fragile, and are discouraged from eating *igunak* (aged walrus meat), because it is a powerful meat that can react badly with medications.[103]

Certain foods are avoided not only because of the health of the people eating them, but also because of the health of the animal. People observe the physical condition of animals, and if they do not seem well, they avoid them. In extreme cases, unhealthy animals have killed people, as in the case of trichinosis, a disease that can affect walrus meat. Some years before my stay in Puvirnituq, people had killed a musk ox not far from town. This animal is extremely rare in the region, and so, one would think, something that would be desirable to eat out of curiosity. People noted, however, that it was not healthy, so some refused to eat it.

People's health and behaviour also has an impact on the animals. Apphia Agalakti Awa, a woman from the Igloolik area, talks about how in earlier times, if a woman miscarried or had her first menstruation, she ought not to tell anybody because then the animals might not come.[104] Awa also cautions that if humans mistreat animals, they, in turn, may suffer the consequences: a man who plucked a duck while it was still alive became covered in sores so that he seemed to be losing his skin.

Animals are also used as a metaphor for a person's health. I was speaking to my former landlady on the telephone after I had left Puvirnituq. I had been ill and unable to shake a cough that dragged on. In the midst of our conversation I was wracked with coughing. She said that I have a Canada goose cough, *nirliujaq.* "When I say this, we know exactly what kind of cough you have."

Food and the animals whence they come are an integral part of Inuit ideas about good health and ill health. As with so many things in the view of Inuit, to separate things, to perceive somehow that cause and effect are not interconnected in intricate ways, is absurd. What people eat and what they are cannot be separated.

Politics and Country Foods

My colleague Kooyoo, with whom I worked in Sanikiluaq, said to me on a July day in 1993 as we were looking out the windows of our office at the motorboats leaving from the harbour, "They should be fishing, not fighting." It was a sunny day with sparkling water and blue skies, the kind of day when anyone would feel pangs at working indoors while seeing others set off for a different world. We had been listening to the news on the radio. War was raging in Bosnia. Somalia was in tumult. Faced with the beauty of the day before us, and the knowledge that people were taking advantage of it to go hunting and fishing, the thought that people were fighting and dying anywhere seemed nonsensical. In a world in which all that seemed to matter was the weather and food, in a culture in which displays of anger are repugnant,[105] the thought that people should want to fight was incomprehensible. All the same, the Inuit world is not free of politics. Tensions over resources and their use exist both within Inuit society and in their dealings with non-Inuit.

In a society that functions based on communal access to resources, the ideal that all food is shared operates within an understanding that the animals that people catch are theirs to share as they choose. Thus, except in exceptional circumstances, people do not have the right to take from the nets or traps of others. If such rules are broken, Inuit habits of non-confrontation prevail, although the individual can eventually receive his or her just desserts. Adamie told me the story of a man who was stealing foxes out of somebody else's traps. Everybody knew about it, "but nobody ever told him because he is big enough, he is adult, he is supposed to have his sense." People knew he would face the consequences one day. Sure enough, when he was dying, people "could hear foxes crying coming out from his mouth."[106]

Although Inuit disapprove of stealing without cause, there are times when the theft of food is sanctioned. Nungak and Arima quote a man from Puvirnituq who tells the story of how once, when people were short of food, they visited a family that had lots of food. They were fed, but did not receive extra food for the people back in their camp who were hungry, so when they left, they stole food for the others. The narrator says this was acceptable, because the people were not treated properly; the hosts should have given food for the others.[107] In most cases, however, socially sanctioned norms and behaviours ensure that within Inuit communities, everyone has access to the foods they need.

It is in their dealings with the external world that Inuit have the greatest cause to be wary. As non-Inuit have moved into the Arctic, Inuit have had to learn how to negotiate their way through systems of understanding the world and how to behave in it that are not of their own making. They have learned something about how they are viewed by others. They have confronted animal rights activists and regulatory regimes that conform neither to their own way of understanding animals nor to their use of them.

When the animal rights movement rose to the fore in public opinion, and Brigitte Bardot helped to convince the world to save the seals, it had devastating effects on the trapping economy of the North.[108] Within a very short time people were no longer able to earn a living from trapping. When the European Union again moved to ban the sale of sealskins in 2008 and 2009, the market for Inuit-produced sealskins was threatened once more. Environmentalists are tarred with the same brush, and are viewed with distrust by many Inuit. Biologists can be perceived with similar misgivings. Their influence on the regulatory systems that affect what Inuit can and cannot hunt has long been a source of strife. In Greenland, Nunavut, and Nunavik, beluga populations have been a significant bone of contention between Inuit and non-Inuit regulatory systems.[109] The biologists argue that the populations are decreasing while the Inuit argue that the sampling methods used by the biologists are faulty: they come for too short a time, which means that weather conditions and other environmental factors are not taken into account; they go to the wrong places or sample in too limited an area; the noise of their boats frightens the animals away. From the perspective of many Inuit, the decisions made by state regulators who are influenced by biologists are deeply offensive.

At a basic level, the various disagreements exist because Inuit view animals in a fundamentally different way. The idea that the land and animals are there to be controlled by humans simply does not make sense from the perspective of most Inuit. As Jamisie explained,

> That's not in our nature . . . to try to own the wildlife. That's something that most Inuit don't like at all, that's somebody who says, "don't harvest this species; don't catch too many; don't go that way; don't go there." It's never been in our tradition and culture. We never had boundaries. And when they try to impose that, naturally, we get angered by this. It's like trying to put up a fence. That's when the problems started . . . in North America, and that's when the problems, the Range Wars started. . . . Because fences, naturally, make people angry. Even today there are wars over fences and boundaries. That's why there *is* war, because of boundaries and ownership to the land.

The regulation of wildlife is essentially the addition of one more invisible fence. These fences have profound implications for the way people use resources. Since the federal government imposed quotas on the beluga harvest in Nunavik in the 1990s, for example, people have had to travel vast distances to unknown waters to hunt in locations predetermined by the Department of Fisheries and Oceans. Sometimes they have been forced to go without, as happened in 2006 in Puvirnituq, because the quota had already been taken by other settlements. What has also happened, I have been told, is that since beluga meat has become scarcer because of the quotas, people are sometimes hiding their catch and not sharing it because they are afraid they will be punished by the authorities. In other instances, they fear they will be reported by people in their community who feel they have a grievance against them. What is most hard for many Inuit is that they are obliged to behave in abnormal ways to adhere to regulations that seem nonsensical. If a specific animal stock is part of a larger whole, it makes no sense to set up laws about methods and tools for hunting it without considering the animal in the larger context in which it lives.[110]

Economics and Country Foods

"Nobody's starving." Those were the words of a woman in Puvirnituq when I asked about welfare in the community. She pointed out that, while people may sometimes lack money, at least they do not lack food. Because everybody knows everybody, they tell people to come and get food from one another when they need it. Such sharing keeps body and spirit alive. Some have told me that, among Inuit, one is considered rich when one has something to eat.

Economics can mean different things to different people. At its most basic, it can mean basically ensuring that the essentials of life — food, shelter, and clothing — are provided for. At a more complex level, it involves the understanding of values and institutions that underpin the production, circulation, and consumption of goods that ensure people's survival. So economic systems entail both the physical manifestation of goods required for survival and the principles that identify why certain things have particular values over other things. These two ways of understanding — physical and epistemological — have expression in the economics of country foods.

Inuit have a logic internal to their understanding of country foods and their role in the world that governs how the food is produced and how it circulates and is consumed. Quantitative studies have been done that discuss the cycling of food in Inuit society. Some have focussed on energy flows, looking at inputs and outputs in the production of country foods.[111] Others have used money as a means of measuring the production, circulation, and consumption of country foods.[112] People measure, for example, the amount of food caught by Inuit and attempt to quantify its replacement value were they obliged to buy the food instead. Such studies have been done across Canada,[113] and they have all found that the monetary value of country foods in Aboriginal economies is vast. Heather Myers cites research on Holman Island in 1989, which found that hunters spent $1 million to produce $10.5 million worth of food.[114] The cost of replacing this food is beyond the reach of many people. Marcelle Chabot cites a study in Nunavik in 1993 that found that a family of four on welfare spent 86-93 per cent of its income (after rent) to feed itself on imported food.[115] Another study found in 2006 that food costs in Nunavik were, on average, 57 per cent higher than in Quebec City.[116] Clearly, country foods provide high-quality foodstuffs that people would otherwise be unable to afford were they obliged to buy something close to its equivalent in imported foods, which do not have equivalent values in non-monetary terms. An underlying economic rationale can be made that country foods make good sense from a numerical point of view. But such arguments present only half the picture.

Seen from a purely statistical perspective, the consumption of country foods relative to imported foods seems insignificant. Most of the food eaten by people in Nunavik is imported. In 1995, 85 per cent of the food eaten in Nunavik was store-bought, 2 per cent came from the Hunter Support Program, and 13 per cent came from outside the market — i.e., through sharing networks.[117] Moreover, a 1992 dietary study of food consumption in Nunavik revealed that younger people get 80 per cent of their energy from imported foods.[118] Chabot found that, on average, households in Nunavik spent $1,000 per month on imported foods, and the amount of these foods consumed is growing.

People's reasons for eating store-bought foods are many, from simply wanting variety in their diet to not having access to country foods. All this would suggest that imported foods are economically far more important to Inuit than country foods, and from a purely monetary perspective this might in fact be the case. Certainly, for most people in Nunavik, eating country foods is now more a matter of choice than a matter of necessity. As we have seen, however, many Inuit value country foods for reasons other than monetary.

Whether or not people consume imported foods, one cannot take this as a sign that they have ceased to set great store by country foods. Of the country foods that people do eat, generally little goes to waste: from the skin right down to the marrow of the bones. And those portions that are not eaten are often given to dogs, or may be used to make clothing or sleeping mats or household tools. While in Puvirnituq, I came to appreciate the superior qualities of brooms made from seagulls' wings.

At the same time, not all country food is created equal. There is a hierarchy.[119] One species may be economically significant in terms of how much it is actually consumed by people, but other species, such as beluga *mattak*, may be far more prized. Some foods have more symbolic than strictly economic significance.

Inuit across the North continue to spend time on the land. They continue to hunt, fish, trap, and gather country foods, and they continue to eat them. As Kublu said to me, "People go camping just to eat. They always come back fatter." Among Aboriginal peoples in Canada, Inuit have the highest consumption rates of country foods,[120] and Nunavik has the highest per capita consumption of country foods of all the regions in the Canadian Arctic, with an average of 284 kilograms per person per year.[121] Yet people are sorely aware that money gets drawn into the country food economy. It costs money to produce the food. This includes equipping oneself to go out on the land and providing the fuel and goods needed to be there. As Jamisie complained, it is "*very* expensive to go hunting. . . . My son went three days, and I had to buy him four hundred dollars of supplies. That's at least a hundred dollars a day, just to be out on the land. That's fuel, oil, parts, and food . . . not to mention the warm clothes that we have to buy every year."

Many people from Nunavik are aware that life in the North is expensive, and protest that they pay the highest prices and taxes of anyone in Canada. They complain that there is a double standard for them as compared to food producers in the South. Farmers can claim tax deductions for the equipment they buy to produce food, while Inuit, who use skidoos to hunt, are not only unable to claim this expense on their taxes, but must pay an added tax on the machines because the government deems them recreational vehicles.

Some people are no longer able to spend time on the land because they lack the funds. Yet many people find ways around that to ensure that they get country foods. One man mentioned that he would not go out by boat because it was less fuel-efficient than a skidoo, four-wheeler, or dog team, so he generally limits his hunting and gathering to these modes of transportation. Others, who lack the money to equip themselves, make arrangements to contribute some money or labour to those who do have the equipment in order to be able to accompany them on hunting or fishing trips. The fact that people may contribute financially to the hunter is simply a reflection of the modern necessity to have cash in order to produce country foods. People cobble together whatever means they can to be able to get that food, which they then share with others. Whatever money people do earn from the sale of country foods, they generally reinvest in the production of those foods. The goal of hunting, fishing, and trapping is not individual self-sufficiency, nor capital accumulation, but a continuous flow of goods and services.

In a study involving three communities in Nunavik, Chabot found that a small minority actually provides country foods for most of the population.[122] Many of these people do not have regular salaried work, but subsidize their hunting and fishing either by part-time work or through the contributions of family members. Otherwise, the majority of people hunt and fish only occasionally, when they have the time or the opportunity to do so.

Some contend that subsistence activities are now merely forms of leisure.[123] After all, people are eating less country food than they did in the past and are relying more on imported foods. Moreover, because of the need for money to equip themselves, those who have the time may not always have the money to hunt, and those who have the money may not have the time. The majority in Puvirnituq are now only able to go out on the land in the evenings, on weekends, or when they are on holidays. Otherwise, the necessities of money, the need to send children to school, the demands of a job, the draw of the comforts of houses, and the desire to be with others mean that people do not live on the land as they did before the 1960s. One might think, then, that these activities are of less importance, both economically and socially, than in the past. But Inuit are adamant that, for them, hunting, fishing, and gathering are not things they do only for fun. As Jamisie put it,

> When down South, when they talk about hunting or fishing, they automatically think about their holidays and the fun they are going to have. Just sport. It's like a baseball game. . . . But when you go to Native communities, we do it not to have any fun, we do it to eat, to survive. We always have, even though now we can order food and food comes from the South a lot now, but still, well over 50 per cent of our diet in the Inuit communities is off the land. . . . Hunting for us, it's not a game.

When they are out looking for food, people do not approach the activity with the relaxed, lackadaisical air of someone who is on a holiday. If there is no food in a particular area, they move on until they find it. Whenever people are able to, they head out looking for food. On weekends Puvirnituq can feel like a ghost town as everyone who is able goes out looking for whatever food happens to be in season and available. At the end of the day, after work or school, people leave the community with guns, fishing rods, or buckets in hand. There is a constant movement of people out of the community looking for country food. This is not for leisure. People are not doing this because they want to take it easy. They do it because ultimately, the food they produce is valuable to them, not just economically, but socially and even existentially.

Conclusion

It must have become apparent, in reading this chapter, that the divisions I have created are, at some level, arbitrary. Who is to say where society begins and environmental relations end? How is time separate from memory? How is land not also part of identity? And how is what people do on the land separate from what they put in their stomachs? These questions reveal precisely why country foods are important to Inuit. To separate the getting of country foods from the sharing and eating of them does not make sense. To separate these activities from the places they occur or the forces that shape these places is also nonsensical. They are all tied up together, and they are all part of the context in which the economics of country foods must be considered. Economics may allow people to calculate that x per cent eaten is worth y dollars, but the economics of country foods is also about things that are immeasurable and intangible. It is about time in place. It is about family and memory. It is about community. It is about health and politics. It is about knowledge and all that is needed to spend time in the world outside your house and beyond the boundaries of the settlement. It is about life and death.

All these things contribute to, and constantly rebuild, place and people's sense of themselves in it. They build up history and confirm memory. They help people affirm their knowledge and reinforce a sense of community. All these things are predicated on a system that stresses that the value of country foods is social rather than monetary. This emphasis on social value has allowed people to survive, and is at the root of how they make sense of themselves in place.

Economies may have physical manifestations, but at their root, they operate because of beliefs: they are only as sound as the beliefs that hold them together. Just as money can only exist if we believe it to have the value it purports to represent, so, at its root, the vernacular economy of Inuit, with its currency of country food, exists based on, and as long as, people maintain the set of beliefs that allow it to operate as it does. Given that the getting and eating of country foods are interwoven with layer upon layer of meaning and import in northern societies, and that at the root of these processes lies the sharing of food, what happens when money gets thrown into the equation? What does it mean to people when they start to see country foods being sold both in and outside their communities?

Heading to Kugaaluk

3
— – —

The Political Economy of Nunavik and the Commoditization of Country Foods

THE PROCESSES OF GETTING, SHARING, AND EATING country foods are central to the construction and experience of place, and they continue to maintain that order. Yet it would be foolish to think that these activities exist in a vacuum. People are not eternally waiting like patient hunters at the floe edge, frozen in space and time. Hunters in caribou skins with dog teams have given way to store-bought parkas and skidoos. They do not go out looking for food without gas in the tank, bullets in their guns, and the knowledge in their minds that there are regulations that ought to be respected. Although at one level country foods are constructed by and construct experience of place, that experience is affected by external forces, so that the iterative process this entails is, in some ways, both circular and spiral. If the previous chapter essentially looked at the circle, this chapter looks at some of the forces that propel the spiral.

Economic systems in the North do not operate in isolation, especially as the state has increased its presence there. Larger regulatory and political processes shape what people do and how they do it. Economic development is not so much an economic process as a political one,[1] so any market development involving country foods in the Arctic must be considered, in part, as the outcome of government policy. We need, then, to grasp the role that government policy and regulation have played in determining economic development in the Canadian Arctic in general and in shaping the commoditization of country foods in particular.

Government Approaches to Economic Development in the Canadian North

In the process of colonization, and later nation-building, the British and then the Canadian governments initially paid scant attention to the Arctic. As territory that had been ceded to the Hudson's Bay Company, it was little more than a blurry image at the edge of the country, left to the domain of traders and the odd missionary. Given what they perceived to be an inhospitable climate, colonizers had no wish to settle there. Governments viewed the Arctic as a hinterland whose raw materials they might draw upon as they wished.

Initially, then, traders were left to their own devices, and from the late 18th century, when they first started to move into Inuit territories, they served as the primary point of contact between Europeans and Inuit.[2] It was not until the late 19th century that the Canadian government started to make its presence felt in the North. In 1870 Canada bought the territories that had been under the domain of the Hudson's Bay Company, and in 1880 it was granted authority over the Arctic islands by the British. Thereafter, it began to assert control in the region by sending ships to patrol northern waters. These voyages were initiated because of concerns about sovereignty in the face of American and European whaling ships and explorers who were plying the lands and waters of the region. The Canadian government began sending ships and police to visit the northern territories and establish its rule over the area. As of 1922, the federal government sent the Eastern Arctic Patrol on annual tours of inspection. It was only later that, in addition to issues of sovereignty, the government became concerned about the plight of the Inuit.[3]

Stricken by diseases introduced by Europeans, and suffering from periodic food shortages, Inuit were at times in need of aid, a situation aggravated by the Depression, World War II, and the closure of trading posts. Trading companies in the Arctic had essentially operated on relationships of debt and dependence. Traders would give Inuit trappers advances at the start of the season which Inuit then had to pay off by the end of the season. Increasingly, traders were unwilling to carry Inuit debt; they felt they had been saddled with providing relief. In the 1920s the federal government started paying for this relief, which, given its limited presence in the North, generally continued to be delivered by traders, although missionaries also served this function.[4]

The "Eskimo problems," as the director of Northern Administration and Lands Branch called it, became a matter of increasing concern to the

Canadian government, and spawned much debate about who precisely had responsibility for addressing those problems and how they were to be addressed.[5] These issues were particularly contentious in Quebec, which had gained territorial responsibility for the area of what is now Nunavik as a result of the *Quebec Boundaries Extension Act, 1912*. Territory was one thing, but people were another. In Quebec, the federal and provincial governments each tried to avoid taking administrative and financial responsibility for the Inuit.[6] In 1939, the Supreme Court of Canada decided the matter: Inuit were legislatively deemed to be "Indians" and therefore fell under the purview of the federal government, which thus had official responsibility for their welfare. The answer to the second component of the debate — how actually to respond to the welfare needs of Inuit — was guided primarily by economics.[7]

Gradually — but not without debate — the government started to provide social transfer payments to Inuit, including Old Age Pensions and family allowance.[8] As with the "relief" payments, these were first disbursed through the Hudson's Bay Company. Later, the Royal Canadian Mounted Police took over the responsibility. Eventually, in the 1960s, Northern Service Officers moved in to administer these programs.[9] Concern about creating excessive dependence on the government purse and Euro-Canadian institutions became a recurring theme in the discussions about how to respond to Inuit needs; it was feared that too much reliance on social transfer payments caused a self-reinforcing cycle of "indolence" among the Inuit.[10] Such fears continue to be debated by various parties — Inuit and non-Inuit— in the North.

Between 1945 and 1951, when the government first started getting involved in northern development in earnest, the amount of money spent on relief to Inuit increased from $11,000 per year to $115,000, with a total for the period of $405,000. If family allowances are taken into account, the total outlay by the federal government was $1,687,000.[11] During much the same period, the price for foxes dropped from $25 to $5 per skin. In the Baffin Island-Ungava Bay area, 53 per cent of Inuit income came from government sources. By 1952, this had increased to 59 per cent, with only 28 per cent coming from earned income — the rest being in unrecoverable debt and relief issued by the Hudson's Bay Company.[12] This trend continued. Between 1965 and 1975, public expenditures on the administration of the North increased tenfold.[13] Various levels of government felt the need to improve the situation, in part to ensure that Inuit needs would not increase the drain on public coffers. How this was to be accomplished, however, was not obvious.

During the 1940s and early 1950s, the approach of the federal government was to promote traditional Inuit activities. This led to the "strategic neglect" of Inuit, based on the belief that it would promote their independence.[14] In 1952, the federal government set up the Committee on Eskimo Affairs whose main goal was to determine how Canada intended to fulfil its responsibilities vis-à-vis the Inuit.[15] As the invitation to the organizational meeting of the committee put it,

> The basic issue seems to be this, are we to regard the Eskimo as fully privileged economically responsible citizens with the right to spend his income as he pleases, or are we to regard the Eskimo as backward people who need special guidance in the use of their income. . . . I personally feel that if we are realistic we must consider the Eskimo to be in the second category.[16]

The committee's first conclusion was to encourage Inuit to live off the land and follow a traditional way of life. Shortly thereafter, in seeming contradiction of this position, Prime Minister Diefenbaker introduced the New National Policy that was to be implemented between 1957 and 1963 and intended to give private enterprise access to northern resources.[17]

Camped at Qapirquktuuq in July

With this in mind, the federal government published fifteen area economic surveys between 1958 and 1967.[18] These surveys were designed to assess the renewable and non-renewable resource bases of the North, and identify the potential and present means of exploitation of those resources. Part of the goal was to suggest how Inuit could use resources more effectively and at the same time tap into their unused potential. Generally, the surveys came up with three conclusions: first, to expand non-renewable resource exploitation by non-Inuit; second, to expand capital investment in such things as airfields, telephones, education, and health services; and third, to improve the harvesting of renewable resources with an eye to improving the lot of the Inuit — for example, by encouraging the harvesting of eider down and the development of tourism, crafts, and commercial fisheries, lumbering, and blueberry picking.[19] There was clearly an interest in promoting commercial ventures related to country foods.

At the same time, in the late 1950s and early 1960s, Inuit were persuaded to move into settlements — sometimes with a carrot, sometimes with a stick. Inuit speak of being told they had to put their children in schools in order to receive the family allowance, for example, and rather than lose their children, the family moved to a settlement. Sedentarization had a number of immediate effects, including increased dependence on the state and increased reliance on motorized vehicles in order to get to now-distant harvesting areas. These greater distances were not only because, for some, the areas with which they were familiar were far from the settlements in which they now lived, but also because, with people concentrated in one area, local resources were soon exhausted, so people had to travel further afield to get them. Another impact of sedentarization was that it drew Inuit into the Euro-Canadian school system. This was by design, since, by the reckoning of the state, Inuit might there learn the skills necessary to take up wage employment.[20] As one Northern Affairs Department projects officer saw it,

> Their true hope for survival is through education. As the caribou and other game dwindle, their hunting skills are dwindling, and they simply cannot live as they used to. They depend more and more on store-bought goods, and their kids, through lack of training, won't be as good hunters as their fathers were. All we can expect to do with the present flock of youngsters; because the time has been so short, is to teach them English — or possibly French, in the French-speaking areas of Canada — and the three "R"s.[21]

The belief that Inuit hunting skills are dwindling has been a recurring theme in the discourse of Euro-Canadians. Given this perception, it is natural to assume they should be replaced with the skills provided by a Euro-Canadian education. The goal in providing this education was, and is, to enable Inuit to look after themselves in the context of a modern, market economy.

The Political Economy of Nunavik

"Born to Hunt, Forced to Work." I saw these words printed on the t-shirt of a man in Puvirnituq. The t-shirt was meant to be worn by a thwarted deer-stalker in the South, but the man in Puvirnituq who was actually wearing it had likely been among the last generation of Inuit to be born when people were more on the land than in communities, and among the first generation of people who, with the move to settlements, had learned the skills required for him to get a job. He really was born to hunt and forced to work.

And work he did, when it was available and he was able. The words on his t-shirt revealed a fundamental misconception: that somehow hunting and work-ing are two separate things. Today, some Inuit are considered "unemployed," negating the traditional and necessary employment of hunting, fishing, trap-ping, and gathering, and the activities associated with them. In that single term, "unemployed," an entire economic form has been swept aside, subject to ideas that cannot see hunting and work as one and the same thing. And so people get misplaced. They are swept into a gulf of ignorance and misunderstanding. When the Puvirnituq man appeared at a community feast wearing the t-shirt, some pointed and laughed, appreciating the irony of the words.

Inuit occupy, at best, a marginal position in the world of wage labour and the world of money that comes with it. According to the statistics that measure their potential to participate in these things, and in comparison to the province of Quebec as a whole, the Inuit face some challenges. Of the 10,000 Inuit living in Nunavik, who represent about one-quarter of the Inuit population of Canada, 63 per cent are under the age of 30.[22] In 2002, the high school graduation rate in Nunavik was 33 per cent, compared to 71 per cent across Quebec, while the "unemployment" rate hovered around 15 per cent, compared with 9 per cent province-wide.[23] Between 1987 and 1994, the youth suicide rate was twenty times greater in Nunavik than in the rest of the prov-ince.[24] Behind these numbers are many stories about how people in Nunavik manage to survive, and how they make sense of themselves in a world geared for wage labour rather than hunting, fishing, and gathering.

Northern economies face numerous difficulties. Immense transportation costs make life expensive. In the short season when northern waters are navigable, sealift boats bring bulky items to settlements across the Canadian North. During the rest of the year, goods must be flown in. In 2006, a comparison of costs in Nunavik with those in the region of Quebec City found, among other things, that food was 57 per cent more expensive in Nunavik and accounted for more than 40 per cent of household budgets.[25] People in the North know that life is more expensive, and they resent it. They know that when they pay the Goods and Services Tax, they are paying more than others because the costs of the goods are higher to begin with. Given that, in 2001, the median income of families was $39,328 in Nunavik compared to $50,242 for the province of Quebec, and given that families in Nunavik are larger than in Quebec, with an average in 2001 of 5.0 individuals compared with 3.1 individuals for the province as a whole, families in Nunavik have less money to spend on more people for goods that are more expensive.[26]

The options are limited for making money in the North, and people are subject to decisions made elsewhere, so northern economies are extremely vulnerable to changes caused by external forces. The region has already felt the impact of one such turn in its economic tides. In the past, economic development of the North was based on the fur trade. In the 1980s, with the boycott of seal skins by the European Union, the monetary economies of northern settlements collapsed.[27] According to the government of the Northwest Territories, 18 out of 20 Inuit communities lost more than 60 per cent of their yearly income following the demise of the fur trade.[28] In 1978, Inuit earned $320,000 from the fur trade; by 1991, eight years after the EU ban, they earned $47,000 from the same trade.[29] Having felt the shock once, people in northern communities make money where they can. This includes guiding for tourists or people working on mining exploration, working at outfitting camps, working for public and private agencies, selling arts and crafts, bootlegging, rummage and bake sales, raffles, bingo, lotteries and gambling over cards, going to the dump to get things that may be re-used, renting rooms to visitors, going to meetings or taking a course for which they receive an honorarium, stealing, selling their possessions, exchanging skills — for example, one person does income tax returns and gets mittens in exchange — and even prostitution.[30] Such forms of bricolage allow individuals to make ends meet.

As the policy of introducing salaried work took hold, people's incomes increased. In Nunavik in 1966, the per capita income was $426; in 1973 it was $1,288; in 1983 it was $15,596.[31] By 1983, salaried jobs were the primary source of money for Inuit in Nunavik. The majority of jobs are in the public sector, accounting for 53.7 per cent of full-time employment in 2005.[32] At the same time, income from social transfer payments has also increased; in fact, it grew more than salaries.[33] In 1993, approximately 60 per cent of working-age Inuit were "unemployed" for most of the year, with underemployment affecting many others.[34] Increased transfer payments are a reflection of the fact that, as the population grows, there are increasing numbers of people of working age compared to the number of jobs available. People's access to jobs has been negatively affected by the demand for credentials whose terms of reference are set by the non-Inuit world.

As the rule-bound system of judging competence to hold a job based on official measures of qualification has moved into the North, Inuit have been unable to qualify for jobs that they would be more than capable of filling. Twice while I was in Puvirnituq the electrical wires were accidentally disconnected, cutting off power to much of the settlement. Despite the fact that there were people in town who had the skills to fix the problem, we were forced to await the arrival of an officially sanctioned person from the South to come and repair the wires. This has led some to feel that the standards discriminate against Inuit.[35] But, as Jamisie pointed out, the hegemony of Euro-Canadian systems of knowledge, and the emphasis on southern ideas of who is and is not qualified, has far more disturbing implications:

> I don't consider myself a drop out. Yes, I dropped out of learning the *Qallunaaq* tradition and culture, but I didn't drop out of learning my own traditional culture. Many of the people my age went all the way, and then they came back and they couldn't work, because they didn't know enough Inuktitut, or they have lost their culture and tradition. They lost their self-esteem. And they were shy. They didn't know how to live here any more. Many have died from depression and alcoholism, and so on. And now their children, the next generation, is even *more* confused. Because *these* people have lost their values, traditional values, and traditional knowledge, which is still very essential here in the North.

As a result of the changes people have lived through, the displacement they have experienced, there are some who are unable to participate in either the vernacular or the market economies — people for whom welfare has become the only form of living they know. People in the North have mixed feelings about welfare. Some view it as necessary, ensuring, at least, that people are not starving. Others see it as crippling initiative and independence. The question is, what alternatives do they have? "We can't very well get rid of dinner when there's no other dinner to be found," Jamisie told me.

Given the difficulties in finding work, and the limited numbers of jobs available in the North, the government is encouraging the development of private enterprise. In 1991, 1.5 per cent of the population earned money from the private sector.[36] By 2005, 37 per cent of full-time jobs were from private business and the Co-ops.[37] Were the Co-ops to be removed from these figures, the number would drop considerably.

Marcelle Chabot notes that, with all these changes in the northern economy, the vernacular economy has lessened in importance. She calculates that, in 1995, 5 per cent of the active population of Nunavik earned a living from hunting and fishing, for a total of 222 people in the region — or, on average, approximately 15 people per village.[38] The people who are participating in hunting, fishing, and gathering appear to be the older members of the community, with the youth showing less commitment to these activities.[39]

Gwen D. Reimer found that there is a gap in the perception of economic processes between the young and the old, with the former seeing cash as the basis of all economic activity while the latter retain a place for subsistence activities in their understandings of economic processes.[40] Richard G. Condon, Peter Collings, and George Wenzel also found divisions in the perceptions of the different generations, with young men placing little emphasis on subsistence production.[41] Some to whom I have spoken challenged this view, saying that young men, in particular, were increasingly interested in spending time on the land, but felt shy about their lack of skills and wished only for the opportunity to develop them by spending time on the land. Jamisie pointed out that, like anything else, there are those who are good at it and interested in it, and those who are not:

> There *are* young ones [who go hunting]. Yes. Those who try. Those who turn off the TV in the morning and do things. Those are the people who go places. It's like all over the world, there are people who prefer not doing hard things and there are people who are active. Those are the ones who *learn*. Those are the *providers* in the community.

Those who are interested do find ways to participate in hunting, fishing, trapping, and gathering when the opportunity arises, accompanying friends and relatives, borrowing equipment, and periodically going hunting and fishing as a paid activity.

From the Eskimo Affairs Committee in 1952 to the Royal Commission on Aboriginal Peoples in 1996, the idea that Inuit should be encouraged to use their traditional economy as a means of promoting economic development has been a recurring theme.[42] As a Royal Commission publication put it, economic development "is about maintaining and developing culture and identity; supporting self-government institutions; and sustaining traditional ways of making a living."[43] In the belief that it makes sense to draw on people's skills and use the resources of an area as a means of earning much-needed money, governments have gone about promoting the commoditization of country foods in the Canadian Arctic.

The Commoditization of Country Foods among Inuit: An Overview

Until recently among most Inuit in Canada, country foods have continued to circulate based on the principles of sharing that are central to their vernacular economy. As a result, the commoditization of country foods in the Canadian Arctic has historically been limited to exchanges between Inuit and non-Inuit. Inuit worked for European and American whalers during the 19th and early 20th centuries, providing country foods to ships' crews and traders. Commercial whaling and fisheries began off Baffin Island in the 1820s,[44] while in Nunavik, the Hudson's Bay Company had commercial fisheries in Kuujjuaq and whaling from Kuujjuaraapik as of 1900.[45] Ungulates were incorporated into the market economy in the first half of the 20th century. In the 1930s, the Canadian government imported reindeer herds from Alaska to the Mackenzie Delta, planning to raise them for both domestic use and export.[46] There was also the practice, which continues today, of selling country foods to itinerant non-Inuit who passed through the area.[47] Throughout these processes, however, many Inuit managed to maintain a distinction between their vernacular economy and the market economy, sharing food among themselves and selling mainly to non-Inuit.

After Inuit moved to settlements, the processing and selling of country foods for export as well as local consumption seemed like a good idea to government. Not only would it provide much-needed cash, it had the additional potential of alleviating intermittent shortfalls of food while providing desirable alternatives to the unhealthy and expensive imported foods that Inuit were eating in increasing quantities.[48] Accordingly, the federal government developed the Specialty Foods Program in 1960 to sell tinned country foods.[49] It also used the burgeoning co-operative movement to provide a mechanism for the production and sale of country foods.[50] These schemes did not meet with success. Perhaps it was because Inuit felt able to produce this food themselves, or perhaps it was because they were simply mystified by the prospect of tinned country foods, or perhaps it was because they were loath to sell food to one another. In any case, a domestic market for country foods did not develop.

Programs have also been developed to encourage the export of country foods on a larger scale, either in the form of inter-settlement trade in Nunavut and Nunavik or in the form of sales to southern markets. Early on, the federal government encouraged the co-operatives in Nunavut and Nunavik to sell such goods as Arctic char or sealskins to southern markets. In Nunavik, projects were developed in what was then called George River (Kangiqsualujjuaq), Port Burwell (Killiniq), and Fort Chimo (Kuujjuaq) in the late 1950s and early 1960s.[51]

Ironically, government efforts to commoditize country foods have been hindered by legal forces created by government. Regulations that limit who may harvest what, where, and when effectively promote the view that Inuit harvesting of animals should be limited to subsistence production. These regulations exist at all levels. In the name of conservation, international regulations such as the Convention on International Trade in Endangered Species of Wild Fauna and Flora, the *Migratory Birds Act*, and the International Whaling Commission either limit or prevent the harvesting of and commercial trade in various Arctic animals. National and provincial regulations define such things as processing standards to safeguard public health, but in the North, where animals are migratory and infrastructure is limited, meeting these standards is prohibitively expensive. Regional regulations — defined, for example, by the James Bay and Northern Quebec Agreement (JBNQA) — limit who may harvest what and to what ends. Under the original terms of the Agreement, with the exception of commercial fisheries, only officially registered beneficiaries were permitted to buy and sell country foods.[52] In addition, the JBNQA defines a hierarchy of harvesting rights, with personal use by beneficiaries being the most important, followed by harvesting by communities (again for consumption by the beneficiaries), followed by harvesting by outfitting camps that allow people from outside of Nunavik to hunt and fish in the region. Non-beneficiaries who go to these camps are only allowed to harvest and export country foods from the territory if they have sport and export permits or they have bought country foods that have been sold with commercial tags and that have met government standards of slaughter and processing. The net effect is that, legally, the commercial sale of country foods is severely restricted. Given these regulations, one cannot help but assume that any efforts to commoditize country foods would essentially be limited to the domestic market.

Forms of Commoditization in Nunavik

International, federal, provincial, and regional regulations have effectively limited the commoditization of country foods in Nunavik. What commercial processes do exist fall into three categories.

First, a limited number of individuals in Nunavik sell country foods commercially. Their operations have tended to be sporadic, piecemeal, and problematic, as it proves difficult for the animal populations to sustain such operations. Arctic char and salmon have been particularly prone to over-fishing. For this reason, at various times, fisheries have had to be shut down in Kuujjuaq, Kangiqsualujjuaq, and Kangirsuk.[53] Further, it is difficult to meet government processing regulations, and the costs due to the lack of infrastructure and transportation can prove prohibitive. For example, in the 1990s in Inukjuaq a local resident tried to develop a joint venture with a Japanese company for the sale of caribou, but it was unsuccessful. Although it met federal regulations, it was unable to make money because of high freight costs and competition from cheaper meats raised in the South.[54]

The second form of commoditization of country foods in Nunavik has been undertaken by the Makivik Corporation, an agency owned by registered beneficiaries under the JBNQA. Makivik is charged, among other things, with managing the funds received by Inuit in return for signing the JBNQA. Part of its goal is to turn a profit with the funds received under the Agreement while promoting development that benefits its largely Inuit membership. It has commercial fisheries operations, and it tried unsuccessfully in the 1990s to establish an inter-community country foods trade project within Nunavik.[55] The idea of inter-community trade was permitted, and therefore indirectly promoted by the JBNQA. At first glance, trade that aims not to maximize production or profits but to supplement exchanges in the domestic economy seems an appropriate form of northern development, since it would merely adapt ideas of sharing rather than replace them. At the same time, it would avoid the conflicts over resource use that can arise from export to faceless markets in the South. Given that northern animal populations are not farmed, large-scale commercial developments of country foods might threaten the long-term viability of the populations for domestic use. No doubt it was for these reasons that, when the JBNQA was signed in 1975, it permitted the possibility of intra and inter-community trade, but, apart from fisheries, precluded the possibility of trade for export.

The failure of the project was owing to a number of factors. In part, it was the challenge of meeting government processing standards in the context of a population of wild animals that is constantly on the move. In addition, communities were concerned about the ability of the caribou to sustain a commercial hunt. In any case, Makivik had difficulty getting a sufficient supply of meat from local hunters. These last two factors suggest that the majority of hunters were placing more importance on domestic rather than commercial production. With a limited number of hunters providing the majority of food in any given community, their commitment appears to have been to produce for, and distribute via, sharing mechanisms rather than the market. Market production also emphasizes convenience while masking the fact that the need for convenience is born either from lack of time, owing to people's participation in wage labour, or lack of access to the goods one needs. In Makivik's view, inter-community trade would appeal to the people of Nunavik because it would allow them to have portions of meat that were manageable rather than having to cut off pieces from a larger section of the animal, which is how animals are normally butchered. This may have been a faulty assumption, however, for people are not yet as removed from the processes of production and consumption characteristic of the vernacular economy that they would buy meat that they could otherwise get for free.

With the end of the inter-community trade project in 1998, Makivik focussed its attention on selling country foods to export markets.[56] Although the project is ongoing, it has been problematic, and has yet to be sustained over the long run since it has to confront the perennial problems of meeting processing regulations, carrying expensive transportation costs, contending with the inconstancies of a migratory herd, and finding and keeping regular, trained employees.[57]

The third form of commoditization of country foods in Nunavik is through the Hunter Support Program (HSP).[58] Created as part of the James Bay and Northern Quebec Agreement, the HSP's goal is "to favour, encourage and perpetuate the hunting, fishing and trapping activities of the beneficiaries as a way of life and to guarantee Inuit communities a supply of the produce from such activities."[59] Thus, it is designed to support both the production and the consumption of country foods, thereby also aiming to avoid the economic marginalization of hunting.[60] Each community in Nunavik receives funding based on its population. Similar programs were established for Cree[61] and Inuit in Nunavut following the signing of the JBNQA,[62] but each operates differently with quite different budgets and modes of delivery. The program in Nunavut is the poor cousin of the lot, receiving limited funding that is not indexed to population. The programs established under the JBNQA, in contrast, have guaranteed funding in perpetuity, with increases based on population. All the same, in comparison to the Cree program, the HSP in Nunavik is less well funded; it covers, on average, 20 per cent of the costs of production, while the other 80 per cent must be found elsewhere.[63]

Each municipality in Nunavik receives HSP funds to support activities that take place on the land, such as subsidizing people for materials to help people to hunt, training young people for spending time on the land, and buying country foods.[64] In practice, this generally means that each municipality pays hunters who are not otherwise employed to supply the community with meat on an intermittent basis. The municipality is then responsible for distributing the country foods to registered beneficiaries under the JBNQA. Although the meat is paid for, and thus has a monetary value, it is not bought by individuals. The HSP's food represents a hybrid — part sharing and part commodity — for it is neither truly involved in market exchange nor truly a reflection of the sharing that has been central to the vernacular economy of Inuit.

Conclusion

How are we to understand all of this? How are we to comprehend the forces of commoditization in the larger context of northern development, not in terms of policy but in terms of reality lived by particular people in a particular place? This is the question I explore in the coming chapters.

As they have settled into fixed communities over the past fifty years or so, Inuit have experienced enormous changes in their ways of living. They have had to adjust not only to changes in the spaces they occupy, but in how they go about occupying those spaces. The commoditization of country foods appears to be a good way of building an economic future on the foundation of customary ways of living. It would appear to mitigate some of the economic challenges people face.

Yet, as I have argued, the getting, sharing, and eating of these foods serve more than simply economic ends: they build place, sustain community, establish identity, help people to maintain a sense of themselves through time, foster the development of knowledge, and determine people's understandings of their relations with the natural world.

In the selling of country foods, there is an encounter between two ways of understanding and operating in the world. One is the world of place and movement, of uncontrollable forces that determine one's survival. It is a world in which things are eternally changing, all is becoming, and the job of humans is to understand and learn to live within the flux of time and the elements. It is a world in which these forces have been alleviated by social systems predicated on respect and responsibility to others that is expressed in sharing. As the environment shares its bounty with humans, so they, in turn, share that bounty with one another.

The other world is contained in the settlements that have sprung up across the North. This world assumes a level of permanence and control over the elements. It relies on predictability to ensure one's means of survival. Once the elements have been understood, they can be tamed to the extent that humans can stay put, have shelter, food, drink, and clothing, as well as other, non-essential things that have become part of life in settlements. The medium by which these things are gained is money. By whatever means it is secured, it pays for the houses, the food, the water, the clothing, and all the other conveniences of life. Flux gives way to permanence and becoming gives way to being.

Of course the world inside settlements is not wholly separate from the world outside them. These two worlds seem essentially different in some of the assumptions that underlie them, but it would be overly simplistic to assume that life in towns exists in a bubble, that the world out there has not found a place in northern settlements. Life for Inuit is not a question of assimilation versus tradition. Rather, it is about the ways in which people have managed to combine things to create hybrids. In the selling of country foods, the world outside the settlement confronts the world inside the settlement. The ethics and behaviours that govern the two meet, sometimes collide, and then come to some sort of adjustment.

4

— – —

Sold Down the River:

THE BUSINESS OF COUNTRY FOODS IN PUVIRNITUQ

History, Economy, and Society

PUVIRNITUQ IS ON THE PUVIRNITUQ RIVER (see map on follopwing page), not far from the river's outlet into Hudson Bay. Like most northern settlements, the site was chosen because of its proximity to trading posts, but the history of human occupation here pre-dates the arrival of the posts by millennia. The surrounding area has long been a source of sustenance to the Inuit and Tuniit (or Dorset people) who preceded them. It is rich with memories and signs of the past. It is a history that lives in the stories told by people through the generations, although most non-Inuit see the history of Puvirnituq as beginning with the arrival of European traders.

The history of contact between Inuit and non-Inuit echoes that of European incursions into the Arctic generally. Such incursions moved like a slow tide across the North, leaving what it touched profoundly altered as, little by little, Inuit were drawn into the non-Inuit economy. In the early 19th century, Inuit around Puvirnituq had limited contact with non-Inuit, seeing them when whalers came through or during their yearly visit to the Hudson's Bay Company trading post at Little Whale River, several hundred kilometres to the south.[1] By the end of the 1800s, however, Inuit were increasingly being drawn into the trading economy.

A number of circumstances conspired to bring this about. At the turn of the 20th century, the caribou population fell dramatically, and people turned increasingly to fox trapping in order to buy imported foodstuffs.[2] Consequently, they became more reliant on the trading posts, bearers of what Jean-Jacques Simard calls "mercantile colonialism."[3] At first, people travelled to Little Whale River, but traders eventually set up posts closer to Puvirnituq. The literature does not wholly agree on the dates, but the accounts of the trading posts in the area indicate that Révillon Frères opened a post in about 1910, while their competitors at the HBC moved into the area later, establishing posts in 1920, 1921, and 1927.[4] In 1936, the HBC bought out Révillon Frères and became a monopoly. The HBC did not stay in one place, but opened and closed its posts as circumstance dictated, moving between what is now called Akulivik (then Cape Smith) and Puvirnituq. So the Inuit, who came only periodically to the post — primarily to trade, but also for special events such as the arrival of the supply boat, or for Christmas or Easter — moved with it.

With a trading post more conveniently at hand, Inuit were more disposed to rely on the goods they might get from it. This, in turn, transformed the migration cycles of the people, who were less inclined to travel inland in search of food.[5] Until the 1950s, people mostly lived in camps at the mouths of the rivers that flow into Hudson Bay, venturing inland to trap and hunt

Location of Puvirnituq

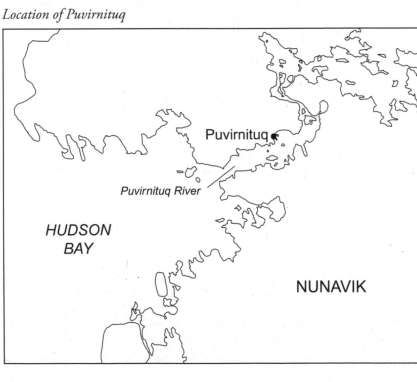

according to the seasons.[6] It was only in the 1950s that people started to congregate near the trading post in what was to become the village of Puvirnituq, although Monique Vézinet's maps of Inuit camp locations in Nunavik from 1900 to 1945[7] suggest that the process of centralization had been gradually taking place for some time. According to Simard, in 1932 the Inuit of Puvirnituq made their last seasonal migration inland.[8] Thereafter, they only went for short trips, often leaving the women and children behind. During this period, trapping increased, and Inuit became increasingly reliant on the trading post for medical treatment, petty justice, intermittent wage employment, credit, and relief in periods of scarcity.

The 1940s and 1950s was a time of crisis for the Inuit of Puvirnituq. The caribou had almost completely disappeared, and seals and other food species were also in decline. In addition, the HBC was progressively withdrawing from the fur trade. The amounts paid out in relief in northern Quebec were higher than in any other Inuit region,[9] reflecting the fact that northern Quebec, having been more deeply integrated into the fur trade, felt the consequent effects of its retrenchment all the more.

Not only was it difficult to get country foods, but people were earning less from trapping, which meant they could not buy imported food to fill the gap. It was a time of great hunger. There are stories of a man and several children starving to death in about 1945, and in 1955 some were begging for food and feared starvation.[10] Tuberculosis was having an impact as well; in 1956 more than one-third of the population had been sent south for treatment.[11]

Aware of the scarcity of food, health issues, and falling income from the fur trade — and compounded by a desire to promote resource development — the Canadian government moved into the Arctic. It encouraged Inuit to congregate in villages all over the North. This brought with it increased access to, and reliance on, government services and other institutions of the non-Inuit world. Between 1952 and 1962, all the camps between Port Harrison (Inukjuaq) to the south and Kettlestone Bay (around Akulivik) to the north of Puvirnituq were abandoned.[12] A settlement was first established at Kangirsurjuaq (or Shallow Bay), about ten kilometres south of Puvirnituq's present location. It was moved when people found that the large ships that supplied the North were unable to enter the river. In 1952 the new location was chosen.

At first, the only buildings belonged to the Hudson's Bay Company, but the government built a school in 1958 and a dispensary in 1960.[13] A Roman Catholic missionary built a chapel there in 1956,[14] followed by an Anglican in 1962. Otherwise, there were only a few houses, with tents scattered here and there. As Taamusi Qumaq puts it, although the Inuit started to live in houses when the non-Inuit first arrived in Puvirnituq, they did not *really* start to live in houses until the 1960s.[15]

As the physical circumstances in which people lived changed, so, too, did their societal ones. With increased centralization, people were brought together to live on a scale they had not experienced before. Two families had generally used the area around Puvirnituq, but, with centralization, people came to settle from other locations. Asen Balikci notes that, when people first moved to Puvirnituq in the early 1950s, there had been five camps based on extended kin groups and functioning as economic and religious units, each with its own lay preacher, camp leader, and boat captain in charge of the communal Peterhead boats. On arrival at the settlement, they clustered their tents according to these pre-established groups, so that when Balikci was doing his fieldwork in 1958 these camps were the social units within which country foods were shared. Balikci argues, however, that the camp settlement patterns were breaking down as people started to rely on income from family allowance, carving, and casual employment.[16] As a result, social structures and power relations were changing. The nuclear family was becoming the most important social unit for the acquisition, distribution, and consumption of food, taking the place of the traditional patterns of sharing that had involved all members of a given camp prior to sedenterization. At the same time, people were developing new group identities based on the trading posts where they settled.[17] Those who traded in Port Harrison (known today as Inukjuaq) to the south of Puvirnituq became known as Port Harrison Eskimos while those who settled near the HBC in Puvirnituq became known as Puvirnituq Eskimos — this despite the fact that there were long-standing familial links between the two populations. Doubtless such appellations were used for administrative purposes, but Balikci does not indicate whether these new identities were self-imposed or used only for the benefit of non-Inuit authorities. People from Cape Smith moved to Puvirnituq in the mid-1950s because of the government-sponsored surveys for tuberculosis that were taking place across the Eastern Arctic, when many people were being sent to southern sanatoria.[18] At much the same time, the HBC in Cape Smith closed, leaving only the post at Puvirnituq open.[19] In 1975, many of the families from Cape Smith moved back to their old hunting grounds to live in the new settlement of Akulivik; however, the links between the communities remain. Although Inukjuaq and Akulivik feature large in the extended families of people in Puvirnituq, social and kin relations spread throughout the region, up and down the Hudson Bay coast, across the Ungava Peninsula and across the water to the Belcher Islands and Baffin Island. These social links among communities continue to influence life in Puvirnituq, including the movement and sale of country foods.

With the centralization of Inuit, the population of Puvirnituq increased exponentially. In the early 1950s, when people were living in camps, there were approximately 30 people in each camp: a core *ilagiit*, or family group, along with other unrelated people who had married into the group or chosen to associate themselves with it. Given that there were five such camps,[20] there were approximately 150 Inuit inhabitants in the settlement when it first came into being. The population has grown steadily, with an almost tenfold increase between 1952 and 2006. Birth rates have also been steadily increasing, with a bulge in the younger population of 860 people under the age of 25 in the 2006 census (see Appendix 2).

Puvirnituq is a regional service centre, which means that there is also a significant, largely itinerant non-Inuit population working primarily for the various services located in the town, such as the school and the hospital. Although some of these people are long-term residents with committed links to the community, many are there for a short time only. They bring with them behaviours and assumptions that reflect their transience, and their presence has exerted a powerful influence on the community. Although some of the non-Inuit have made friends with, or married, Inuit in the settlement, for others, the kinds of isolated and parallel existence that Hugh Brody so effectively described in the 1970s[21] continue to exist today, with Inuit and non-Inuit communities living side by side but meeting only occasionally outside the work setting, each with different ways of understanding and behaving in the world. Jamisie lives next door to the Northern (formerly known as the HBC) staff house:

> And they change staff every four months, so every four months we have new neighbours. . . . Some are quite friendly. But some weren't. Like my next-door neighbour, she's living there since three months now. I see her all the time; I don't even know her name. There are people like that. They only come here to make money. . . . She has a pet, eh? A dog. I think our dogs know each other more than we do.

To ignore one's neighbour, or treat one's dog as offspring — Jamisie heard her call it "Baby"— seem preposterous from an Inuit perspective. So people have had to accept the ways of the *Qallunaat*, and tolerate, for the most part, that they function according to a different set of principles and beliefs, which can seem ridiculous at times, or truly annoying. For some Inuit residents, this provisional population is a source of income: people to whom they sell carvings, knives, and food. For others, they are a source of frustration: hunting in ways that frighten the animals, bringing in drugs and alcohol, seducing local people, or simply being unfriendly. For many Inuit, for whom getting access to money can be such a challenge, it can be difficult to see the comparative wealth of *Qallunaat*. They see the revolving door of non-Inuit who come to their settlements to work for organizations that are essentially creatures of the non-Inuit world, and who seem to have lots of money, and they resent it. As Simigak said,

> They've got enough — they've got more rights than the common people up here. You know, they live in houses that they don't pay for and they have free trips South, and they have cargo allowances, plus they have a guarantee of an income by being here. How about us? We don't have a guarantee — I have to fight for every dollar that I get. . . . And there's never any guarantee. If I don't work, I don't make any mon ey.

Simigak's reaction clearly reflects his awareness of the value of money. It also reflects the fact that those who come north are seemingly guaranteed work while many Inuit must struggle to qualify for employment. In 1991, the per capita income of Inuit in Nunavik was $15,765, while that of non-Inuit was $82,269.[22] This situation has changed with time. By 2001, the per capita income of Inuit over the age of 15 was $19,345.50, while that of non-Inuit in the region, who represent 10 per cent of the population, was $46,886.50.[23]

The non-Inuit population is viewed as transitory. As Kublu observed,

> People who like open country tend to stay up here more, and work longer here. We have people who have come up here for years and years and years now. Sometimes people tell stories, like, since he's been coming up here year after year after year for many years now, we think that he lives in this town. But when he will have to leave, for sure, he will be gone. Because there's very few *Qallunaat* that die in this region and are buried here. Most of them go back South and die with their relatives.

Despite the generally temporary presence of individual non-Inuit, their impact on the indigenous population has been profound and lasting.

If the population of Puvirnituq has changed significantly in the past fifty years, so, too, has its economy. Until their move to settlements, Inuit participation in the market economy had largely been limited to seasonal employment by non-Inuit. Having moved to settlements, however, Inuit moved by default into the economic system that underpinned those settlements, and came to rely more and more on money to provide the necessities of life.

One of the ways they earned money was through carving soapstone sculptures, with Puvirnituq being among the most well-known sources of Inuit carvings in the Canadian Arctic. The success of Puvirnituq sculptors meant that per capita relief payments fell steadily, and Puvirnituq moved from being one of the areas receiving greatest relief to the lowest in the region.[24] In 1966 the average payment was $12.07, compared to $53.66 for the region as a whole.[25] As sculpting grew in importance, there was a corresponding de-emphasis on trapping. Despite dropping fur sales, the overall purchasing power of the Inuit was rising. As a result, the Hudson's Bay Company served less as a trading post and became simply a store,[26] and sales made to Inuit rose steadily.[27]

Although starting in 1953 people sold their sculptures to the HBC in Puvirnituq, by 1958, with the help of an Oblate missionary living in the settlement, they created the Sculptors' Society of Povungnituk, which eventually became a co-operative in 1960, and later branched out into other services.[28] The Co-op opened a *Caisse Populaire*, or credit union, in 1962 (which has since closed); it operated a hunting camp for tourists (which is now privately owned); and today it runs the largest hotel in town, operates the gas station, and is the local cable television and Internet service provider. Puvirnituq's was among the earliest and most successful co-operatives in Nunavik, and received a good deal of support from the federal and provincial governments, which were keen to promote economic development in the North.[29] To understand the importance of the co-op movement in Puvirnituq, we need to understand something of the circumstances which led to its development.

It has been argued that government concern to promote the well-being of Inuit was essentially a by-product of the state's desire to have access to the resources of the North.[30] In the case of northern Quebec, the trajectory of the relationship between local and state development took on a particular shape.[31] As the policy of *maître chez nous* — masters in our own house — developed in the 1960s in tandem with the Quebec separatist movement, so the province took an increased interest in establishing its own presence in the region. Already during the 1950s the provincial government had started doing assessments of what natural resources might be developed in the area; bauxite and iron ore mines along with hydroelectric developments seemed promising. For the Quebec government, the presence of federal government agents in Kangiqsujuaq, Puvirnituq, and Inukjuaq to oversee the development and delivery of services to Inuit meant that the province could not ignore the Indigenous residents of the region. In 1963, the provincial government set up the *Direction Général du Nouveau-Québec* and took over responsibility for the delivery of education, social service benefits, and health services in the North.

In 1970, the Neville-Robitaille Commission toured the settlements of Nunavik to hear community opinion about the change from federal to provincial delivery of services in the region. It found that Inuit were reluctant to change to the new provincial administrators. Some people in settlements continue to feel suspicion toward the province of Quebec; they have been told by their parents not to trust francophones. This stems from people's memory of the sudden closure of Révillon Frères trading posts in the region, which resulted in the death by starvation of some of the Inuit who depended on these trading posts.[32] This mistrust of the province meant that, prior to the Quebec referendum of 1995, the people of Nunavik voted in their own referendum to separate from Quebec and remain with Canada should the majority of Quebeckers opt to separate from the country. Yet Inuit recognize that their territory has been the stomping grounds for both provincial and federal interests in the region.[33]

Whether federal or provincial, one of the effects of increased delivery of state services to the region has been a growing presence of Euro-Canadians and their institutions. Inuit have developed their own means of responding to this presence, including two institutions which have been influential in charting the course of development in the region: the co-operative movement and the Northern Quebec Inuit Association (NQIA).[34] The first two Inuit co-operatives were initially founded independently. One branch, under the sponsorship of the federal government, was founded in Kangiqsualujjuaq (then called George River) in 1959.[35] Another was established in Puvirnituq in 1960 by the carvers' association with the help of both the resident Catholic missionary and a former HBC employee.[36] The two branches merged in 1967 to form the *Fédération des Co-opératives du Nouveau-Québec*.

At both the economic and the political level, the co-op movement has played a vital role in the development of Puvirnituq and the region as a whole. For Inuit of the settlement, it was clear that the co-ops would enable them to extend their economic activities beyond hunting and fishing and allow them a measure of control over how this expansion would occur. It was evident to the residents of Puvirnituq that their economic well-being required them to expand their participation in the market economy beyond that of simply fishing and hunting, and that to be successful in doing so, they should take matters into their own hands. In 1962, two years after its founding, three-quarters of the population of Puvirnituq were members of the Co-op, which realized a profit of approximately $112,000, making Puvirnituq the wealthiest village in the region.[37] The co-ops have also had a significant impact on the political development of Puvirnituq and Nunavik. Through the co-operatives, Inuit sought "to learn about how [the] forces of government could be controlled and used to our advantage rather than to our detriment."[38] Inuit sought to use co-operatives as a vehicle to promote greater self-determination via the establishment of their own government; in 1970, they entered into discussions with the provincial government to establish an autonomous regional government.[39]

As the co-operative movement started in two separate camps, the movement for Inuit self-determination was similarly divided. The Northern Quebec Inuit Association was founded in 1972 under the leadership of Charlie Watt (now a senator) and with the backing of the federal government. According to some Inuit residents of the region, the federal government encouraged the establishment of the NQIA because the Canadian government interpreted the provincial support of the proposal for regional self-government as a manoeuvre on the part of the province to establish its own jurisdiction in Northern Quebec.[40] The NQIA thus represented a means by which the federal government might have an indirect influence on the development of the region. The mandate of the NQIA was to represent Inuit political interests in Northern Quebec. In the same year, shortly after the establishment of the NQIA, the government of Quebec announced its intention to build the James Bay Hydroelectric Development. The NQIA was given sole authority to represent the Inuit of Northern Quebec in the land claims negotiations that were spawned by the proposed hydro development. It urged Inuit to sign the James Bay and Northern Quebec Agreement, thereby extinguishing their land rights. Prominent members of the co-operative movement, however, argued that Inuit should not give away their land; no monetary compensation could make up for its loss.[41] They founded *Inuit Tungavingat Nunamini* (The Inuit who Stand Up for their Land). By the time the JBNQA was signed in 1975, the split between these two movements had resulted in a stalemate: two-thirds of the Inuit population of the region opted to sign the agreement while one-third — made up of Ivujivik, Puvirnituq, and a portion of Salluit — refused to do so.[42]

One cannot understand the social, economic, or political character of modern Puvirnituq without understanding that its leaders were, and are, keen to promote their own economic and political independence, and that the co-operative remains integral to this aim. It has been a source not only of economic growth, but of political action and community pride.

At the opening of its new shopping centre in December 2002, after the Co-op had burned down in May of that year, Alashuak Nutaraluk, one of Puvirnituq's founding Co-op members, said, "It's just like in the South, but it's not run by *Qallunaat*. It's 100 per cent Inuit owned. . . . This means a lot more freedom for Puvirnituq."[43]

Early on, the federal government decided that Puvirnituq was to be a model of what government-sponsored community development could be in the North.[44] As a result, it was chosen to act as a regional centre on the Hudson Bay coast, with a hospital, a school, a courthouse, and other services. In 2005, Puvirnituq had, after Kuujjuaq, the second highest rate of full-time jobs in Nunavik, with 10 per cent of all the full-time jobs in the region.[45]

Opening of Puvirnituq Co-op Shopping Centre, December 2002

Smaller settlements generally have higher rates of full-time employment relative to their populations because there are fewer people to take the jobs necessary to maintain northern settlements. By 1999, Puvirnituq had 30 employers who provided 417 regular full-time and part-time jobs (see Appendix 2, Table 6). Three-quarters of these jobs were with public and para-public agencies, with the rest being mostly in the private sector, and a few with non-profit organizations. Approximately 70 per cent were held by beneficiaries under the JBNQA.

The median household income in Puvirnituq in 2005 was $46,656, compared with $58,687 for the province as a whole.[46] To understand these numbers better one should take into account the fact that, owing to a housing shortage, there are more people per household in Nunavik than in the province as a whole. In 2005, there was an average of 4.9 people per household in Puvirnituq compared to 2.3 people per household in Québec as a whole.[47] The Puvirnituq numbers include the non-Inuit population. Were they to be removed from the sample, the average number of people per dwelling would increase while the income would decrease. In fact, 19 per cent of households in Nunavik live below the US poverty level.[48] All the same, individual incomes in Puvirnituq have been growing despite the fact that unemployment rates have been fluctuating. In 1998, there were approximately 100 welfare recipients,[49] but I was told informally that these numbers are decreasing. It would seem, then, that the economic situation in Puvirnituq is improving, as far as wage employment and income are concerned. Yet, with a growing and increasingly young population, there is a growing need to create more employment.

What the statistics do not reflect is the extent to which people use informal ways of earning ready cash — for instance, selling *ulus*, mittens, sculptures, or even contraband. The sale of country foods fits into this category of informal earnings. Those involved generally take part on an intermittent basis, as theirs or the buyers' needs dictate. Most are hunters or fishers without regular jobs who are obliged to adopt a mixed strategy for earning money, taking temporary or seasonal work that will enable them to continue to spend time on the land while meeting the daily expenses of life. As economic life has changed in Puvirnituq, so have the ways that people have made a living. In 1995, 10 per cent of the non-monetary income of a household in Puvirnituq came from hunting. Compare this with the 1968 figure, which shows that 63.3 per cent of the non-monetary incomes of Inuit in Nunavik as a whole came from hunting.[50]

The morality that governs the vernacular economy dictates that people must not sell country foods, but they do. Community members exchange the food for money in various ways, each on a different scale and therefore each involving somewhat different levels of commoditization — and, as a result, each eliciting different reactions from community members. At one end of the spectrum, with the Hunter Support Program, hunters are paid for their produce, but the consumers do not pay for the food. At the other end, producers are straightforward merchants. What is clear is that, at some level, what is important to people in these various processes is not that the food is exchanged for money, but who is exchanging what with whom.

The Commoditization of Country Foods in Puvirnituq

A commodity is anything that is intended for exchange. Marx emphasized that this exchange takes place in a market, so a commodity is a good that is produced not for immediate use but to be brought to market. There is also a social component to it: a commodity is an alienable product that is exchanged between people who are reciprocally independent. Putting these various components together, a commodity is a thing that is exchanged, generally in a market, and is thus removed from exchange based on reciprocal social relations. This means that the process of turning things into commodities and linking them to the market entails particular kinds of social relations and particular ways of perceiving those things. In the case of the Inuit, at issue as country foods are turned into commodities, is what this means both in terms of how they perceive those foods and how this process affects existing social relations.

With the introduction of markets, the institutions of a vernacular economy can be transformed. Karl Polanyi identifies a number of changes in vernacular economies that accompany the introduction of markets: the motive of subsistence (i.e., production for use) is replaced by that of gain; all transactions become money transactions, with money as the medium of exchange; all incomes are derived from the sale of something; prices are self-regulating, which means that markets must be allowed to function without interference; nature becomes interwoven with processes of commoditization as its products become fodder for the market; and eventually social relations become embedded in the economy rather than the economy being embedded in social relations.[51] Are such changes inevitable? As Inuit in Puvirnituq undertake the commoditization of country foods, will they inevitably go down the road

Polanyi sets for them? And, as discussed in Chapter 2, given all the ways that country foods are tied into larger processes, how might these processes be affected by the commoditization of country foods?

The notion of food as a commodity is not new to Inuit. They have been involved in the commoditization of country foods in one form or another since the whalers arrived in the 19th century. Since that time, they seem to have grown accustomed to trading in country foods with non-Inuit who came from another world and generally stayed within it, even when they were in the North. At first, "sales" of country foods might have been through a straight exchange of goods — i.e., barter. Then they turned into a debit and credit system through the trading posts. Eventually, sales of country foods came to include money. Today in Puvirnituq, the commoditization of country foods incorporates various forms of exchange, including the sale of food to non-Inuit and the institutions that people perceive to be embodiments of the non-Inuit world, as well as wholly new forms of exchange that involve trade among Inuit. The former is far less controversial than the latter, primarily because of the role country foods play in a place-based economy.

Since the vernacular economy of Inuit is predicated on notions of common property and reciprocity, both among humans and between humans and animals, there is an underlying belief that, through sharing, people ensure

Opening of Puvirnituq Co-op Shopping Centre, December 2002

their own and others' survival. Through sharing, the environment provides the necessities of life. Through sharing, people establish and maintain social relationships that build community. If sharing stops, survival is threatened. Most people to whom I spoke in Puvirnituq expressed dismay at the notion of Inuit selling country foods to Inuit, for this would break with the ethical precepts that have held their society together. Everyone said they would not sell country foods to another Inuk, but would give it away. As discussed earlier, such sharing is varied, and extends to many within the community who might otherwise go without country foods. People share among friends and relatives. If they go out with others to hunt or fish, and the others are not successful, they do not return empty-handed, because those who have been successful share with them. That is what they were taught and that is what they continue to do. Yet, although country foods continue to be shared, they are being sold in the community as well.

This contradiction reflects the human condition, which rarely fits into clearly defined boxes. People may be conditioned by unspoken impulses born from what we have chosen to call culture, but we are also individuals with our own set of beliefs and desires generated from experience. As with the rest of the world, there is no monolithic Inuk who reacts with one voice to *anything*. The many voices I heard in Nunavik reflected the variety of responses people had developed as they tried to make sense of themselves in the world, as they tried to understand how their way of living before the coming of settlements fits into the world in which they now find themselves.

The Sale of Country Foods to Individual Qallunaat

Although officially the sale of (uncertified) country foods to non-beneficiaries is prohibited under the James Bay and Northern Québec Agreement, such sales do, in fact, occur. Non-Inuit who are in the community to work buy such things as fish or caribou from local hunters or fishers. Teachers, tourists, hospital employees, construction workers, or crews from the sealift boats all represent potential customers for Inuit wanting to exchange country foods for other commodities. In most cases, the exchange involves money. In some instances it may involve a trade of goods, such as prepared southern meats or alcohol. All these exchanges are informal and irregular; they occur as the opportunity arises or when the producers are in need of cash or the good being exchanged.

The sale of country foods to non-Inuit can occur in two ways. Either someone will come to people's doors asking if they would like to buy, say, some Arctic char or caribou, or else the non-Inuit will have regular suppliers who, following a successful hunting or fishing trip, and after taking meat for their own families, will ask their customers whether they would like to buy some country food. In the former case, the producers are generally strangers to their non-Inuit customers. In the latter case, they are known. One such customer told me that when she bought caribou, her supplier would tell her where they had got the animal, the circumstances in which it was killed, and other details that made her believe she was getting the story of the meat, and so a piece of the place, as she felt Inuit would do among themselves. She felt that, despite the exchange of money, there was also an exchange of relations. At the same time, she expressed the thought that her supplier was interested in selling her meat, not on a regular basis, but when their family needed cash for other things.

That these non-Inuit customers are generally treated as a source of needed goods is a continuation of the relations that have existed between Inuit and non-Inuit since the latter first started to appear in the North. On a social level, the relations between the two groups are fairly distant. Lacking the kind of kin relations that would enable them to have access to country foods, non-Inuit gain access to them via the socially distanced and distancing instrument of cash. Davidie, who periodically sells country foods to *Qallunaat*, said that when he returns from fishing and is unloading his catch, non-Inuit people come up to him, and even though he would be prepared to give some fish to them, they ask, "How much?" They always assume that things can be got only with money.

The economy of Inuit has been associated in the literature with the notion of the economy of the gift, and central to the notion of the gift are the acts of giving, receiving, and reciprocating.[52] There is great variety within this dynamic and much debate about its accuracy as a model. The time between these various actions can differ, and there is not always equivalence between giving and reciprocating. In some instances, gifts are given without an expectation that they be reciprocated.[53] This is why, some prefer to use the term "sharing" instead of "reciprocity," because the former implies not simply exchange, but a host of moral values such as hospitality and land-people relations.[54] By giving and receiving, we are linking ourselves to others. What is important in these interchanges is that they aid in the building up and maintaining of social relations over time. For Inuit, part of the value of country foods, over and above their value as something to be consumed, is that they reinforce social relations. The focus is not simply on production but on reproduction, with the connections forged through a gift sustaining communal relations that ultimately enable social reproduction. In his willingness to give meat to non-Inuit, had they only asked, Davidie is showing how centrally important are the social connections and community building inherent in the production, exchange, and consumption of country foods.

The assumption by the non-Inuk that food can only be acquired via an exchange of money shows the extent to which they function within the paradigm of the market, where one cannot assume that one can get much without money changing hands. One need not have social relations with a person in order to get things; one need only have money. In Davidie's world, one stores value in human relations; in the non-Inuit world, value is stored above all in money. This has profound implications for how people live in society. For Davidie, the basic supposition is to turn strangers into group members

Inside the HSP meat house just before Christmas

through the sharing of food. Sharing represents a social contract by which people implicitly agree to adhere to the morality that governs the collective, and the individual is thereby incorporated into the community. For non-Inuit, the basic supposition is that one is an individual living in a world of strangers from whom one can only get what one wants by means of money.

So it is that, for Inuit, non-Inuit fall into an odd category. As they are accustomed to buying and selling, Inuit have grown accustomed to buying from and selling to them. This is not the only form of relations between the two groups, though, for Inuit have not exiled non-Inuit from the morality that rules their economy. Those non-Inuit who have established social relations with Inuit in the community may periodically be treated by some as members of that community: getting meat after outings with people, receiving a call to ask if they want some spare meat, or being accepted to appear uninvited at someone's house to share in a meal. But non-Inuit with no such links in the community may be viewed as outsiders, and thereby fall into another category of being and behaviour. This has led to some rather aberrant behaviour.

On December 12, 2001, I went to the buildings where the HSP stored its country foods. The door was locked. I turned to see some fishers approaching with a large catch. I later wrote in my journal:

> I just saw all sorts of huge Arctic Char — two *qamutiit* worth — being unloaded in front of the Hunter Support building. . . . The char came from between Akulivik and Ivujivik. "When you throw a net in, within seconds there are fish," one of the men unloading the fish told me. They'd been gone for "weeks." A week??? I don't know. It wasn't clear. . . . As I left, the guy said they'd be for sale.

I wrote these words rather innocently, yet that one event spoke of many things. That the buildings where the HSP stored its country foods should be locked came as a surprise. I had been under the impression that it was open to people at all times. I had approached it rather timidly, thinking that I did not want to intrude. After trying the door, and finding to my secret relief that it was locked, I turned to see the arrival of the two *qamutiit* bearing fish, accompanied by men of various ages. The oldest among them, a man recognized by the community as a serious hunter, looked on in silence as I engaged one of the younger men in conversation, trying to do my research in a friendly, informal way. I was curious about what it was like to be on the fishing trip. I wanted to know what they would do with all those fish. As I asked my questions, the older man threw the fish into the doorway of the meat house, listening but not saying a word. When the younger man said that some of the fish would be for sale, I thought he assumed I was looking to buy fish. I wasn't, so I left them to their work, thinking that I would return another day to see the buildings.

When I did, not many days later, I found the door unlocked and the manager of the Hunter Support Program inside cutting *mattak* for the Christmas and New Year's festivities soon to be held in the community gymnasium. I asked if he would show me around. There was more than one building, and I was curious to see what they contained. He was hesitant. Thinking to excuse myself, I mentioned that I would have shown myself around, but when I came once before the buildings were locked. This surprised me, I said, as I had been under the impression that they were always open. Unbeknownst to me, as he eventually explained, my comments were poking at events that had caused some distress in the community.

Some of the younger men in the settlement had been taking Arctic char from the facilities to sell to non-Inuit. Because of this, the HSP made a rule that only two Arctic char would be allowed per household, and had decided, moreover, that when there was food in the meat houses, they would only be open for a specific period at lunchtime and at the end of the afternoon. Otherwise they would be locked. In discussions with others in the community, I learned that this had also happened with people's personal supplies.

Behind each house in Puvirnituq is a shed where the occupants store things, including country foods. Because people generally did not steal, these sheds have traditionally been left open. If people had only to ask for meat and they would receive it, why would anybody steal it? The very notion of sharing is based on larger ideas of equality, respect, and personal responsibility to the collective. Robbery has no place in such a value system. But things are changing. Some of the younger generation had started to take fish without informing the "owners" in order to sell it to non-Inuit.[55] As a result, some had taken to locking their sheds.

The presence of a largely separate community of non-Inuit has had the effect, in part, of changing age-old patterns of behaviour. People have told me, "We did not steal until the *Qallunaat* came." This seems to me a kind of shorthand for all the changes Inuit have lived through that have collectively contributed to the wearing down of the social norms associated with life on the land.

This is not to say that stealing was unknown before the arrival of Europeans, but robbery was rare because the maintenance of social connections among people was of fundamental importance, and breaking the social contract was to ignore one of society's basic precepts. Stealing also places individual desires above the collective good. The sharing of food can only function among Inuit because they have internalized a set of moral principles that reinforce an individual's commitment to the community as a whole, such as the notion that one's success as a hunter relies on one's sharing the bounty offered by the animal. That people should have started to steal and sell country foods reflects their abrogation of these principles. It is also linked to the fact that once money becomes a medium of exchange, people become distanced from the goods themselves and ultimately from one another, since they need no longer have social relationships and responsibilities in order to attain the things they want.[56] Money becomes a shortcut for obtaining things that bypasses people's involvement in the production of those things. Consumption gains a primary role, whereas access to modes of production and distribution can be circumvented and their importance is undermined.

If people have taken to stealing country foods to sell to individual non-Inuit, whom they perceive as outside the circle of morality that governs relations within Inuit communities, they have also extended this practice to the institutions that they perceive to be foreign. People have stolen fish, for example, to sell to the hospital. The hospital chef, like other itinerant workers in the community who might have bought country foods from people at the door, probably knew nothing about the situation. He lacked the linguistic skills to understand what was being talked about on the community radio, and he lacked the social relations with Inuktitut speakers to learn that such thefts were taking place. Further, Inuit have historically tended not to let *Qallunaat* know when they did not agree with them. As Rachel Attituq Qitsualik explains, *ilira*, or passive silence and compliance, was a reaction that Inuit developed to avoid conflict.[57] Despite the fact that many Inuit knew that non-Inuit sometimes buy stolen goods, the non-Inuit community remained ignorant of this problem.

While the sale of country foods to individual non-Inuit has long served as a mechanism whereby Inuit gain access to other goods, through either direct exchange or money, it has also resulted in some problematic behaviours that have challenged the moralities that bind Inuit together. Yet sales to individuals represent only one channel by which country food has moved into the commodity sphere.

Various formally constituted institutions such as the catering company, the Co-op, the fish-smoking plant, and the HSP also buy country foods. Each has particular motivations and mechanisms for acquiring those foods, and each has particular impacts upon the workings of the vernacular economy of Puvirnituq.

The Catering Company

The catering company operates out of the local hotel, providing meals for hotel guests and seasonal construction workers. Though it has been buying country foods for some time, it has only recently formalized its transactions, weighing the fish before paying for them. Before that, fish sales were informal, with the fishers receiving whatever amount they needed at any given time. If they needed $50 they would sell the fish for that amount, but if they needed less, the same quantity of fish would cost less. The people selling country foods were not out to make a profit. Rather, they had more immediate needs to fulfil and the money was a means to an end.

In Marxist analysis, the logic of such pre-capitalist exchange is rendered C-M-C: a person takes a commodity and transforms it into money, which is then used to acquire another commodity. Therein lies a strange mixing of values. One of the basic distinctions between different forms of value is that between use value and exchange value. Generally the former involves value that is established based on a thing's worth as something that is used, and the latter is established as a result of processes of exchange. Whereas use value is based on the concrete and the particular, exchange value is abstract and general. Whereas use value represents non-alienated labour, exchange value entails labour that is separated from the end product. Whereas use value involves production as a means to an end (being human use), exchange value implies production as an end in itself. In either case, value can be a social or cultural construction; however, the simple fact that something is produced for direct use generally means that it is less prone to intangible constructions of value that are not grounded in fact. The danger in exchange value is that it can be grounded in an abstraction. The stock exchange is replete with examples, from the tulip craze in 17th-century Holland to the dot com craze of the 20th century. Money generally serves as the means by which use value may be transformed into exchange value.

It would seem that, by selling their fish to the hotel, the sellers are making a straight shift from use value to exchange value. But the shift is only partial. They may well have produced the meat for exchange, and thereby its value becomes defined in terms of exchange, but in fact that exchange value is simply a proxy granting them access to money as a means of meeting other needs. The use value of the fish is shifted along slightly, and the goal continues to be use value. They have not become capitalists, aiming to make money with which to make more money, and they did not produce the fish only to make money, but to enable them to meet other uses.

Although the suppliers did not demand it, eventually the catering company decided to pay standardized and generous prices vis-à-vis the other potential local markets for the food (see Appendix 3). The company decided this was only fair, given that the company was making the best revenues in town from the purchase and resale of these foods. The company also felt that it was providing support to local hunters and fishers. By adopting standardized pricing with an eye to fairness, the owners of the catering company are part of the process of normalizing money as a medium of exchange and reinforcing its importance as an absolute measure of value.

Although some of the people who supply country foods to the hotel do so only when they need money, others are more regular. The latter have, in a sense, internalized an understanding of exchange value and of the need for money as a store of value. They are therefore more conscientious and consistent in their willingness to exchange fish for money, which will be used to meet the ongoing needs of life rather than the more immediate needs of the intermittent sellers. One might argue that such people are in fact more alienated from the produce of their labour, but the dynamic is more complicated than that.

Those deemed to be trustworthy are the people on whom the company relies, buying food when they come selling or, when in need, contacting them to ask if they would go out and get meat. The company owners encourage them in their work ethic. However, there is a complicated issue of power here, power that works at many levels. One of the company owners said that he tried particularly to encourage people who face otherwise difficult circumstances in life. So at one level, those who have access to money and the power money gives them are choosing to encourage those who have less power to gain access to money, and thereby gain a measure of power both in material terms, since they are able to meet their physical needs, and in social terms, since to be able to hunt or fish gives them a certain standing in the eyes of community members. The company owners are thus using their economic power to reinforce one community-based notion of power: the capacity to produce country foods and potentially share any excess with other community members. At the same time, people with less power may be more willing to adhere to the work ethic required to be dependable workers for the company. It is also the case that those who are less dependable have perhaps incorporated a sense of powerlessness that has come with the welfare state, and so have lost the work ethic required to be productive members of society. In this whole dynamic, it is difficult to identify who is the master and who is the slave.

Despite the catering company owners' public-spirited approach to buying country foods, they also recognize that there is a level of resentment in the community about selling country foods to them. If those who provide the company with country foods are not capitalists, they recognize that the company owners are, and they dislike it. The latter are taking money to buy a commodity from which they are making more money — M-C-M in Marxist terms. As one of the owners told me, "a lot of them . . . would never sell here, because they know it's to make a profit. While they sell at Mikikatiit [the local HSP], they know it's going back into the community." Thus, for many, the commitment even in selling country foods is to the collective good rather than to the good of individuals. This view is reflected in Nunavik as a whole. Of the country food sold in the region in 1995, the vast majority went to the HSP.[58] So people seem reticent to sell country foods on the private market. It would seem that, for some in Puvirnituq, the HSP falls into a different category of institutional exchange, one in which control remains in the hands of the Inuit, and so is less threatening to the social structures that have governed the exchange of country foods.

Mikikatiit (The Hunter Support Program)

The Hunter Support Program was created as a result of the James Bay and Northern Quebec Agreement, so it falls into an odd category. On the one hand, it is one more institution that has been introduced to the North that reflects non-indigenous ways of perceiving human relations and how to operate in the world. Formal institutions with budgets and bureaucrats were not part of Inuit society, which functioned on a far less formally codified basis and on a much smaller social scale. On the other hand, the HSP is the offspring of Inuit land claims, and so there is a sense of ownership of the program that must surely never have been there with other alien institutions. It treads a fine line, and nowhere is this more apparent than in the commoditization of country foods. As the first and most widespread instance of the commoditization of country foods among Inuit in Nunavik, it was the cause of some debate.

The notion that the food at the HSP is given away is important to people. If people start selling food, Imalie told me, then "it's just for money." But she felt that the HSP was acceptable because the hunters were not paid for the animal, but for their gas and their labour. The food was given away. To her it appeared that the HSP is simply an extension of the practice of sharing. This seems to be supported by the fact that, although some people sell country foods to the program, others periodically give it. Jamisie argued that the HSP was a form of government assistance that resembled farm subsidies in the South. Financial support that invests in production as opposed to, for example, social assistance, which is designed to support consumption, has some unmeasured benefits that spill out into the community. Each dollar spent has a multiplier effect on a household's income through the resulting production and distribution of food.

Caribou meat waiting to be loaded into the HSP meat house

The program has not been without its glitches. When the HSP in Puvirni-tuq first started buying country foods, it sent out a blanket request saying that it would buy from anyone. It soon changed this approach, for some people were killing animals and taking only the parts they were able to sell to the HSP, leaving the rest of the carcass behind; or they were killing inappropri-ately — taking, for example, skinny animals, or females who should be left to reproduce; or they were simply stealing food from people's shacks in order to sell to the HSP. The moral order that governed the vernacular economy was being threatened. Such dangers are inherent in the move to market exchange as the motives of production become exchange value and gain. Unlike free markets that, by definition, should operate unfettered, the HSP retains con-trol over the process of commoditization. As George Dalton points out:

> It is not alienation from the means of production which is socially divi-sive, but rather the dependence on impersonal market forces unrelated to indigenous social control, the separating of economy from society by divorcing resource allocation, work arrangement, and product disposi-tion from expressions of social obligation. And to be sure, the conse-quent loss of socially guaranteed subsistence, as well.[59]

In order to retain control over the means of production, the municipality decided to hire people who are known to have good hunting skills to go and get food and thereby ensure that, in the getting of country food, at least Inuit rules of appropriate killing would be respected.

Davidie, a man in his fifties who sells country food to the HSP, told me he appreciated the fact that the HSP has limited funds to buy country foods, and that only a few people were able to supply it. As he saw it, were the HSP to provide country foods for the community on an on-going basis, people would get lazy. Because the food is only occasionally available, people are still forced to go out hunting for themselves. He argued that the Hunter Support Program in its current form was able to avoid affecting the system of food sharing that has been the basis of the vernacular economy of Inuit.

Certainly, the HSP was conceived of as a way to subsidize hunting, fish-ing, trapping, and gathering while perpetuating the notion of sharing the produce from those activities. One might argue that the HSP is simply one of many newly introduced institutionalized approaches to sharing — for ex-ample, people who are members of a church now give food to other church members — yet there is some debate about the ways in which the program has affected food sharing. Some assert that the HSP allows food-sharing relations to continue.[60] However, Nobuhiro Kishigami points out that the patterns of sharing have changed, so that people are no longer so reliant on pre-established reciprocal obligations to share food.[61] Moreover, with changes in the economy and way of living among the Inuit, some young men are now no longer participating in, or contributing to, the vernacular economy, which means that they take food from the HSP without providing any for the community. Such forms of behaviour would have been unlikely a generation ago. Yet, with the advent of wage labour, the HSP has served, in part, to provide food for people who might otherwise not have the time to get it themselves.

Not everyone in the community shares the view that the HSP has not affected food sharing. Alurut, who has periodically sold country food to the HSP, expressed some reservations,

> For some, the first time when we was making a decision if we should get the Hunter Support money, some people didn't agree. Like *myself*, I didn't agree to get the Hunter Support money at that time. . . . I was scared to lose our tradition. Like, we share our catch. That's our tradition. We've done that for thousands of years, like our ancestors. And they never buy or exchange any food. So I was scared that if we started to use Hunter Support money when it would be starting to pay for food, I was scared that we were going to lose our tradition.

For Alurut, the HSP was a slippery slope. Not only were hunters not dividing their catch — "He's not going to share with *anybody*, because he prefers to have money" — but he feared that Inuit would soon be selling to Inuit:

> They're going, for sure, they're going to start to do that in the coming years. Because the Hunter Support Program started that in the past years. It started. That's what I was afraid of. It's going slowly but slowly, and Inuit are going to start to sell to their fellow Inuit people.

Others to whom I spoke expressed a similar misgiving: that with the advent of the HSP people shared less than they had in the past. Despite this concern, people recognize that they face a predicament. Though they try to maintain the tradition of sharing, they also acknowledge that hunters need that subsidy to be able to continue to hunt, fish, and gather. As Jamisie put it, "Those who have food give it away for free for those who need. And that's something we're still proud of doing. But if we can get paid for doing it, well then, that's acceptable too, since there's no other work."

According to some, then, the requirement for money is not to the exclusion of sharing. As one person said to me, "If you want to buy, I'll sell it to you. If you're asking for it, I'll give it to you." As for the exchange of country foods among Inuit, Benjamin, an older man, said that, although he sells to the HSP, that does not prevent him from sharing with others. The shack where he stores meat is open to anyone who needs it, and when he goes hunting or fishing with others, he shares with those who accompany him. The two systems of exchange operate in tandem, and people switch back and forth between them.

Processes of commoditization do not produce all-or-nothing situations; it is not necessarily the case that a thing is either a commodity or is not a commodity. It can move in and out of commodity status, or it may be viewed as a commodity by some and not by others.[62] Depending on the situation, a thing may be a commodity produced for exchange on the market, or it may be something that stays in the vernacular economy outside the market. Sometimes the market realm and the vernacular realm are able to coexist, and sometimes not; sometimes they complement one another, and sometimes they are at odds. Many argue that economies, particularly those that have been associated with subsistence production, are in fact a mixture of vernacular and market forces, and that to make a clear-cut distinction between the two is at best inappropriate and at worst unfair, because it has been used to keep such production out of the market realm, whether or not Aboriginal peoples might wish it otherwise.[63] The relationship between vernacular and market economies is dialectic, not absolute.

Commoditization ought to be viewed as a process of becoming rather than an all-or-nothing state.[64] The process of commoditization operates at two levels: first, making a given commoditized thing exchangeable for more and more other things; and second, making more and more different things more widely exchangeable.[65] Money, although it does not embody all forms of value, tends to be applied to more and more things as a measure of value and serves to concentrate the range of values into fewer and fewer varieties.[66] Thus, for example, where once things like air and water were generally inalienable public goods, they are now products that can be bought and sold on the market. The rise of lawsuits, the growing domains of human existence that can now be insured are all indications of how the range of values linked to our lives have been gradually reduced to money. But some people take exception to the notion that money is a measure of all things, and try to put brakes on the rush to commoditization. One way is by securing portions of their environment as "sacred," thereby ensuring that it is not commoditized. In other instances people allow goods to operate with the realms of both market and non-market exchange. Societies the world over grapple with such issues. So Inuit are struggling to come to terms with what it means to desecrate their traditions by selling rather than sharing. Benjamin has done so by ensuring that he operates within both the market and the non-market exchange; his sharing has, of necessity, adjusted to the modern economy. When commoditization clashes with individual ways of thinking or cultural principles, it can result in "anomalies in cognition, inconsistencies in values, and uncertainties in action."[67]

Davidie saw the fact that the HSP only offers food to people intermittently as a good thing, because it prevents people from getting lazy. Not everybody shares this view. Some see the HSP not only as promoting laziness, but as eroding the core of Inuit culture:

> It's difficult now to find anybody who's willing to finance his own hunting trip. If they have to go a great distance, they'd rather wait for money from the Hunter Support Program. It's not a way of life. You can't call anybody a hunter if he waits and refuses to go hunting until he gets paid. People still take trips close to the village to do ice jigging, but if they have to go hunting for walrus their supplies are financed by the Hunter Support Program and they are paid for every day they are out. They waste a lot of animals because, in order to get paid more, they stay out much longer than they would really need to. They kill too much, much more than the village requires. . . .[68]

Others echo these fears of dependency. Seeing the introduction of codified institutions that are supposed to mimic informal ones, they argue that they cannot be anything but pale imitations of the original, imitations that bring with them hidden costs. As Malachi said of the HSP,

> It's taking away the spirit of the people. Initially the fish that they bought was supposed to be for widows and people that didn't have anything. But in recent years it's been fish for everybody. And it's *free*. Because you're a beneficiary, from the Hunter Support Program, once these fishers have been out, everybody can go and get fish without paying for it. And that's killing the spirit of the people.

Malachi went on to say that the HSP did not reflect the Inuit tradition of sharing:

> It is a program. And there's no spirit in it. *Before*, it was real sharing . . . and you *depended* on these people that were hunting. And you appreciated that, for that reason. There was spirit in it. There was real sharing. But this is not real sharing. It's a program, and there's no spirit in it. There's no life in it. There's no heart-felt appreciation in that kind of thing.

Some people remember what it was to live outside of communities with all their services. They have often mentioned to me their fears about Inuit dependency on these services, which they see as promoting a lack of initiative, responsibility, and self-respect. Yet, I believe that at the root of this is the loss of the value and affirmation of ways of living and making a living that have been part of the vernacular economy of Inuit until recently. For generation upon generation, people developed knowledge and ways of living that were geared toward hunting, fishing, and gathering. Such skills were central to people's understandings of what it meant to be a fully functioning adult in society. These skills and ways of living continue to be useful to people, but life in communities and the wage economy that goes with it does not generally validate such talents, and for many, they have not been replaced by any viable form of earning one's way. This is why, in the eyes of some people, welfare has had such debilitating effects. Although hunting, fishing, trapping, and gathering have waned, some of the new generation do not seem able to participate in the market economy that has taken its place. As some people have lost the ability or the willingness to contribute productively to society, they seem also to have lost the motivation for respecting the conventions that allowed the vernacular economy to function. During a conversation I had with Salamonie, I asked whether he thought people would always be willing to share. "It's very hard to tell," he responded. "Like those young guys, in their age, we used to be inland with our parents, with our uncles. But today they're not. They're not inland. They're hanging around in the Co-op, in Northern, waiting for the welfare cheques. But not *all* of them."

OCTOBER 30, 2001: A couple of nights ago there was an old guy talking on the local radio. I was listening, trying to practise my Inuktitut. He was speaking very passionately, and I knew he was talking about the past, and about animals and his parents. Yesterday I asked someone what exactly he'd been saying. He said the old guy was talking about how it was here in the past. How hard people had had to work to make ends meet. About how people relied on the animals, about how people had to get up at three in the morning to prepare their dog teams to go out hunting, and about how young people now have no idea what it was like. During the last month, two young guys have killed themselves, one young guy was murdered, we had a woman and her two kids staying with us who was fleeing her abusive boyfriend. . . . I think about the kind of violence and unhappiness that lies beneath the surface here and it amazes me. You wouldn't know it. I feel like the ignorant Hudson's Bay factors working at the trading post on the Labrador coast whose journals I used to read in the HBC archives. They wrote of distant troubles off somewhere out on the land that they would hear about, and discover only later that whole camps had died of disease. But all I can see are happy, smiling people. That old man who was talking on the radio, eventually they cut him off and started to play music. I remember being at a meeting a couple of years ago where we spent about three days discussing "Inuit identity in the 21st Century." At the end of the meeting the Inuit participants were talking about how Inuit were worried about the gap between elders and youth. At the time, I thought they meant the younger generation was afraid of losing its connections with the past as the elders died. But the Inuit participants corrected me: it was the elders who were afraid that Inuit were losing their future. Since I've been here I've been using the adult education centre as a space to work in. As far as I can tell, they're learning literacy and numerical skills. They're learning computers and the Internet. But somehow it all seems so out of whack, if you think that such a short time ago people were in tents and igloos and getting up at three in the morning to go hunting. . . . Boy oh boy, the accommodation of the past with the present, and those who somehow try to plan for the future, is a challenging thing! And meanwhile there's a great deal of trauma.

One of the guys I've talked to a fair amount here was the first person who had to deal with what to do when the boy was killed. We were talking about it and he said that the abuse of power that Inuit had experienced when non-Inuit first moved here in big numbers, the violent changes that they experienced, had transformed into violence that people turned inwards within the community.

Some among the older generation fear for their juniors, whom they see as not understanding where they are from, and so they spoke of how some of the younger generation had been affected by the sales of country foods. They talked about the fact that some were taking food from individuals or the HSP to sell it, or were killing animals inappropriately. They also referred to a scheme in the past to sell caribou antlers to Asia for medicinal use. In their eagerness, some of the younger people had gone out looking for antlers and got lost. Some older people, laughing at past experience, said that they feared that if there were more sales of country foods they would spend more time looking for young people lost on the land.

Yet, as Salamonie mentioned, not all of the younger generation is un-schooled in the ways of the land. In any community there are those who are taking their place in the vernacular economy. The HSP is hiring them to get country foods and holding a training program to bring them on the land to acquire the skills of previous generations. Some people saw the selling of country foods as a fitting alternative to welfare for young people. At least they were being productive; they were doing something to help the community and to help their families.

Coming from a society in which, just a short time ago, generally all were involved in productive activity, the notion that people should not contribute to society as a whole simply does not make sense. At the same time, there have always been those who, for whatever reasons, were more successful at what they do than others. One man pointed out that some of the grandchildren of those who depended on his father are now depending on him. Though people may not always like it, such one-way sharing is a feature of life in Inuit society.[69] It is because he shares what he has, like his father, and like countless generations before him, that they are able to make ends meet. The ideal is that when they can, the haves help the have-nots. But there are limits to this ideal.

Some researchers argue that giving can create or sustain social ties and confer prestige, even power, on the giver.[70] To be sure, the capacity to provide food for others potentially grants an elevated status to the giver, and the ca-pacity to give food does potentially contain elements of power. As Jamisie put it, being able to give food to others gives a person prominence, but it does not give them dominance. One woman mentioned that she thought some-times the abusers in her settlement could get away with it because they were also providing food, but such notions of power imposed on others are not how Inuit ideally conceive of giving food. When I asked Adamie, who likely receives more country food than he gives, about whether the giving of food conferred power on the donor, he replied that to give food is not about power. Rather, the person who gives food should do so because he or she wants to do so. The feeling such an act should elicit is pride in being a provider, and pleasure at being able to give to others without question.

Generosity is the ideal. It is the spirit with which Inuit endorse the sharing of country foods. That being said, the ideal is not always followed. Jamisie acknowledged that some families are known to be more generous than others, even through the generations, and it used to happen that some people were known to give people poor cuts of meat to make the recipient feel small.

Over and above social distinctions being made in the process of sharing, there are instances when it simply does not occur. In the past, in extreme circumstances, the sharing of food did fall by the wayside. One man from Sanikiluaq, in his 50s, told me how, as a child when his father was in the South for medical treatment, he was left in a camp with only females. Although others knew of their circumstances, it was not until they were starving that an uncle brought them to live with him. Today, although there is certainly food insecurity in Nunavik, such extreme circumstances no longer exist. With fewer people involved in getting country foods, though, the demands for it can sometimes become difficult. The same person who continued to share food and support people, as his father had before him, also expressed some irritation about it, sometimes giving away his less good *misiraq* (a sauce made from aged beluga whale fat) and reserving the best for himself. Another person told me that, when they ask someone for meat, they can sometimes hear the matriarch of the household in the background demanding, "Who's asking?" Depending on the answer, she will give a better or worse cut of meat.

In the past, the ethic was that food was shared with the elderly, the infirm, and women without a productive man, under the assumption that the rest of society was essentially able to meet its own needs. Today, however, given the expense associated with outfitting oneself and going hunting and fishing, and given the fact that fewer people are able to participate in these activities while the demand for country foods still needs to be met, the challenge grows for people to get these foods.

Originally, as Malachi observed, the HSP was conceived of as a means of providing country foods to those who were otherwise unable to get them, such as the elderly or those without hunting equipment. This caused some debate within the community. Some argued that, as JBNQA beneficiaries, they should have access to these foods regardless of their age or financial circumstances. Alurut explained:

The HSP is for *hunting*. That's what that's for. . . . So at the beginning, we didn't buy any food from the hunters. . . . But people started to complain. And we wanted to help elders. So we started to buy food from hunters to distribute to the elders. That's how it started: for less fortunate, for those who doesn't have hunting equipments, we used to do that. If a person had hunting equipment, we didn't give out the food. But the people who have good hunting equipment started to complain. . . . They said, "I'm also a beneficiary. How come I don't get anything from Hunter Support?" . . . That's what I was afraid of. Even today, even now, they're, "How come we could not sell food to Hunter Support?" They're asking. Even *today*.

Access to HSP food at Puvirnituq thus became open to all beneficiaries within the community, although at certain times — for example, when country food is most difficult to get — the administrators of the program will limit access to the elders and those in need. Here again, the introduction of non-Inuit institutions, with rigid definitions that dictate people's access to services, is a new thing, and one that has some significant implications. In the past, food was to be available to all, based on need and people's willingness to share. With the introduction of legal definitions through the HSP, now sharing has become at once a legal right for those to whom it applies and a means of excluding those to whom the law does not apply. People are not people; they are beneficiaries, with privileges that accrue to them. So Inuit find themselves caught within the limits of "dogmatic law."[71] The give and take that has been associated with custom gives way to the rigidity of rights associated with the law. In the process, people's understandings of themselves change.

When the administrator of the HSP told me that the meat house was locked in order to prevent people from taking fish and selling it to non-Inuit people, there was a second reason. Some weeks before, a group of non-Inuit workers had been passing the HSP buildings one evening when they saw people getting fish. Seeing that fish was there, the non-Inuit joined in and helped themselves. At the time no one voiced any objection, but later some community members did object. As a result, access to the meat house was monitored to ensure that non-beneficiaries did not take what they did not deserve.

When I mentioned this to one woman, she was scandalized. "But that's not Inuk!" she said. To be Inuk is to share meat with anybody, no matter who they are. The notion that things should be shared is based on the belief that all humans are equal. Refusing to share with certain humans goes against the tenet of equality. Some people are more equal than others, though, and what serves to put people in one camp or another is a legal construct that has come only since the signing of the JBNQA in the 1970s. People are no longer all equal; rather, some are beneficiaries and some are not. So the HSP has, for some, affected not only how they understand who they are, but also the morality that has governed their membership in society.

For all the debate that has taken place with respect to the HSP, many see it as a useful program that contributes more good than ill to the community. People recognize that hunters and fishers need money to go out on the land or the sea, and it represents an acceptable way of paying them to do so. It prevents the purely individual self-interest that can come with the selling of country foods, and it underscores sociality. The commitment of the HSP to providing a subsidy to hunters which then spills over into the rest of the community was made apparent to me in a conversation I had with someone who had been involved in Makivik's now defunct inter-community trade project. Given that the prices paid by the HSP ended up costing more per pound than the meat sold by the inter-community trade project, he wondered why administrators of the HSP did not simply buy the meat produced by Makivik's project rather than paying more to individual hunters in the community. As he pointed out, it would cost the HSP less in the end, and enable it to have more meat. That man's cost-benefit analysis was done purely on the basis of money, and it missed the fact that administrators of the HSP were presumably more interested in providing support to community members and sustaining their local economy than in getting cheaper goods. The HSP was, in fact, also doing a cost-benefit analysis but it was measured against not only money, but society. People's commitment to common property and to the social relations that are at the root of the gifting economy is, at some level, holding sway. Although the sale of country foods represents the privatization of resources, by using the HSP to finance hunters as much as possible, administrators of the program are demonstrating their commitment to ensuring that productive hunters continue to be able to get food for the community. The money provided by the HSP subsidizes and encourages productive hunters to continue to hunt, not only for the program, but for meat that is redistributed among community members via customary means. So commoditization is used to support local cycles of exchange in ways that do not necessarily cause the vernacular economy to crumble.[72]

The Co-op

The co-operative is further along the continuum of commoditization. Like the Hunter Support Program, it is essentially an institution whose origins are from the South, yet it has a long history of support in the community, and has been enthusiastically adopted by most people of Puvirnituq. Like the HSP, it is a quasi-Inuit organization that is involved in buying country foods from the local population for resale within the community. It is this second component of the commodity equation that is somewhat different from the HSP.

The sale of country foods among Inuit through the medium of the market has a history in Puvirnituq that predates the Co-op. According to Balikci, the Hudson's Bay Company trader in Puvirnituq tried to set up a system of exchange between carvers and fishers that would compensate the fishers for the constant supply of fish they gave to the carvers. The trader would buy fish and sell it to the carvers. As Balikci saw it, "Thus the traditional sharing patterns were to give way to formalized inter-Eskimo trade relations, reflecting the occupational differentiation within the community." The system seemed only to work under the trader's watchful supervision, however. Once he relaxed control, Inuit reverted to sharing the food.[73]

In the 1960s, despite the fact that the Co-op had been selling country foods since the 1950s, such sales were nominal in its overall accounts.[74] Almost 40 years later, in 2001, the manager of the Co-op told me that a similar trend had persisted, with the store having only a limited budget for buying country foods, although he mused that, given Puvirnituq's growing population, the demand was likely to increase in the future.

Though it has sold other country foods in the past, for the time being the Co-op limits itself to Arctic char. Such fish is hard to come by, particularly in the winter, when they are in lakes at a distance from the settlement, and people are unwilling or unable to face the hardships involved in getting them. So, because it is in short supply, the Co-op buys fish mostly in the winter, and has no problem selling it, particularly given that the HSP supplies are limited and go quickly. As the manager observed, Puvirnituq is big now, so the meat does not stay long at the HSP.

The price that the fishers receive for their fish has not greatly changed over time. As one Inuk bureaucrat observed, people's revenues have not noticeably increased over time, but the costs of procuring the food have steadily increased — he cited fuel and equipment in particular — and people's returns are getting smaller and smaller. All the same, people continue to want to sell fish to the Co-op. They do so, not because they want to make a profit, but simply in order to try to get some money for gas or groceries, and they generally only sell after they have kept some of the fish for themselves.

If the fishers make little in the way of profits, the same is true of the Co-op. As the manager informed me, the store buys fish mostly as a means of providing support to those who wish to continue to make a living from fishing. The Co-op prefers to respect its underlying mandate, which is as much social as economic. This explains, perhaps, why no one expressed any reservations about the sales of county foods by the Co-op. Like the HSP, people see the sale of country foods as contributing to a larger collective social good.

Pitsituuq (The Smoked Fish Plant)

Of the various structures involved in the commoditization of country foods in Puvirnituq, the one that most closely resembles the capitalist mode of production as it is commonly conceived is Pitsituuq. It was set up in about 1985 by the municipal government. It changed hands several times until finally it came into the possession of its current owner, an Inuk from the settlement.

For the time being, because of regulations that restrict the sale of non-commercially tagged fish to beneficiaries residing in Nunavik, his sales are limited to Nunavik. However, he wishes to expand the business and has built a new plant that he is in the process of having certified to ensure that the fish will comply with provincial and federal regulations.

Regulations have affected the business in other ways. In order to sell his fish outside the region and to non-beneficiaries, he is obliged to buy fish through commercial quotas. But owing to over-fishing in the past, commercial quotas in Nunavik are limited, and therefore difficult to come by. He gets around this problem in two ways: first, he buys Arctic char from commercial fishers in Nunavut; second, he gets fish from an island which is located in the waters between Nunavik and Nunavut, which makes their regulatory jurisdiction open to debate. He started fishing there so as to avoid competing for fish with subsistence fishers in Puvirnituq who, having noticed that the char were getting smaller, wanted to ensure that they were protected.

Not only do local residents buy his products, but so do various institutions such as the Co-op and the catering company. Given that Inuit tell me that an Inuk should not sell country foods to another Inuk, I was curious how people in the community perceived his business. No Inuit of whom I asked this question expressed reservations about the fact that Pitsituuq was making a profit from the common pool of resources. Nor did they say that the owner of the business was breaking social norms. Despite people's reticence to speak ill of the operation, as the first business in town in which an individual Inuk is selling country foods to other Inuit, the owner does face some challenges; he has had to confront his own and other people's reactions to the breaking of social norms about the sharing of food. As he informed me, people had given him a hard time, and in order to develop his business he had had to close his ears and his eyes.

So, should I take the fact that people did not express any reservations to me that Pitsituuq was selling char to Inuit as an indication that they had come to accept such behaviour? It is hard to answer this question with certainty. Perhaps the best one can do in understanding how it might feel to be engaged in such activities is to acknowledge the observations of the majority of Inuit to whom I spoke who repeatedly said that selling country foods among Inuit was deplorable.

Selling Country Foods among Individual Inuit

Despite people's reservations — spoken or otherwise — it would seem that the selling of country foods to both Inuit and non-Inuit has taken hold in Puvirnituq. Nonetheless, time and again people in the community would differentiate selling by institutions from selling among individuals. To sell to one's neighbour was anathema, but to sell to the various organizations in town was tolerable. So, for example, one person who sold to the HSP said that he was shocked and disgusted when he heard people on the community radio offering to sell meat or bannock. They were asked to stop. Others told me that such sales did not happen in Puvirnituq, but occurred in other communities in Nunavik and Nunavut. Another said that Inuit who sell country foods to other Inuit are thinking only of themselves, which points to an important thing: in the sharing of food, commitment to the collectivity is both built up and sustained. And community is part of what has ensured Inuit survival. Thus, anything that threatens that sense of community threatens people's notions of survival. Yet the same people who said these things would also affirm that people need money and are justified in trying to get it in order to spend time on the land. That conundrum poses a difficult problem, and how people manage to resolve it can be complex.

One way they do so is by selling things other than country foods. Among themselves, money comes into the equation via other means. The administrator of the HSP said that, although people did not sell country foods in the community, sometimes what they will do is pay for gas to go out with someone else, and then they will split the catch.[75] Although there was an exchange of cash, the food itself was not commoditized, and so social norms were not threatened. In fact, in order to ensure that these norms are adhered to, people talk on the community radio about the importance of sharing. They fear that without such discussion, the younger generation might not understand or respect its importance.

Yet, for all that, people, both from Puvirnituq and from other towns and villages, sell country foods to various institutions, from which local Inuit then either buy or are given it. The local coffee shop used to sell dried fish, and another restaurant planned to buy caribou to cook and sell to its patrons. In the past, someone in the community clandestinely sold beluga *mattak* to others in the community. It caused a stir, but the municipality could not stop it because it recognized that it did not have the money to pay the hunters who got it so that it might be distributed to the community as a whole, and the hunters needed to recoup some of their expenses.[76]

Inconsistencies also crop up which have to do with scale. Kublu told me that on occasion he buys char from people in town when he knows they have some to spare. Surprised, I asked him how he could tell me with one breath that Inuit did not sell country foods to one another and with the next say that he bought fish from an Inuk. He explained that it was a question of quantity and designation. Were he to get only a couple of fish from a fisher for his own consumption he would ask for and be given it. In asking for more than two fish for the purpose of sending them to his sister in another settlement, however, both he and the fisher find it wholly acceptable that they be paid for. The scale of the exchange, both in quantity and spatial extent, means that each party involved in the exchange finds the move from one realm of value to another wholly legitimate. If used for personal consumption, the use value of the fish along with the maintenance of social capital in the giving of it mean that they are given freely and the expectation that they be thus given is wholly legitimate. Their use value becomes less clear, however, once the quantity increases and their destination removed from direct social interaction, and so, they move into the realm of exchange value.

Conclusion

Clearly, the commoditization of country foods in Puvirnituq is not simple. In trying to make a living, people must find ways to get money. Participation in the market economy has become an integral component of making a living for Inuit, and the most direct means of participation is through wage labour in the various institutions that have developed in Puvirnituq since it was founded in the 1950s. And yet, relative to what preceded them, for most Inuit those institutions, along with the skills and conceptual frameworks that structure them, are as new as the settlement that spawned them. Those who wish to continue to hunt, fish, and gather as their main occupations face great financial challenges. On the one hand, they need money to undertake these activities and, on the other, they are morally prevented from selling their food to Inuit. How they have managed to combine these contradictory requirements reveals something about how age-old ways of living have combined with relatively new ideas about what is and is not permissible. In the process, people manage to respect conventions while breaking them.

Truck parked outside the Co-op

5

— — —

"If you want to buy, I'll sell it to you.
If you're asking for it, I'll give it to you."

CHANGE AND CONTINUITY

THE WORDS THAT GIVE THIS CHAPTER ITS NAME were uttered to me by someone in Puvirnituq who was explaining how I, as a non-Inuk, might get access
to country foods. They are telling. They reveal something of the dual and parallel worlds in which Inuit live. These worlds are, more correctly, multiple and
intersecting, and depending on the situation, people move among them with
more or less ease. They are also evocative of debates that have been prevalent
in discussions about how Indigenous peoples are dealing with the increasing
presence, and influence, of non-Indigenous institutions in their lives.

This debate comes down to discussions about acculturation or adaptation.[1]
As they confront the presence of non-Indigenous institutions, are Indigenous
peoples being swallowed up by them, thereby losing their customs, or are they
modifying their customs and managing to keep the values that are at the heart
of them? Answers to this question have vacillated between one view and the
other, and say as much about intellectual trends and people's larger needs for
clarity in responding to the "Other" as anything else.

When confronted with institutional processes that challenge our patterns
of behaviour, we may feel deeply unnerved, for these institutions can provide
"the principal way we explain ourselves to ourselves."[2] When confronted with
unsettling complexity, then, we may feel the need to call upon pristine es-

sentialisms. But what I hope I have demonstrated is that they are just that — essentialisms — and in fact how we live, give meaning to our lives, and behave are deeply ambiguous. By focussing on the commoditization of country foods, I have also sought to demonstrate that the act serves as a fundamentally important touchstone for far larger questions about how all of us, not just Inuit, construct our worlds and lives. Again, how people react to the commoditization of these foods reflects the degree to which they are coming to terms with the presence in their lives of the "Other" in all its manifestations.

The previous chapters suggest that, in the selling of country foods, there seem to be contradictions. How can people both oppose the commoditization of country foods and accept it? What has gone on in their minds and in their lives that has enabled them to sustain these seeming discrepancies? The reactions of people in Puvirnituq in confronting these issues reflect something of the variety that exists in the world.

Selling off the Commons: Evolving Systems of Belief and Behaviour

Land is the basis of human existence. From it we get food, clothing, shelter, and all the other physical necessities of life. Land determines how people live, and, concomitantly, the institutions that we develop to give order to that existence, be they economic, social, or political. "To isolate it [the land] and form a market out of it was perhaps the weirdest of all undertakings of our ancestors," writes Karl Polanyi in *The Great Transformation*.[3] Yet this is precisely what is involved in the commoditization of country foods. As described in Chapter 2, the land, sea, and sky, and the things they contain, have been central to the economic life of Inuit. They have also been integral, whether conscious or unconscious, to how people made sense of themselves in the world, to their understandings of appropriate behaviour, and to their notions of what constitutes a proper life. Fundamental to this view has been the widely held belief among Inuit that resources are common property. No one individual has more or less rights to access those resources than another. If people meet with success, they have done so because they have acted appropriately and shared those resources, and in continuing to share them they will continue to meet with success. Inherent in this view are beliefs that must be respected about the correct ways to share resources with others which are, in turn, guided by correct ways to treat the land, water, and animals.

In the abstract, the selling of country food would seem to assume that what was once common property can now be taken by one individual and sold, thereby excluding others from the resource. I corresponded with Pilitsi King-warsiaq, whose letter to *Nunatsiaq News* appeared in Chapter 1. His response reflected this view: "I personally think that the sale of country food should not be allowed. The animals are not ours, so who are we to sell them?"

I asked several people if the selling of country foods somehow implied that people were beginning to think they owned the animals. I used the private fish-smoking plant as a case in point. To some extent, people's responses were indicative of the view that the animals are common property. Thus, when I asked whether people resented the fact that Pitsituuq was taking fish to sell, Jamisie said, "That's not in our nature . . . to try to own the wildlife. . . . It's never been in our tradition and culture."

Kublu's perspective was more ambiguous. When asked whether people got upset about the fact that common resources were being taken and sold, he responded, "No, not really. Even though they have noticed that the business owner is sending much of his cooked fish out of town . . . they don't complain, because they know that there's more fish out there that hunters can catch."

Some, then, accept the sale of country foods, because they have faith that there are enough resources to meet their needs. Yet not all tolerate this with such equanimity. Alurut remarked that people adjust their behaviour to make allowances for the fact that people are earning money from country foods, but they can also resent it:

A few times I have been hunting with a friend, in the past, who's hunting to sell, and me, hunting not to sell. We would have divided *equally* if we're not — if both of us wasn't going to sell. . . .

Alurut was also uneasy about the school's scheme to employ people to take students hunting. Although he supported the idea that children should learn to hunt, the leaders of these groups — who were being paid — often occupied the best hunting and fishing grounds, which was unfair to those who were hunting and fishing not to earn money, but to put food on their tables.

Joseph made similar observations about the distinction between money-making and sharing. When people from Puvirnituq went to another community for beluga, and then came back and sold it in Puvirnituq, it caused some friction. "It was not right," he said. "I mean, they don't mind you go hunting there and give it to the community. . . . But not to make money off of it."

The experience of being on the land, then, seems to be different when people are after money. The fact that people are making money from hunting, fishing, and gathering causes people to behave differently so they do not share in the same way. When people hunt together the standard practice is that each receives an equal share of the harvest. As money comes into the equation, that standard share is changed and the practice is transformed. And so the presence of money challenges customary practices that have regulated people's activities.

Give and take is an important aspect of common property systems. In the case of Inuit, people are willing to accept the sometimes disproportionate acquisition of resources by others because, in essence, all will be evened out eventually through the process of sharing. Yet in the commoditization of country foods, the division of products from shared hunting is transformed, and people's willingness to share becomes marked with a measure of ill feeling as they discern that there is a lack of equality in the basic framing of their access to resources. The presence of money causes an imbalance in the neat equation of give and take, with some giving more so that others may take more.

If the implicit privatization of the commons inherent in commodized country foods has affected relations among people, what of their relations with the other-than-human world of the animals? As discussed in Chapter 3, one of the concepts that has sustained ideas of sharing among many Inuit was that animals were, in fact, sharing themselves with hunters or fishers, who, out of respect for the animal and in order to ensure their future success, then shared their catch with others. What goes around comes around, both in the human world and in the world of humans and animals. If people started to sell the animals rather than share them, then, would the animals react badly?

The response I received to this question was generally a concern that is reflected in the literature of non-Inuit about the commoditization of country foods: namely, that the selling of country foods might affect the sustainability of the animal populations.[4] This reflects the concern of most Inuit that animal populations continue to be viable. People are worried that selling country foods might threaten their stocks. They had seen this happen with Arctic char; they knew that the caribou had been gone for a long time, and were concerned that it not happen to other animals. One person who sold to the Hunter Support Program said that limiting the sale of country foods to the HSP was a good thing because it prevented over-harvesting or the taking of animals at inappropriate times in their reproductive cycles. Many people also said that, in hunting or fishing for the HSP, they were careful never to take more than they needed. Despite people's concern that the commoditization of country foods might affect animal stocks, one person said that the caribou *should* be sold, because this will help to prevent a crash of the population.

I wondered whether, over and above issues of sustainability, people thought that the selling of country foods affected the metaphysical behaviour of the animals. I was tentative when I posed this question for, as Inuit have told me, the power of animals is so great that people are unwilling to talk about it. Most people stuck to issues of sustainability. From those who were willing to talk about the metaphysical nature of animals, however, I received different replies. Salamonie had told me how selling country foods would be a good thing, because it would bring money to the community and provide an income for those who might otherwise be on welfare. All the same, I wondered whether this might affect the animals. "Maybe," Salamonie allowed:

> In the past our grandfathers were hunting. There were lots of caribous everywhere. There were not many people hunting, but there were lots of caribous. They knew they had lots of meat to catch, and . . . they only take the best part: the back and the best skin in the back. The fur. And when they did that the caribou disappeared for forty years. They didn't come back for forty years. They were killing more than what they need.

I asked Benjamin, an older man who sells country food to the HSP, whether he thought selling country foods affected the relations between humans and animals. He responded that, in the past, hunters used to take all the available animals and store the meat for the winter:

> But today they don't do that. . . . Before they were using dogs, and they had to feed also the dogs and they had to catch almost everything that they could catch because they were feeding the eating machine dogs. And today it's different now. They don't have the dogs. They catch only what they need.

When I asked if the animals themselves behaved differently, Benjamin said that when the HSP has asked people to get meat to sell to the program, "the meat they want to catch usually disappears. When it's time to catch . . . it's kind of disappeared or moved away."

These responses suggest that, when animals sense they are being mistreated, it can make them go away. Others to whom I spoke had no such concerns. Kublu said that people locally had never really thought about it, and the fact that the animals are being sold has not affected the animals' behaviours:

> For sure, they know that certain animals have spirits 'cause they don't hunt them without having the animal *notice* the person first. Or they don't kill them. For example, polar bear, they have to see you first before you kill it. . . . 'Cause the polar bear has a spirit and that's the way it is. Our fathers before us have taught this. For polar bear, you have to notify the polar bear to kill it, 'cause if you don't, you can lose the bear.

From Kublu's perspective, certain animals do possess powers, but the fact that they will be sold does not appear to have affected how they react to those hunting them.

In the morality of Inuit, sharing food should always take precedence over selling it, but in the case of selling, there are ways and ways of going about it. What is clear, however, is that in trying to understand the commoditization of country foods, we need to understand its impacts on the social systems associated with it.

Social Processes: Sharing, Community, and Identity

As I have argued throughout this book, for most Inuit, country foods are inextricably bound up in social relations, and social relations are similarly bound to country foods. So it is not surprising that people should remark on the fact that the selling of country foods is having an impact on Inuit society. As they express their fears about the effects of selling on sharing, they reveal their notions of community and identity.

The social relations so tightly connected to country foods, and particularly the requirement to share those foods, evolved as a way of ensuring stability.[5] Through getting, sharing, and eating country foods, people were able to survive, both physically and psychically, in challenging circumstances. In getting food, sharing it, and eating it with the people who move in and out of their lives, Inuit are able to build and make sense of the world they inhabit. The social relations that such sharing engenders has held people together and ensured their continuation. One must wonder, then, as the processes that regulate the getting, sharing, and eating of country foods are commoditized, have the social relations at the centre of these processes also been affected?

Polanyi argues that, as labour becomes a commodity, as it is separated from the other activities of life that take place in the cycle of survival from morning to night, from season to season and from year to year, its inclusion in the market somehow destroys these "organic" forms of existence. Instead, individualistic, atomistic forms of life replace it. With this, he argues, come other changes. Rather than behaviour based on responsibility to the collective, society starts to be arranged by contract between individuals. Kinship and community suffer as a consequence. As labour becomes a commodity, as people start to sell their toil, "traditional institutions must be destroyed, and prevented from re-forming, since, as a rule, the individual in [pre-capitalist] society is not threatened with starvation unless the community as a whole is in a like predicament."[6]

In some ways, Polanyi's words are convincing. The legalistic forms of social relations that are part of the market relations he describes have begun to appear in Puvirnituq. As discussed in Chapter 4, some say that, as beneficiaries of the James Bay and Northern Quebec Agreement, all have an equal right to the country foods provided by the Hunter Support Program. Why should only the needy have access to these rights? Clearly for some, their identities as far as the social relations around country foods are concerned have altered; they see themselves in officially authorized terms defined by an agreement signed with the governments of Canada and Quebec, rather than in the communal terms defined by life prior to the appearance of Euro-Canadian governments. The reciprocal bonds of community appear to be giving way to the associative bonds of society. But I am inclined to think that such a view applies primarily to the formal institutions that came with that agreement, institutions that are seen by people as somehow external to their own ways. As people insist, they still share country foods, among many other things.

It is frequently argued that, as people start to produce goods for the market, workers become alienated from their produce and start to see both their labour and the products of it as objects. This is because, as Georg Simmel writes, they are producing for "unknown and indifferent consumers who deal with [the producer] only through the medium of money. [Their] work is thus objectified. . . ."[7] This, certainly, is not the case in Puvirnituq. In fact, the difficulty that Inuit face in selling country foods is that they generally know who consumes the produce of their labour, and it is only to non-Inuit and their institutions, who are outside the realm of social relations built into country foods, that they generally feel comfortable selling those foods.

Tim Ingold makes the interesting point that, in industrial society, as labour comes onto the market and is socially disembedded, society starts to place more emphasis on consumption than production.[8] Work becomes separate from the rest of our lives — what Simmel calls the "whole life system" — rather than being incorporated into it. It is something we feel obliged to do in order to survive. In the process of earning a living, we must give ourselves over to an alien will that compels us to act in particular ways at particular times in order to have the wherewithal to buy the things we need to survive and thrive. Thus, we produce only to the extent that it enables us to consume things, and as a result, the social relations that had been present in productive processes are dissolved.

In some ways, this does appear to be occurring in Puvirnituq. Certainly, those who sell country foods to various buyers do so in order to get cash and have access to other goods. But such behaviour is limited. In fact, many people sell country foods as a means of subsidizing their production in order to share it with others. In other words, they sell a portion of their catch and retain the rest for other ends which are very much guided by their commitment to share food.

The sociality that is part of the mainstay of country foods is also being challenged, some argue, as a result of changes in technology.[9] With the introduction of guns, for example, Inuit are no longer obliged to hunt communally; they are no longer forced to work together to herd caribou so that they might kill them collectively. Certainly, people go out alone to get food, as they always have, but the fact remains that the production of country foods continues to be deeply embedded in social life. People *do* go out to get country foods together, whether for their own consumption or for sale, and the getting of country foods continues to be a communal experience. In part, they do it in order to be safe, but they also do it out of the pleasure of being together on the land. Many people go ice fishing in a group in the spring; in the late summer, women and children gather to go berry picking or to fish when the Arctic char are returning to the lakes. Many Euro-Canadians, heir to the belief that true nature must be devoid of people,[10] go into the wilderness to experience being in nature in its purest form. When they come across others, they steer a wide berth so as not to sully the illusion of remoteness from humanity. Inuit do the opposite. Should they come across others, whether on land, ice, or sea, they will go out of their way to meet them, to share a conversation and perhaps a cup of tea and a bite to eat, to hear the latest news, and just to be together. Being on the land is a social event. For Inuit there is no wilderness; the land is home.

The emphasis on sociality in the getting, sharing, and eating of country foods is nowhere more apparent than in the statistic that in 1995, 99 per cent of the country foods produced in Nunavik stayed within the region, and 85 per cent o f the total production stayed within the vernacular economy.[11] This means that only 15 per cent of the total production was sold on the market. Generally, very few people in any given community provide the majority of country foods consumed in that community.[12] In most cases, these people came from households where the male head of the household did not have full-time work. Instead, he subsidized his activities with the help of periodic part-time work, with sales of meat to the HSP, and with financial contributions from others with full-time work either within his immediate or extended family.[13] The hunters, in turn, distribute food among people in the community. Those men who have full-time work are less able to go hunting, fishing, and gathering. However, many of them spend what time they can spare doing this. This came out in a conversation I had with Jamisie when I asked whether selling food interfered with sharing:

> Not really. We don't let it. We do like to sell our catch too. I mean, it's good to have money for what you've caught, especially when you're fishing. . . . But most of the time we don't even sell our catch, we share it, myself especially. Now that I am working full-time I only go out on weekends mostly, and I still try to catch more than I need to be able to share it with elders and people who are less fortunate than I am. That's our tradition, and that's something I want to preserve and promote forever, and that's the reason we have survived in the harsh environment we have over thousands of years. It's something we must keep and preserve and promote.

By hook or by crook, many wish to find ways to ensure that there are enough country foods available to allow for its redistribution within the community. People with cash to spare ensure that this takes place, and those with the inclination and the time are willing to forego the possibility of earning an income via other means. Given that so few people are involved in the production of country foods, which then get shared within the community, the sale of country foods threatens their supply to the community, and occurs only minimally. But such sales also threaten people's notions of community, for the sharing of food is one way that people have of sustaining social relations.

Community is an important component of the vernacular economy of the Inuit, and it means many things. Part of what is involved in the construction of community is the accretion of life experience that people have shared with one another. On the whole, there is none of the anonymity that marks the lives of so many who live in southern Canada. Until not very long ago, Inuit lived in small groups on the land. The composition of those groups changed depending on such things as people's inclinations, the seasons, the availability of food, or social obligations, but everyone knew everyone, and everyone was required to get along, for the alternative was profound isolation. The move to settlements did not occur that long ago, and many of the social structures and understandings that developed when people were living on the land have persisted. As people pass one another, they are not passing strangers but people they have known their whole lives, people whose lives they have shared in from one generation to the next. They are related to one another. They know the stories of their ancestors. They know who went out with whom. They know that this person's father once had a really fast dog team, or that person's sister has married the cousin of a friend of theirs and moved to another settlement. They know both the good and the bad that have occurred in people's lives, and they know the good and the bad of the people themselves. Generally they have no choice but to accept people as they are, and accommodate this knowledge in their interactions, because they will continue to meet these people in the course of daily life. It is necessary to maintain an acceptance of one another to ensure that sense of community. It is community that has enabled Inuit to survive. It is this commitment to the group that ensures their continued understanding of themselves. One expression of this is the sharing of the necessities of life.

One of the great markers that divides Inuit from the non-Inuit who inhabit their settlements is the fact that Inuit just drop in on one another unannounced. There is no knocking on doors, no need to ask permission to join people in a meal or a cup of tea. People just arrive, walk into the house, and join, or not, in whatever happens to be taking place. Many shake their heads at *Qallunaat* formalities, and know that a knock at the door means a foreign person waits outside.

I noticed Jamisie and his wife remarking, on their return from another settlement, that nobody visits there. I have noted others, in Puvirnituq and elsewhere, remark with distress that no one visits them. In such words, people are observing the fact that basic ideas of community are not being observed; they are referring to the breakdown of, or their exclusion from, some of the social processes that define Inuit understandings about themselves. One of these understandings is that with notions of community, with the idea that people belong to society, come obligations to help one another and to share food.

Such sharing is an expression of responsibility to, and for, the group. When I first arrived in Puvirnituq and talked to the board of the Hunters', Fishers', and Trappers' Association to explain what my research was about, some members said they supported the idea of selling country foods, citing people's perennial need to find ways of earning.money. Others pointed out that, if people started selling country food more than they were doing at the moment, people without money would not have access to it, which would mean that they would get less of it than those who have money. The board members remarked that, as things stand, people can go on the local radio and ask for meat, but they worried that these people might not receive it if others were to start selling meat in a more concerted way.

Now, when people go out to get beluga or walrus, on their return to the community they share much of what they have got — hence the big crowd that turned out to welcome the beluga hunters back. If these hunters were to start selling their catch, only those who could afford it would get beluga or walrus. It would be a "disaster to lose the tradition of sharing," one of the board members said, and people could not call themselves hunters any more.

In places where the sense of social belonging is great, the sharing of country foods is more prevalent, and in places where that sense of belonging is less great, it seems that sharing also is diminished. Generally, for Inuit in the eastern Canadian Arctic, society remains deeply embedded in the economy of country foods, and is generally disembedded only in so far as it is linked to what appear to many as non-Inuit organizations, such as the Co-op or even the HSP, or to non-Inuit individuals. The selling of country foods among Inuit continues to be frowned upon, and the stricture remains, at least in public discourse, that Inuit must not sell country foods to one another. So it was that those people who sold country foods to such organizations as the HSP or the Co-op were adamant that they should not sell country foods to one another. Some people view the communities where Inuit have taken to selling country foods as having lost something of their Inuitness. So, for example, one person speculated that in the communities where the selling of country foods between Inuit does happen, it is because Inuit have been too long with non-Inuit, and the sense of community has been eroded. This is an example of Marshall Sahlins's point that central to subsistence production is the "principle that one does not exchange things for food, not directly that is, among friends and relatives. Traffic in food is traffic between foreign interests."[14]

Scale is important in this directive. Both Marcelle Chabot and Dominic St-Pierre found that people in larger communities shared country foods less than those who lived in smaller communities.[15] With the move to settlements, Inuit have had to confront what it means to live with people for whom they may not feel a sense of kinship because they are from distant, not closely linked camps. In the process, they have had to learn both how to sustain the sense of community that has been part of their understandings of themselves and how to adjust to new forms of it. Given these changes, food becomes even more important as a medium by which people try to maintain social relations.

Inuit who have chosen to sell country foods to other Inuit face the difficulties that come with having moved, in some ways, into a world of foreign interests. What Polanyi calls the "whole man" — a member of a family and a community — is faced with real difficulties. As Malachi revealed, such people must confront deeply seated ideas about how others should be treated,

> [W]e've always been told to share as much as we can, and not to sell at all among ourselves. That was our tradition. But, if we keep that tradition, nobody's going to start any business in country food. And it's been very hard for *me* in that area, where, in my tradition we're supposed to be providers and share among the needy. And now since there's hardly anyone in need, because of the other programs, and welfare. . . . I've had to . . . turn a blind eye in order to stay in business. . . . Like, even selling to relatives is a no-no in our tradition, but is the kind of thing that I have to overlook. Because I can't stay in business if I just keep on giving everything away. So I have to change. I have to change my tradition. . . . I have to be as if I had a cold heart.

Malachi argues that, with the change in the circumstances in which Inuit now live, he must change his ways and develop new modes of behaviour in order to be financially successful. As Simmel sees it, money and the pursuit of money lead to impersonal relations between people, which in turn, affects the degree to which people are dependent on, or independent of, social obligation.[16] In the process, people's social relations change from personal ones to objective ones, and hierarchies develop that contain within them new forms of domination and subordination. This, Simmel argues, is a general trend that happens as economies move from barter systems to money systems.

Some argue that economic inequalities have appeared among Inuit in the Canadian Arctic in ways heretofore unseen, which, in turn, have led to social differentiation.[17] There are those who drive big cars, skidoos, and boats, and those who must walk. The walkers may be dependent on the drivers for many things, including food. On occasion, the same people who have shared food and told me what a pleasure it is to do so have also expressed resentment about doing it.

Generally among Inuit, however, economic power and societal respect are not synonymous. In fact, an individual's social status does not apply to all domains of life. People with particular skills to get a particular job done are given the respect they deserve for their capacities in that realm, but this does not necessarily extend into other areas of life. In December 2009, one of the principal hunters in Puvirnituq died. His funeral was held in the community gymnasium, which was full to overflowing. A bag-piper came from the South to mark his departure. I asked the dead man's niece who was the most important person in town now. She replied, "We don't think that way."

Inuit have no tradition of hierarchy that applies across the board.[18] The fact that one has money or occupies a position of political power does not necessarily mean that one has social status in all spheres; it is just a sign that one has succeeded for the time being in one aspect of life. This reflects a sense of equality among people that has deep roots in Inuit society. Anyone who is in a position of political or economic power generally knows that this is only one aspect of what it means to have status in society, and, moreover, that their position can change at any time if they do not have community support. Moreover, those with economic power are participating in social structures that are founded on relationships of obligation, so people with money are often called on by members of the extended family to subsidize them. They subsidize the vernacular economy both politically and financially. When the phone call comes from someone asking for something, people spare what they can. This extends beyond food to money.

Money and Processes of Valuation

To understand something of Inuit reactions to money, we need first to know something of their history with it. Prior to the arrival of Europeans, Inuit had nothing that served the set of functions that money generally serves: put simply, as a store of value, a unit of account, and a medium of exchange. They produced what they needed to meet the requirements of survival. For certain specialized goods that they were unable to produce themselves, historically Inuit acquired them through trading across larger social or spatial distances.[19] When money started to appear and be used, Inuit saw it in quite different ways from the Europeans who brought it. The word in Inuktitut for "money" — *kiinaujaq*, or "which looks like a face" — reveals something of its foreignness. Seeing the head of a monarch: that is what money was.

Money stores value. Rather than having to produce all we consume, money allows us to do other things to earn it, and then use it to acquire what we want at some other time. The very notion of money is predicated on the assumption that the future is predictable and the world is a place that can be controlled.

Inuit, in contrast, have an abiding awareness of how unpredictable the world can be. Rachel Attituq Qitsualik argues that traditional Inuit culture reflects this view, going so far as to say that Inuit culture *is* the environment.[20] Thus, Inuit have developed what she calls a "survival mind" that has allowed them to endure in the face of an often dangerous and overwhelming world. Such a mindset determines how people perceive the world and their place in it, and is based on people's awareness that environmental conditions can change from one moment to the next, so people must constantly be attentive to what is going on, and react accordingly. They do not assume they have control over the forces of nature, nor do they assume the future is predictable. They live very much in the present: what is past is past, what will be is hard to foresee. As hunters, trappers, fishers, or gatherers, people must live like that. This is not to suggest that the vernacular economy does not require of Inuit that they plan for the future; they certainly did and they certainly do. They would not have survived otherwise. The caches dotted across the Arctic are physical proof of it. But at a fundamental level, in order to be productive as hunters and fishers, Inuit must focus on the moment, for, as far as natural phenomena are concerned, they cannot count on the future as something that is predictable. They have had to watch what goes on in minute detail in order to understand it and use it appropriately. Such watching is not in the speeded-up time of a nature show, but in the real time of wind and sun and snow, in the flick of a tail and the blink of an eye. This affects the kind of society that has developed and how people react to new situations.

"The spirit of the Inuit was always that of contentment, even through hardship," Otokiak writes. "It's reflected in the saying '*Ajurnarmat*' (which means 'it can't be helped'). Inuit were quick to accept the natural occurrences in life and move on.[21]

Awareness that one cannot assume one has control over the environment is born of their knowledge and experience: to make such assumptions is fool-hardy. The world is full of flux and ambiguity which must be acknowledged, respected, and responded to appropriately. The uncertainty and the trans-formative forces that people have always known are present in the environ-ment translate into the primacy of social relations over financial ones that is at the heart of the edict not to sell country foods among Inuit. If the world is an unpredictable place, then at least food is a necessity which, if not always available, is at least very real. Money, in contrast, is a figment of people's im-aginations. It can only have meaning if we believe it does.

Without money, the major way Inuit were able to store value for the long term was by establishing and respecting social relations. If you do not know what the future holds and survival is uncertain, you can always hope that others will look after you in times of need. You, likewise, will look after them. It was social capital that people had an interest in building up, through shar-ing and co-operation, and, above all, through the exchange of food, one of the most basic necessities of life, and sometimes the most difficult to find. In the selling of country foods, social capital and financial capital come head to head. The question is, has one given way to the other, or have they reached some form of accommodation? Have the values of sharing that are at the root of the vernacular economy given way to the individualizing, objectifying forces of money?

From a functionalist perspective, money is an abstraction of value, a standard of value, and a method of storing value. It serves all these functions despite the fact that it is not valuable in and of itself. From this abstraction, a host of attributes follows. As money is applied to more and more objects, the objects themselves become increasingly distant from the people acquiring them, yet, all the while, people are able to acquire more and more objects.[22] Although money allows people to have increasing numbers of objects, they are less and less close to the objects themselves, and in the process of acquir-ing objects they can become more distant from one another. Although it does not embody all forms of value, money tends to be applied to more and more things as a measure of value, which serves to concentrate the range of values into fewer and fewer varieties.

In order to understand the impacts of money, one must understand how a given society defines the situations in which it may be used and how it may be used. The symbolic representations of money are linked to culturally constructed notions of production, consumption, circulation, and exchange.[23] There are instances in which money can be embedded in economies that are themselves embedded in social systems, and are not devoid of the moral imperatives under which those systems function. Money simply becomes one more means by which socially sanctioned views of morally appropriate behaviour can be expressed. So, a particular worldview gives rise to a particular understanding of money.[24]

Certain people do express concern that money has caused a distance among Inuit. This is particularly noteworthy among those who knew life on the land before the move into settlements, with its increased reliance on wage labour and money. As Apphia Agalakti Awa, who was born in 1931, puts it,

> As Inuit, we would trade things. We didn't pay each other. Paying makes you distant from your relatives. . . . If my husband needed kamiks and I didn't have any bearded seal for the soles, I would ask someone, "My husband is out of soles, can you give me soles?" And of course that person would say, "Yes, come and take what you want." There wouldn't be any talk of payment. That is how families were kept together. Asking for things, it is not part of our life anymore. I never thought we would end up thinking so much about asking for things. Now we are trying to be like the *Qallunaat*. *Qallunaat* want things to be paid for right away.[25]

Jamisie observed that money is not like food and so is not shared in the same way. Instead, people are constantly after it. Dorothy Mesher, who grew up in Kuujjuaq, also complains that, compared with the past, money has come to dominate people's behaviour too much. "They have moved, in just a few years, from a world in which nothing that people did for one another had a dollar value to a world where it's commonplace to think that *everything* has a dollar value."[26] Like Awa, Mesher believes that the corruption comes from *Qallunaat*.

> October 31, 2001: On *Newsworld* they just had a financial reporter talking about how to teach your kids how to deal with money. She said to start teaching them at three — to give them an allowance at three. And then she said financial knowledge was "the greatest gift you can give

your child." At least the weather woman challenged her. She thought love and safety and happiness were the important things, and money was down on the list. It's amazing how early we're taught things and how early we learn them.

Several people to whom I spoke about the selling of country foods commented on the fact that young people were behaving in distasteful ways: stealing food from the common pool, or killing animals ineffectually or inappropriately in order to sell them. People also remark that they are working to ensure that young people do not get rewarded for such behaviour, talking to them in person, or on the radio to ensure that they learn to behave correctly. Malachi thinks that the younger generation may well break with tradition, despite people's attempts to socialize them otherwise:

> [I]t's changing now. It's a new generation now, and they understand the principle of achieving. . . . And of course, we were educated in English, and our way of thinking is much different than the traditional way. So we're going to be businessmen. We're going to break some rules, our traditional rules.

This may well be true. But for many people, at least for the time being, money appears to be no more than a tool that has immediate use when and where it is needed. The idea that money should be saved for future use, to maximize profits, or to accumulate wealth is not a deeply ingrained consideration.

Money seems a transitory and illusory thing compared to the necessities of life. The immediacy of life — living in the moment — which Inuit have been taught, and which comes from their understanding that the world is constantly changing, extends to the ways they live with money. To some extent, this explains Chabot's findings that people in Nunavik live with fairly significant debt. While part of this is attributable to people's ideas that money is a thing to be used when and how they choose, she also notes that there is another rationality to this debt. People often acquire and juggle debt in order to be able to spend time on the land. For many, this is of greater value than the requirement to pay back the debt.[27] This is another explanation for the impression, held by many non-Inuit, who are involved in buying country foods, that Inuit are only selling these foods when they need money for a particular thing. They do not sell them on a regular basis to get money on a regular basis, nor are they interested in making a profit or accumulating capital. Kublu echoed these views, saying that people sell country foods to get money, which is generally in short supply, but they want money simply to get other things; profit is not the issue:

> You make money to buy your cup, your tea, your sugar, your bannock, or flour. And people . . . didn't really try and start selling meat just to make money or just to have money. It's when they *really* needed something, that's when I started noticing, when I was a younger person, it was because they really needed something.

Certainly, things have changed in the North, but "monetization of the mind"[28] seems not to have set in. Rather, money appears to have been assimilated into forms of behaviour and understandings that have existed among Inuit long before the advent of money. Their existing worldviews have given rise to particular ways of understanding and using money. For many, money continues to be something that is shared, like the other goods in life, in the interests of the collective rather than the individual. In fact, there are social pressures to redistribute money, and those who do hang onto it can meet with resentment.

Along the waterfront in Puvirnituq

For many people, social relations affect how their money is redistributed, family and extended family being the primary recipients of their largesse. It is not only family, however, that benefits from the financial generosity of others. As in the days that existed prior to life in settlements, sharing can extend to any number of people with whom an individual has established social links.

The superior value that sharing has over money is clear in people's self-imposed limitations on selling country foods. By selling only 15 per cent of their total catch and keeping 85 per cent for their own use, Inuit in Nunavik lost potential earnings of $3.9 million for the region as a whole.[29] Some people will actually buy food in a store in order to be able to give away country food.

It would be overly simplistic, however, to assume that people do not know the value of money, and, within limits, do not seek to maximize their access to it — or what it will allow them access to. When the administrators of the Hunter Support Program started to implement the HSP in Puvirnituq, they found that the hunters were asking for as much money as they could get. Eventually, having called other communities to consult them on prices, the administrators in Puvirnituq adjusted the prices they paid to be on a par with what hunters got elsewhere. The amount of effort required to get different foods also plays a factor in the prices, which is why the Co-op pays more for fish in the winter than at other times of year, and why the HSP pays more per pound for ptarmigan than for caribou; the former has less meat on it, but requires more effort per pound to acquire (see Appendix 3).

It looks as if Adam Smith's — and later Marx's — labour theory of value holds true in the selling of country foods. It is argued that, in subsistence production, neither labour nor its products have a monetary value; these are applicable only to commercial cultures.[30] Inuit have maintained the values inherent in their vernacular economy while at the same time allowing for the appearance of commercial notions of value. All the same, the latter is secondary to larger issues of value inherent in the former. For many, the social value of country foods continues to outweigh its monetary value. Igor Kopytoff provides a useful way of understanding this process. He suggests that people develop distinct spheres of exchange, each with its own set of values. Often, he argues, there is a lack of common measures of value between the different spheres. As a result, "When a thing participates simultaneously in cognitively distinct yet effectively intermeshed exchange spheres, one is constantly confronted with seeming paradoxes of value."[31] Perhaps this is why, as one businessperson suggested, in order to be able to be economically secure, the injunction against Inuit selling to Inuit must give way:

. . . it's changing slowly. But it was not always like that. You know we hear people, when I was getting started in business, even my uncles, I heard them on the radio, that we shouldn't be selling to one another, because it's breaking up relationship; it's breaking up family. They said, "We are always the ones that were sharing and providing." But in doing that we'll never start businesses. We'll never become independent financially. We'll never have any . . . aspirations. In fact, if we stick to those traditions we're condemned . . . not to do *anything*. We wouldn't be business people at all.

When I pointed out that Inuit tradition doesn't come with money, the person went on to say that Inuit

just don't know that nothing's free any more. Especially today. It might have been . . . when it was a small community. There was no money involved. . . . *I* share. I share my own food. I share . . . my own resources with my family, with my immediate family, or to those that are my friends. But, when it comes to business, it's a different thing. I say, "Business is business." . . . It doesn't involve the emotions at all. It doesn't. But that doesn't mean that a person is heartless. It's just a principle, you know.

Such is, indeed, part of the rationale of the market. Money does not grow on trees, and so "nothing is free." Instead, we must sell our labour or the products from the land. This is life in the market. In such a context, the idea that the more you give the more you get, which lies at the heart of the vernacular economy of Inuit, becomes reduced to time and money, and the essentially social relations that lie at the heart of this edict among Inuit are swept aside. In part, this is because, with money, people are no longer quite so reliant on mutual support to meet their material needs.[32]

Yet the social relations that underpin the vernacular economy do not vanish as easily as that. To take on the principles of the market is a struggle. At some level, this person appears to be both promoting the development of a new ethic for Inuit, and feeling the pressures to preserve the ethic of sharing. Such an ethic is developing, he remarks. All the same, the push and pull of two spheres of value are manifest in his words. Business may be business, but he still notes the importance of sharing among family and friends.

For Inuit, the value of country foods is very real. Death by starvation exists within living memory, so food is not something that people take for granted. It is literally a matter of life and death. Money, in contrast, is an abstraction of value and the potential of something in the future. It may be that, for Inuit, the promise of the value inherent in money is, to some extent, questionable, because it is not real in the way that country foods are. The value of country foods — survival at a basic level and social reproduction at a more removed one — are still more important than the abstraction of value that money represents. They refuse to replace something of real value with promises of value. For this reason, they are trying to preserve the injunction against selling country foods among Inuit. At the same time, they know that money is a useful tool, one that is worth having, so they have found ways to get around the injunction to sell country foods by selling them to individuals and institutions that exist outside the spheres of valuation that place primacy on the sharing of country foods and the social relations inherent in that sharing.

How precisely this is done comes down to issues of scale. What is clear is that, with the introduction of money to societies that had no such tool, there is no simple trajectory from forms of value that are purely embedded in society to ones that are purely disembedded.[33] Culture plays an important part in this process, and the particularities of place are an important component of the processes of valuation. In attempting to maintain the notion that country foods must not be sold among Inuit, they are trying to preserve values that remain embedded in community and larger notions of how society ought to work, and reflect their experiences of the natural conditions in which they live. In the case of money, at the local level — that associated with place — it, too, generally reflects values that are indigenous; thus, like other things, money is shared and is used to sustain social relations and ideas of community. And for many, money functions in disembedded ways only at the larger, more impersonal scale, in the space out there that is inhabited by non-Inuit and the institutions they brought with them.

Scaling the Boundaries of Place

Scale, both physical and metaphysical, plays an important role in determining the course of events. Its impact has been both negative and positive — serving, for example, to shelter people from some of the psychic distress that accompanies the breaking of rules, and causing some grief for those who wish to sell country foods. As with most things in life, the good and the bad are mixed together.

At a physical level, it is clear Nunavik's distance from large commercial centres where people might sell country foods, and the lack of infrastructure linking Nunavik to these centres, make the commoditization of country foods expensive for anyone wanting to undertake such a venture. Yet this distance also protects people. Because the commoditization of country foods is essentially taking place locally, it allows people more control over how it is done, enabling them to apply local norms to the process. Thus, they are more able to preserve local ideas of how the land should be used, who should have access to country foods, and how those foods should be obtained. With such control, people are less dependent on impersonal market forces to regulate how the food is commoditized, and so are able to control the extent to which economic systems become separate from the social systems within which they operate. Having experienced the impact that animal rights activists had on the fur trade, Inuit have learned the hard way what it means to be economically dependent on external markets.

No less important than physical scale, however, is metaphysical scale. This comes down, essentially, to the ways in which people are able to keep a mental distance between themselves and the processes in which country foods are commoditized. How is it that the same people who hunt or fish to sell their produce to the HSP or the Co-op are also able to say that they would never sell country foods to other Inuit? They can do so because they make a distinction between the two spheres of exchange that operate within the vernacular and market economies. The former is predicated on processes of valuation that place an emphasis on social capital, whereas the latter emphasizes financial capital. In 1969, Nelson H. H. Graburn argued that people would soon be unable to sustain such a separation, as the pressures of acculturation and world markets bore down on them.[34] Yet, more than 40 years later, people in Puvirnituq have managed to sustain that separation. Those who sell country foods and those who consume them are still able to make some distinction between the two economies, and to participate in both.

The ability to isolate themselves from the influences of non-Inuit may have become harder as people spend more time in settlements, in schools, watching television, and otherwise participating in the Euro-Canadian culture. But such influences are not recent. Even prior to sedentarization, Inuit understandings of the world had been influenced by contact with various non-Inuit institutions that accompanied the arrival of traders, missionaries, RCMP officers, and bureaucrats who progressively moved into the Arctic. Yet the basic explanations that frame the non-Inuit institutions of money and business are foreign, which means that the ways in which Inuit react and adapt to them are less tied up in the non-Inuit traditions associated with the market. People are thus able to adopt, adapt, and live with the contradictions more readily because they can much more readily erase them epistemologically. There is not the depth of time and meaning associated with them. Instead, in various ways Inuit have taken these forces and shaped them to their own ends, imposing their own culturally framed meanings on these institutions, thereby maintaining their autonomy.

People accept that they should share foods among one another, but they also accept that they may have to sell to, and buy from, the institutions that are part of the economy that came with non-Inuit; the one involves friends and relatives while the other is relegated to the world of strangers that exists outside the local realm. As people like Paul Bohannan and Marshall Sahlins observe, generally, market relations among people who are subsistence producers, particularly related to food, can only develop when people have a certain social distance among themselves.[35] The commoditization of country foods through such institutions as the Co-op or the Hunter Support Program provides people with that sense of social distance.

I explored this thought with Jamisie, who said, simply, "The people who sell [to other Inuit] will be the bad Inuit according to our tradition." The ones

High school in Puvirnituq

who sell to the Co-op, on the other hand, are not seen as bad Inuit "because they have to make a living to buy more fuel, for instance. If they're selling fish, they need nets; nets are very expensive. Also machinery, it's double the price when it gets here. Fuel is triple the price."

In continuing to emphasize the importance of sharing country foods, many Inuit are sticking to a world of values that they have always known, a world that is predicated on an awareness of uncertainty, a world in which survival depended upon people's connections with one another. Life within communities has changed that. As people readily acknowledge, they need access to cash in order to have the goods they appreciate and to which they are now accustomed. This conundrum — how to adhere to one's principles while getting cash — is not unique to Inuit. Most of us do it in one form or another. I, for example, have fairly strong moral principles about how to behave toward people and the environment: they should both be treated with respect. Were I to live fully by these principles, however, it would be difficult to participate in the world. It would be difficult to travel to the Arctic and other distant places. It would be difficult to eat or buy clothes. To live wholly according to one's principles can be an onerous task, so we find ways that allow us both to feel that we are respecting them and ignore the ways in which we violate them. We need to live, so we learn to ignore the contradictions, finding ways to justify them or developing cognitive and teleological blind spots.

Jonathan Parry and Maurice Bloch have provided a useful way of thinking about how people are able to contend with these kinds of contradictions.[36] Scale plays a part in their explanation, not in terms of space, but in terms of time. One must consider how short-term cycles of exchange — which involve the domain of individual activity that often focuses on acquisition — are linked to long-term cycles of exchange that commonly aim to reproduce the enduring social and cosmic order. Short-term individualistic transactions are morally acceptable to the extent that they do not threaten the long-term cycles that focus on the collectivity. In fact, short-term cycles may be desirable if they yield goods that are transferred to the long-term cycles and used to maintain them. The process resolves the sometimes contradictory interests of the individual and the collective, for it provides an ideological space in which individual interests may be justified in the name of the collective. These activities, however, are conceived of by people as operating in a separate sphere subordinate to the sphere of activity that promotes long-term production. This is necessary for two reasons: first, because the short-term sphere often provides the material goods required to sustain the reproduction of the long-term sphere; and second, because the long-term order can only be maintained by the contributions of individuals. So people make sense of the existence of individual self-interest. It is only if this short-term order of individual self-interest threatens the reproduction of the larger, long-term cycle that it is condemned. Money is generally associated with the short-term cycle. In societies that place a premium on reciprocity, short-term, individualistic transactions are morally acceptable as long as they do not threaten the long-term cycles of exchange that focus on the collectivity; in fact, they are desirable if they yield goods that are used to maintain this over-arching order. This is why, for many, the HSP is an acceptable means of commoditizing country foods, because it gives people access to cash while allowing sharing ideologies to persist. The same is true for sales to the other institutions that come from the outside world. So, for example, sales to the Co-op are acceptable because it is conceived of as "a new way of sharing."[37] In these cases, goods from the short-term cycle are transferred to the long-term cycle, and individual interests serve to sustain those of the group. It is the group sustaining the interests of the group that has ensured that individual Inuit have been able to survive.

These two spheres must also be understood in terms of physical scale, so that it is acceptable to sell outside the local scale to the impersonal realm beyond a community and its institutions. By these means many people have learned to create a distance between the needs and interests of the individuals who sell country foods and the collective requirement that they be shared. The individual, short-term necessity for money is used to sustain the long-term necessity that country foods should be distributed to any who need or wish to have them. Behaviour that threatens this long-term order, such as the direct selling of country foods, is met with censure.

The Commoditization of Country Foods: Scale, Value, Identities, Community, and Futures

Clearly the commoditization of country foods is closely linked to people's notions of how community should function. People have depended on one another for their survival. The Arctic can be an unforgiving place. When a storm hits, when food cannot be found and supplies are running low, people can be powerless to protect themselves against nature's forces, particularly if they are alone. Connections with others and the sharing of resources, in good times and in bad, have helped people to overcome these uncertainties. If the world is an unpredictable place, at least people could generally rely on one another to counterbalance it. This is why community is so important, and this is at the root of why people wish to maintain it. This is why they place a premium on sharing country foods, for it is an expression of community, and part of the bulwark that they have built to protect them in the face of life's uncertainties. And this is why the commoditization of country foods can pose such a threat to people, for it threatens the ideal of sharing. For many, the value of social relations far exceeds other values, and so must be preserved.

People do not assume they can control what goes on, but preserve enough flexibility to adjust to whatever comes. Money presumes that things behave in predictable, controllable ways. A monetary economy does everything it can to ensure that this is the case, and when, for some reason, the world turns out to be uncontrollable — as in the crashing of planes into the World Trade Centre — monetary economies teeter in very much the same way as the structures they produce. Just as market economies develop regulatory systems, such as quality controls and laws against counterfeiting, Inuit have developed regulatory systems, such as the sharing of food, for the same reason: to ensure stability.

The knowledge and behaviours that have been vital to Inuit survival are built into the vernacular economy at many levels. They have developed over centuries and are expressed in people's capacity to survive on the land. They come out in people's abilities to navigate their way over the land, water, and ice, in knowing that particular kinds of environmental circumstances indicate particular kinds of behaviours in the animals, in knowing how to kill and butcher an animal, in knowing what meat is good and what meat is bad, in knowing the stories that are held in the land and sea, in knowing when to act and when to sit back, in knowing that responsibility and maturity often mean not interfering with others, in possessing the various components of a "survival mind," such as stoicism, cynical humour, easy-goingness, and non-paranoid wariness.[38] All this knowledge, and all these behaviours, have been integral components of people's ability to participate in life on the land.

With the move to settlements, the importance of that economy and of the institutions associated with it seems to have diminished. Yet those institutions and their knowledge, understandings, and perceptions remain. They are not always manifest in the money economy that is built into the functioning of life in settlements. Many of the institutions associated with Euro-Canadian society, with market systems, with wage employment, assume that the world is a predictable, and therefore a controllable, place. In the face of this, people must act forcefully. In the face of this, money can allow us to meet many of our physical needs. And in the face of this, many of the skills and understandings that Inuit possess find no room for expression — in fact, are actively discouraged. I had a conversation with a teacher who told me that he spent much of his time trying to get his students to plan ahead, not realizing that this contradicts the broad requirement among Inuit to be flexible, to wait until circumstances seem right, and then to act. The monetary economy is all about standardization and control, while the sharing economy of the Inuit is about irregularity and not having control.

Built into the commoditization of country foods, then, are some powerful forces. Put simply, the world of behaviours, understandings, and knowledge that developed with life on the land meets the world of behaviours, understandings, and knowledge that came with the move to settlements. How is this being played out? How have people learned to accommodate these different ways of knowing, behaving, and understanding?

There is no simple or single answer to these questions. What I have heard from people, what I have observed, and what I have learned is that Inuit, like other peoples, reflect variety and contradiction. In trying to understand these things, the words of Kopytoff have served as a useful directive: "Commoditization . . . is best looked upon as a process of becoming rather than as an all-or-none state of being."[39]

In this process of becoming, people express concern that the commoditization of country foods will affect people's ability and willingness to share those foods. For a few, this concern remains, but others have found a way of accepting the necessity for some to sell country foods while preserving the requirement to share them. Thus, people continue to subsidize the hunting, fishing, and gathering economy by whatever means they can, whether it is by sharing what food they have with others or by discussing publicly the importance of continuing to do so with those who might be inclined to break with this imperative; whether it is in providing money themselves to subsidize others' trips on the land or by lending support to the various institutions in which people may sell country foods.

These institutions exist in realms that are essentially outside the mental or physical domain of the vernacular economy. Inuit sell to non-Inuit and to the institutions they brought with them, but they try to preserve the notion that such sales should not take place within the Inuit world. By selling country foods to the HSP, or the Co-op, or the hospital, or the catering company, they are able to get much-needed money while preserving their notions of appropriate behaviour. Such a mental split in people's perceptions is of great symbolic importance, for it allows them to continue to be Inuit; to live as members of a community; to reflect the importance of relationship, both among Inuit and between Inuit and the natural world; to act as morally responsible adults; to confirm their knowledge and express their values.

Some are less able to retain a clear mental separation between the Inuit and non-Inuit worlds. Things creep in. The moral order appears to wear away, so that the self-regulating, morally-defined mechanisms regulating economic behaviours become eroded, and aberrant behaviours start to appear.[40] In expressing reservations about the commoditization of country foods, people are, in a sense, reflecting their concern that the moral order that has governed Inuit society is being challenged. They fear that values of sociality are giving way to individual self-interest, and, in the process, the very community on which their survival has depended may appear to be fracturing. So they mention the appearance of theft in the community. So they say that people are sharing less than they used to. So they say that some of the youth seem to be losing the skills and behaviours that are necessary to live on the land. So they say that people are lacking a sense of initiative and are floundering in their dependency on non-Inuit goods and services. Such services might be an attempt to replace the knowledge systems associated with the vernacular economy, but they are not a true replacement. They do not allow people to feel productive in ways that give them a sense of pride or responsibility. As Simigak said,

> As long as the people were attached to the land, they had *respect* for it, they had self-respect from living off the land. But now everything's provided for them. Housing. Welfare. . . . Even if you don't put in an effort. So why the hell should people make an effort to go out and hunt any more? Or to go out and get a job? It's genocide. We're witnessing genocide *right out* in the open, but nobody's saying anything about it.

Malachi expressed a similar view when he told me that he wished people would do more on their own:

> Even if they don't have *fancy* roads, I would prefer that they would do it themselves instead of getting governments to do it for them. Even if they have not very good housing, I would prefer that they would have done it themselves and built it themselves. From their own resources, from their own money. Because they would . . . be *real* people then. And

that's what I want to see. If government stops all their subsidy coming in to the Inuit people, it would be a blessing in disguise because they would have to try and do it themselves. . . . Like before. They would be independent, and I'm very certain that with God's help, they would be able to do it. But the way things are going now, with all kinds of subsidies left and right, coming from the back and under, right and left with the Hunter Support Program, people are *dying*. They don't *have* to do anything. All they have to do is watch TV and listen to the radio. People don't *need* to do anything. And that kills people.

As an entrepreneur selling country foods, Malachi acknowledges that he must confront head-on the gulf in values between the vernacular and the market economy. He believes that change is necessary. Times are changing, and people must change with them. Such a view was, in fact, an important component of the perspective of the dissident movement in Puvirnituq. Part of the reason the residents of the village refused to sign the JBNQA was, they argued, because the Agreement cast them only as hunters and fishers, whereas they believed that Inuit should be allowed to expand their economic practices beyond these domains into other areas.[41] Moreover, the dissidents maintained, such development was best managed by Inuit themselves, rather than by the non-Inuit institutions established as a result of the Agreement.

So, Malachi argues, the plethora of government services that have been provided to Inuit in an attempt to help them deal with these changes are debilitating. This is why he thinks Inuit must start to produce their own destinies. For him, business is one way of doing this. As a businessperson, his commitment to doing this can sometimes come at the expense of breaking the rules that governed society. But if this is the price that must be paid, then so be it. At least he is being productive. Financial success is the new gauge of productivity, and, as many recognize, it is also a requirement for other forms of production.

Malachi says that nothing is free, but is money the only way that Inuit have found to express and reflect notions of what is involved in making a living? For some, the answer is yes, but for others, the answer is complex and rooted in the richness of their experience. To be sure, money is part of it, but people take that money, use it, and choose to be able to do what they *really* value. As Jamisie told me,

We're a big community. We're well off money-wise; we're well equipped. But there's just not enough money to go around. And it's . . . not in our tradition to sell to one another. I mean, we try to keep our traditions, traditional values, as best we can. And sometimes it's not the best . . . thing for us to do. But still we try to keep our tradition alive. That's why you've never seen a skinny Inuk, even though a lot of people don't practise their traditional hunting and fishing too much anymore. A lot of young men [on welfare], under the age of forty don't bother. . . . And you can't afford a skidoo or a canoe on your welfare cheque *anyway*. You need to have a full-time job to have those things. You need to work all year round to be fully equipped. And those of us who *are* only have a chance to work [hunt] on weekends now. . . .

A lot of the men who work five days a week go on Saturday. . . . That's how we live. . . . We're still living off the land.

Closing the Circle?

This book grew out of a wish to find out how people were surviving in the North. I wanted to understand something of how the economy indigenous to the North was faring in the face of the newer economic systems that have moved into the area. Despite all the changes that Inuit have experienced, they cannot avoid where they are from. How, then, are they to make sense of these changes? This is what I set out to discover.

I embarked on this journey with a certain reticence. I knew that, for all my focus on the vernacular economy, today there is much more to the economy in the North than that. I feared, when I started doing this work, that I was helping to perpetuate fixed ideas of Inuitness and stereotypical notions of how they survive (as I was asked, as a child moving to Britain from Canada, whether I lived in an igloo).

Today, like other Canadians, Inuit are part of the market economy, so they need money. These days the vast majority also live in settlements, in which the skills associated with hunting, fishing, and gathering continue to be valued — as too is the ability to use computers, fly aeroplanes, and balance budgets. Not everybody is interested in hunting, fishing, and gathering, so I am loath to give the impression that that is all there is in the North; far from it. Yet, all the same, it has been only a short time since Inuit have moved into settlements; people and their ways of life do not quickly shed their roots. The forms that people's lives take, the ways in which they think about the world and participate in it, are reflections of the ways of living and institutions that they developed in living on the land. Where the past takes people is, to some extent, a matter of the choices people make, both formally and informally, as individuals, as communities, and as a collective.

I learned a great deal in Puvirnituq. I learned a great deal about the world in which I live and what it means to live in the North, both in a settlement and outside it. What became clear to me was that some people were having a hard time making the adjustment. The changes they have gone through are enormous. Ideas about how to behave, knowledge that was required to survive, the spaces that people occupy, notions of time, the social scale in which people now live are only some of the ways in which people's lives have changed. I have tried to identify some of these effects, because what people have known in terms of life on the land, and what they are experiencing now in settlements, all contribute to the ways in which they are reacting to the commoditization of country foods. In thinking about these things and listening to people, three things became clear to me: first, that ideas of community are central to the ways in which people think about country foods; second, that notions of time and place are the foundation upon which they construct these ideas; and finally, that in commoditizing country foods people must deal with the fact that these things are being altered.

Anyone who has ever lived in a more natural setting — on the other side of the glass and steel and heating and cooling systems that insulate so many Canadians from the world outside — must know that life is a transient thing, constantly changing, subject to the wind and rain and sun. Inuit developed their society and their understandings of the world in recognition of this flux, a recognition closely tied to how they live in place. One way in which they have learned to deal with the instability of life is by accepting and encouraging their reliance on one another. If all is impermanence and uncertainty, then one of the means of providing stability is the social relations people create. This is their wealth. This is why things that challenge the links that people have worked so hard to forge are deeply disturbing to their notions of how to live.

At the same time, people are envcouraged to live very much in the present. I was once on a spring ice-fishing trip with people from the Belcher Islands. It was my first time camping with Inuit, and we were together, many families spanning many ages. It was May, and what snow remained was getting soft, so that as the skidoos with their heavily laden *qamutiit* were travelling from one white patch to another, they would sometimes get stuck, sinking into the snow. When this happened we would all get off and help the skidoo on its way. At one point, as we headed to a lake, we were confronted by a very steep hill. We let the skidoos speed to the top while everyone else walked up after them. Wanting not to slow things down, thinking that people were anxious to get there, I kept up a steady pace, walking to the top of the hill as speedily as I could. Looking at the others, however, I was struck by how relaxed they were — talking, smoking, taking their time. The contrast between my behaviour and theirs has stayed with me. In the years since, I have come to realize that, for many Inuit, the awareness of flux means that they place a great deal of emphasis on process. Life is not about getting from here to there to get something, because, as they well know, they cannot count on being able to do that. The forces of nature do not allow them to assume that humans are in control. So they have learned to live in the here and now, to accept what they have at any given time, and to be flexible enough to act when the moment seems right.

As I spent time in the North I started to wonder what the here and now *are* for those who have been born and raised in settlements. For some, the here and now is reality from a box — MTV and *Fear Factor* — or from the end of a bottle. But for countless generations, reality has been out on the land, living in and with the elements, relying on others and doing all you could to ensure that they were well. This reality is about place. It is not time in the abstract — a fantasized present or some deceptively controllable future — but *now*. Life is lived in the here and now. Everything is a string of nows, for it is true that you can never step in the same river twice. This is the world in which Inuit developed the various institutions — social, psychic, political, economic — that enabled them to live, and this is the world that has had to come to some form of accommodation with life in settlements, with jobs and money and fixed buildings, predicated on notions of permanence, with a fixed present and a future that can be controlled.

In the commoditization of country foods, these two forms of life come together. Permanence and impermanence, control and unpredictability, the forces that bind community and the forces that dissolve it must be negotiated. And negotiate it they do. Many people are trying to navigate their way between the need to share and the need for money. This passage is not without problems, but for the time being, many people are nonetheless determined to stick to it.

As I listened, read, and thought, I came to see that, to varying degrees, sometimes consciously, but generally unconsciously, we *make* our livings. We construct the ideas and institutions that enable us to meet the requirements of life. This is what many Inuit are doing. Mostly they make these choices automatically: they have been raised to share food. But sometimes they make them deliberately: in choosing whether or not to adopt the Hunter Support

Program or to sell country foods to one another. In both cases, they are constructing the institutions and adopting structures of belief that establish the form of their existence. These choices are not easily made. In some cases, among those who have chosen to promote the sharing of country foods, individuals forego certain goods — be they in the form of food, time, money, or comfort — in the interests of the collective. In others, those who have chosen to sell country foods must choose to sacrifice social opinion in pursuit of what they deem to be valuable and constructive to society in the long run.

We live in a world in which society must increasingly fit into what seems to be economically rational. What I came to understand is that many Inuit seem resolved to live in an economy that is socially rational. And so, at a fundamental level, they make their livings, as do we all.

Country Foods Eaten in Puvirnituq

FOOD	INUKTITUK	MONTHS HARVESTED	COMMENTS	WHEN EATEN (Past, Today)
Airaq (plant)	Airaq	Jun.-Sep.	Eat roots; has yellow flowers, leaves have many blades, hair.	P & T
Arctic Char	Iqaluppik	All year	Found all over area, although for a couple of weeks in summer they're offshore near islands in Hudson Bay.	P & T
Beluga	Qilalugaq	All year*	Some overwinter in Hudson Bay.	P & T
Black Guillemot	Pitsiulak	Aug.-Sep.	Eat young.	P & T
Black-berries	Paurnguaq	Sep.		P & T
Blue-berries	Kigutingirnaq	Aug.-early Sep.		P & T
Caribou	Tuktu	All year	There's also a shorter-legged one that may have bred with rein-deer.	P & T
Caribou: aged	Pannirk		Put in skin with fat and meat and buried.	P
Caribou fat	Tunuuk			P & T
Clams	Uviluk	Jul.-Sep.	Get only when seas are rough and they wash up on shore. Today people get them from trawlers.	P & T

* Recently harvesting seasons have been severely curtailed by government-imposed quotas.

FOOD	INUKTITUK	MONTHS HARVESTED	COMMENTS	WHEN EATEN
Cloud-berries	Aqpik	Aug.-early Sep.		P & T
Cod	Uraq	Oct.-Apr.	Eaten when other fish can't be found. Like to eat tail as it has no bones.	P & T
Common Murre	Aqpak	Jul.	From Salluit, not in Puvurnituq; not desirable.	P & T
Cran-berries	Qimminaqau-tiit	All year	Generally eaten after snow has gone, but sometimes dig under the snow to get them; also eaten fresh; used to treat infected throat.	P & T
Cranberry flowers	Qimminait	Jun.-Jul.		P & T
Dog	Qimmiq	All year	When starving in past, but would raise puppies for special occasions; considered a delicacy.	P
Duck: Black	Mitirqluq	May-Jun.; late Aug.-Sep.		
Duck: Common Eider	Mittirq	Apr.-Jul.; Oct.-Nov.	Hunted during its spring and fall migrations.	P & T
Duck: King Eider	Mittukluq; Amaulik (male with bump on beak)	Apr.-Jul.; Oct.-Nov		P & T
Eggs: Black Guillemot	Pitsiulak-maningiit	mid-Jul.		P & T
Eggs: Canada Goose	Nirlikman-ingiit	May-Jun.		P & T

FOOD	INUKTITUK	MONTHS HARVESTED	COMMENTS	WHEN EATEN
Eggs: Plain Ptarmigan	Aqikjituinaq-maningiit	May-Jun.	Very hard to find.	P & T
Eggs: Rock Ptarmigan	Nitsiatuq-maningiit	May-Jun.	Very hard to find.	P & T
Eggs: Seagull	Nuraaluk-maningiit	May-Jun.		P & T
Eggs: Snow Goose	Kanguk-maningiit	Jun.		P & T
Eggs: Willow Ptarmigan	Aqikjivik-maningiit	May-Jun.	Very hard to find.	P & T
Fish: mixed dish	Urutulik		Squeezed of liquid and mixed with blackberries and seal fat.	P & T
Fox	Tiririniaq	Oct.-Apr.		P & limited T
Goose: Canada	Nirlik	Apr.-May; Jul.-Sep.	Not eaten while it's nesting; eat goslings before they can fly.	P & T
Goose: Giant	Isaqtuq (one who moults)			P & T
Goose: Ross	Nirlinaq	May-Jun.; late Aug.-Sep.	Hunted during spring and fall migrations; don't nest in area; over-hunted by *Qallunaat*.	P & T
Goose: Smaller (without white on neck)	Nirliaaqtuk	Apr.-Jun.; Oct.	Hunted during spring and fall migrations.	P & T
Goose: Snow	Kanguk	Apr.-May; late Aug.-mid-Sep.	Hunted during spring and fall migrations.	P & T
Grass (not clear what kind)	Ivik	Aug.-Sep.	Eat roots; grows as tall grass on shoreline and riverbank.	P & T

FOOD	INUKTITUK	MONTHS HARVESTED	COMMENTS	WHEN EATEN
Hare	Ukalik	Oct.-Mar.	Smelly in spring, so not good to eat.	P & limited T
Herring	Muruitulik	Oct.-Mar.		P & T
Lake Trout	Isurqlitsaq	All year		P & T
Merganser	Akpanajuq	May-Jun.	No commonly eaten; not eaten while nesting.	P & limited T
Mountain Sorrel	Qunqulik	Aug.-early Sep.		P & T
Mussels	Ununajuk	Sep.	Harvested only when seas are rough and they wash up on shore.	P & T
Narwhal	Alanguak		From Iqaluit	T
Oldsquaw	Agiakanaq	Sep.-early Oct.	Hunt when they're learning to fly; not eaten while nesting.	P & T
Polar Bear	Nanuk	Winter when the coat is good, or any time it interferes with the camp.	Not eaten if it has been tattooed or tranquilized	P & T
Ptarmigan: Plain	Aqikjituinaq	All year, except when nesting.	Not a species recognized by *Qallunaat*.	P & T
Ptarmigan: Rock	Nitsiatuq	All year, except when nesting.		P & T
Ptarmigan: Willow	Aqikjivik	All year, except when nesting.		P & T
Sandpiper	Luviluvilaq	May; Sep.	Used to put hundreds in a pot and boil them; name is based on its call.	P
Scallops	Tallurunaq		Only found where tides are high; not around Puvirnituq	P & T

FOOD	INUKTITUK	MONTHS HARVESTED	COMMENTS	WHEN EATEN
Sculpin	Kanajuq	Jul.-Oct.	Larger kind, no spikes on head, greenish. People eat it "once in a while," when one has a craving for it.	P & T
Sculpin: Baby	Kunajuraq		Smaller kind, spikes on head, almost brown.	P & T
Sea Cucumber	Amumajuq		Eaten as a last resort; only good where tides are high, so rare in Puvirnituq.	More P than T
Sea Urchin	Mirqulik	Jul., when netting in Hudson Bay	Eaten as a last resort.	More P than T
Seabeach Sandwort	Malitsajuq	Jul.-Aug.		P & T
Seal: Bearded	Ugjuk	All year.		P & T
Seal: Ringed	Natsirq	All year.		P & T
Seal: Freshwater (land-locked)	Qasijiaq	All year.	Good fur for boots; prized for food.	P & T
Seaweed	Kianiit	Sep.	From Salluit and salty water away from river; only in fall when seas are rough. Good with mattaq.	P & T
Shrimp: giant	Kinguralak		From further north.	
Shrimp: normal	Kinguk		From further north.	
Snowy Owl	Upiaaluk	Sep.-Mar.	Also eat nestlings before they can fly.	P and limited T

FOOD	INUKTITUK	MONTHS HARVESTED	COMMENTS	WHEN EATEN
Starfish	Akajaq	Jul., when nesting in Hudson Bay	Eaten as a last resort, though eggs are good. Akajaq also means "gloves."	More P than T
Walrus	Aivik	Aug.-Oct.	Hunted when flies have gone, to prevent infestation by maggots.	P & T
Walrus: aged	Igunak		Put in skin with fat and meat and buried.	P & T
Whitefish: aged	Qirnivinirk		Put under rocks to age; stomach not removed.	
Whitefish: larger	Kapisilik	All year	Some are also found in salt water.	P & T

Employment, Population, and Earning Statistics for Puvirnituq

Table 1
Population Statistics 1996 – 2006
(Source: Statistics Canada (n.d.b.)

Characteristics	PUVIRNITUQ	QUEBEC
Population in 2006	1,457	7,546,131
Population in 2001	1,287	7,237,479
Population in 1996	1,169	7,138,795
2001 – 2006 population change (%)	13.2	4.3
1996 – 2001 population change (%)	10.1	1.4

Table 2
Population Statistics 2001
(Source: Statistics Canada (n.d.a.)

Age Characteristics of the Population	PUVIRNITUQ			QUEBEC		
	Total	Male	Female	Total	Male	Female
Total: All Persons	1,290	655	630	7,237,480	3,532,845	3,704,630
Age 0-4	165	90	75	375,765	192,275	183,490
Age 5-14	320	165	155	915,810	466,790	449,020
Age 15-19	130	70	65	462,070	235,855	226,215
Age 20-24	120	55	70	487,405	246,140	241,265
Age 25-44	350	180	175	2,165,760	1,077,480	1,088,280
Age 45-54	115	55	60	1,109,945	548,085	561,865
Age 55-64	50	30	20	760,905	370,960	389,945
Age 65-74	20	15	15	547,185	248,740	298,445
Age 75-84	10	5	5	318,180	120,940	197,240
Age 85 and over	5	5	0	94,450	25,580	68,870
Median age	20.9	20.6	21.0	38.8	37.8	39.8
% Age 15 and over	62.0	61.1	63.5	82.2	81.3	82.9

Table 3
Population Statistics, 2006
(Source: Statistics Canada (n.d.b.)

Age Characteristics of the Population	PUVIRNITUQ			QUEBEC		
	Total	Male	Female	Total	Male	Female
Total: All Persons	1,460	745	715	7,546,130	3,687,695	3,858,440
Age 0-4	215	95	125	375270	191,565	183,710
Age 5-9	190	110	85	398,980	203,985	195,000
Age 10-14	175	95	85	478,255	243,595	234,655
Age 15-19	150	70	75	475,005	242,185	232,820
Age 20-24	130	70	55	472,170	238,440	233,730
Age 25-29	110	60	55	492,870	245,335	247,540
Age 30-34	95	45	50	467,325	232,800	234,525
Age 35-39	90	45	45	502,300	250,340	251,960
Age 40-44	75	35	35	619,120	308,570	310,550
Age 45-49	55	30	25	644,040	318,145	325,895
Age 50-54	50	25	25	588,085	289,780	298,300
Age 55-59	50	30	20	524,350	257,790	266,560
Age 60-64	20	10	10	428,070	208,805	219,270
Age 65-69	15	5	0	315,560	150,165	165,395
Age 70-74	10	5	5	268,145	121,940	146,205
Age 75-79	10	0	5	220,530	92,485	128,045
Age 80-84	0	5	5	156,775	58,075	98,695
Age 85 and over	5	0	5	119,285	22,695	85,585
Median age	19.8	20.4	19.3	41.0	39.9	41.9
% Age 15 and over	60.1	60.8	59.4	83.4	82.7	84.1

Table 4
Puvirnituq: Distribution by Job Type, Status, and Sex (1998)
(Source: Employment and Training Department, 1999)

Characteristics	Regular Full Time	Regular Part Time	Seasonal	Occasional (Casual)
Total occupied jobs	244	78	7	20
Held by beneficiaries	160	71	7	16
Held by non-beneficiaries	84	7	0	4
Held by men	147	50	7	9
Held by women	97	28	0	11

Table 5
Earning Statistics, 2001
(Source: Statistics Canada, n.d.a.)

Earnings in 2001	PUVIRNITUQ Total	QUEBEC Total
All persons with earnings	495	3,815,265
Average earnings (all persons with earnings)	$25,521	$29,385
Worked full year, full time	210	197,0175
Average earnings (worked full year, full time)	$38,779	$39,150

Table 6
Earning Statistics, 2005
(Source: Statistics Canada, n.d.b.)

Earnings in 2005	PUVIRNITUQ Total	QUEBEC Total
Persons 15 years and over with earnings	655	4,225,875
Median earnings (persons 15 yewars and over)	$16,800	$25,464
Persons 15 years and over with earnings who worked full year, full time	175	2,136,705
Median earnings (persons 15 years and over who worked full year, full time)	$42,453	$37,722

Table 7
Work Statistics, 2001 and 2006
(Source: Statistics Canada, n.d.a., n.d.b.)

Characteristics	PUVIRNITUQ		QUEBEC	
	2001	2006	2001	2006
Participation rate (%)	56.3	63.5	64.2	64.9
Employment rate	49.4	51.2	58.9	60.4
Unemployment rate	11.2	19.4	8.2	7.0

Table 8
Income Statistics, 2001 and 2005
(Source: Statistics Canada, n.d.a., n.d.b.)

Characteristics	PUVIRNITUQ		QUEBEC	
	2000	2005	2000	2005
Persons 15 years and over with income	720	810	5,506,245	5,876,975
Median total income of persons 15 years and over	$13,424	$16,800	$20,665	$25,464
Composition of total income	100.00	100.00	100.00	100.00
Earnings as percentage of income	80.2	76.9	75.1	73.2
Government transfers as percentage of income	17.9	21.0	13.9	13.9
Other money as percentage of income	1.9	2.0	11.0	12.9

Table 9
Number of Jobs in Puvirnituq by Employer, 1999
(including full time and part time employment)

Employer	Number of Employees
Air Inuit,	7
Kativik Transport	6
Ali`s Café	2
C.N.V. of Puvirnituiq (Municipal Office)	29
Municipal Housing	6
Mikikatiit (Hunter Support Program)	1
Municipal Garage	4
CKPV-FM Radio	1
Co-op Puvirnituq	18
Cable Person (and telephone)	1
Ski-Doo Repair Shop	1
Hotel Co-op	4
Daycare Centre	7
Hydro-Québec	2
Inuulitsivik Hospital	225
Social Services	8
Youth Protection	8
KRG Education and Training Department	3
Kativik School Board (Regular School)	52
Kativik School Board (Adult Education)	5
Naturaait (Women's Committee)	3
Northwest Company (formerly HBC)	13
Pitsituuq (Smoked Fish)	2
Qumaluk's Taxi	1
Surasiviq (Arcade)	2
Tulugak Enpterprises	2
Niuvirpiapik Kuananack (convenience store)	1
Niuvirpiapik Angiyou (convenience store)	1

Employer	Number of Employees
Christian Bookstore	1
Nuvalingaq Hotel	1
TOTAL	**417**

Comparative List of Prices Paid for Country Foods in Puvirnituq, 2001

Individual Non-Inuit (According to a Regular Buyer)

- Caribou: $20/back strap; $50/rear leg (four years ago was $35, then three years ago $40)
- Fish: (I do not know what kind) was $10/fish, but they were very small so she stopped buying them

Catering Company

- Caribou: $50/rear leg (which equals approximately $2.50/lb.); $30/back strap
- Canada Goose: $10 (if not plucked); $20 if gutted and plucked
- Ptarmigan: $5
- Arctic Char: $3/lb. if not gutted; otherwise $3.50; $8/lb. if filleted
- Speckled Trout: $2.50/lb for the whole fish

Hospital

- Caribou: $25/rear leg according to one informant; $50 according to another (however, that may have been for two of them)
- Arctic Char: $2.50/lb. and $8/fillet from Pitsituuq; another informant told me he paid $2/lb.

Note: The hospital chef does not buy birds because they are too much work to prepare; he already has to disinfect the kitchen when he cooks caribou. He serves raw country food to patients only on request, because regulations forbid serving it in the cafeteria.

Mikikatiit   (Hunter Support Program)

- Arctic Char: $2.30/lb.

- Lake Trout: $2.25/lb.

- Whitefish: $1.85/lb.

- Seal: $2.95/lb. without fat; $1.15/lb. with fat

- Caribou: $2/lb.

- Ptarmigan: $5 each

- Rental of ski-doo or canoe: $75/day

- Hunting for the day: $165 with equipment; $90 without equipment

Note: The difference between how much a hunter is paid for a day's work depending on whether he has equipment is because the HSP essentially pays rent to the hunter for the use of his equipment.

Co-operative

- Arctic Char: $2-2.50/lb., depending on the season

Pitsituuq

- Arctic Char: $2/lb.

Table I

Comparative List of Prices Paid for Country Foods in Puvirnituq, 2001

Species/Activity		Individual Non-Inuit	Catering Company	Hospital*	Mikikatiit	Co-operative	Pitsituuq
Arctic Char	Whole fish/lb.		$3 if not gutted $3.50 if gutted	$2.50 or $2	$2.30	$2-$2.50 based on the season	$2
	Fillet/lb.		$8	$8			
Whitefish/lb.					$1.85		
Lake Trout/lb.					$2.25		
Speckled Trout/lb.			$2.50 (approx.)				
Ptarmigan (whole)			$5		$5		
Canada Goose (whole)			$10 if not plucked $20 if gutted and plucked				
Seal	With fat/lb.				$1.15		
	Without fat/lb.				$2.95		
Caribou	Rear leg	$50	$50 (approx. $2.50/lb.)	$25 or $50			
	Back strap	$20	$30				
	Per pound				$2		
Rental of Ski-Doo or Boat/day					$75		

* Prices vary based on differences reported by the two individuals at the hospital with whom I spoke.

Glossary of Inuktitut

agu: hood of an *amautik*

ajurnarmat: it can't be helped

akisussaassuseq: a sense of responsibility to the land and to everything that lives there (Greenlandic)

amautik: hooded parka for carrying babies; plural *amautiit*

angunahuarniaqara: I'll try and catch it (in speaking of hunting game)

angutjuak (angujjuaq): big male polar bear

angusiaq: godson

anirniq: breath soul

apputainaq: hummocks of snow over open water

arnaliaq: goddaughter

atiq: name soul

igunak: fermented walrus meat

ilira: passive silence or timidity that is induced by a form of fear

ilagiit: extended family group

inuk nammineq: personal independence and individual strength (Greenlandic)

inuksuk: stone marker or figure; plural *inuksuit*

kamik: seal-skin boot

kiinaujaq: money

kiinaujatigut makittarasuarniq: economy (literally, "by money try to stand by itself")

maqaiqatik: hunting partner

mattak: beluga skin

minnatuq: opening a food cache

misiraq: sauce made from the rendered oil of whale or seal

nani nunaharpit?: Where are you from? (literally, "Where do you have land?")

nikuk: dried caribou meat

niqituinnaq: country food

nirliujaq: cough sounding like Canada goose

nirimatut: communal meal

niujuattuq: sharing food with a hunting partner

niujuqtissijuq: communal sharing of large game, e.g., beluga

niujuliuqti: person responsible for distributing meat

nukauq: big young polar bear

nunamut ataqqinninneq: a sense of pride in knowing the land (Greenlandic)

pajuttuq: sending a gift from one house to another within a camp/community

pijurutik: gifts to a *sanajik* from his or her *arnaliaq* or *angusiaq* marking the first time a child achieves a particular act; marking a rite of passage

pitsiatuq: doing something nicely/well/with honour, respect, and awe (used in relation to the treatment of animals)

pualuk: mitten

qaiqujijuq: inviting kin or non-kin to share a meal

qajaq: kayak; plural *qajait*

Qallunaaq: White person; plural *Qallunaat*

Qallunaatitut: the White people's way

qamutik: sled pulled by dog team or ski-doo; plural *qamutiit*

qinuajuaq: rough-legged hawk

qulliq: soapstone lamp

sanajik: godparent

sauniq: namesake or bone

sila: weather, outdoors, atmosphere

silatujuq: a wise person

tarniq: individual soul

tiggaq: seal in rut

tigutuinnaq: transfers of food from a subordinate hunter to superior kin

tukkussuseq: generosity and hospitality (Greenlandic)

tuktuviniq nikkuk: caribou jerky

tulugaq: raven

Tuniit: Dorset Eskimos

ulu: half-moon-shaped woman's knife

umiaq: women's skin-covered boat used for transporting large numbers of people and goods

uqutsaq: the annual migration inland from Puvirnituq at the end of summer to harvest caribou for the winter (literally, "to get something warm")

Notes

Notes to Chapter 1

1   Chipeta, 1981; Mazzucato, 2001.

2   Gudeman, 2001.

3   Ross and Usher, 1986.

4   Moeran, 1995.

5   Egede, 1994; Kalland, 1994.

6   *Cf.* Goldsmith, (1992) 1998; Illich, 1981.

7   Polanyi, (1944) 1957a.

8   People in the Eastern Canadian Arctic call themselves Inuk in the singular, Inuuk when there are two of them, and Inuit for three or more people.

9   *Cf.* Brice-Bennett, 1977; Freeman, 1976.

10 *Cf.* Brascoupé, 1993; Lyall, 1993.

11 Polanyi in Goldsmith, (1992) 1998, p. 379.

12 Narotzky, 1997. In fact, Narotzky's use of the term "global" in this sense is problematic. It implies that this economic system exists throughout the world and is part of the natural order of things, somehow not an expression of particular sets of human beings from a limited area and of a fixed historical period. What is called "global" reflects instead the domination across much of the world of a particular set of beliefs that are very much local in character and linked to Western, liberal ideologies.

13 Makivik Corporation was founded by the Inuit of Nunavik (i.e., Northern Quebec) upon the signing of the James Bay and Northern Quebec Agreement. It received money ceded to the Inuit following the signing of the Agreement. Today its primary responsibilities are to represent the economic and political interests of the Inuit of Nunavik.

14 Nunavik is a semi-autonomous Inuit region occupying the northern portion of the province of Quebec (see map, page 8). It is not to be confused with Nunavut, which is a separate Inuit region that lies mostly to the north and west of Nunavik and occupies what was formerly the eastern portion of the Northwest Territories (NWT). The Inuit of Canada, because they were split into different provincial and territorial jurisdictions and subject to different forces of development, were obliged to negotiate, at different times, a series of separate land claims agreements with the different jurisdictions in which they found themselves located.

Thus, going from west to east the Inuit jurisdictions are: The Inuvialuit Settlement Region in the western portion of the NWT, Nunavut, Nunavik, and Nunatsiavut which occupies the northern reaches of Newfoundland and Labrador.

15 George, 1999.

16 Pilitsi Kingwarsiaq, "Country food shouldn't be sold," Letter to the Editor, *Nunatsiaq News*, 10 Aug. 2001.

17 *Cf.* Geertz, 1973.

18 *Cf.* Sahlins, 1976.

19 Denzin, 1997.

20 Collignon, 2006b.

21 See, for example, Agnew and Duncan, 1989; Buttimer, 1980; Carter, Donald, and Squires, 1993; Casey, 1993 and 1996; Cresswell, 2004; Entrikin, 1991; Eyles, 1985; Feld and Basso, 1996; Gupta and Ferguson, 1997a and 1997b; Hall, 1995; Harvey, 1996; Hiss, 1991; Jackson and Penrose, 1993; Johnston, 1991; Malpas, 1999; Massey, 1994, 1995 and 2005; McDowell, 1999; Nast and Pile, 1998; Relph, 1976 and 1985; Richardson, 1984; Rosaldo, 1988; Rose, 1995; Sack, 1997; Silberbauer, 1994; Tuan, 1974, 1977 and 1984.

22 Sack, 1997.

23 For example, Iglauer ([1962] 2000) describes people's confusion with the concept of interest when they were first setting up the co-operative in what was then known as George River (Kangiqsualujjuaq); see also Arbess, 1967. In contrast, I, having been born and raised in a society where the concept seems always to have been present, accept it as natural, and so I do not think about what an odd concept it is.

24 Polanyi, (1944) 1957a and 1957b.

25 Gregory and Altman, 1989, p. 1.

26 Polanyi, (1944) 1957a and 1957b.

27 Wilk, 1996.

28 MacDonald, 2000.

Notes to Chapter 2

1   Lynge, 1998. Although this quotation is in Greenlandic rather than the Inuktitut of Nunavik, it nonetheless reflects perceptions that are widely held among Inuit across the Arctic.

2   For an in-depth discussion of the translation of *niqituinnaq* see Usher et al., 1995, pp. 121-126; and Wenzel, 1991.

3   In Inuktitut, the generic term for white people is *Qallunaaq* (singular) and *Qallunaat* (plural).

4   Chabot, 2001.

5   Usher et al., 1995.

6   *Cf.* MacDonald, 1998, p. 195-196.

7   Adult Education Centre, 1989, p. 27.

8   Balikci, 1964.

9   Qitsualik, 2003a.

10   This is not to suggest that Inuit are not also aware of the future and the need to plan for it. In the days when they relied exclusively on country foods for their survival, they were very aware that they had to harvest and conserve enough food to carry them through periods of scarcity; hence, the caches that dot the Arctic landscape. But at the same time, awareness of uncertainty and the changeableness of the world is built into how they live.

11   Sandra Pikujak Katsak (born 1973), in Wachowich, 1999, p. 219.

12   *Cf.* Brody, 2000; Little Bear, 1998; Sioui, 1992.

13   Qitsualik, n.d., n.p.

14   Ingold, 1986.

15   Eqilaq, 2002, n.p.

16   Berkes and Farvar, 1989; Ingold, 1986.

17   Ingold, 1986.

18   Saladin d'Anglure, 1984.

19   *Cf.* Wenzel, 1994.

20   Saladin d'Anglure, 1984; Saladin d'Anglure and Vézinet, 1977.

21   People in their 50s still know of these family trails, but the younger generation in Puvirnituq does not.

22   Qitsualik. n.d., n.p.

23 Collignon, 2006a.

24 *Cf.* Andrews, 1994; Brody, 1976; Wenzel, 1994.

25 Berkes and Farvar, 1989.

26 Ingold, 1986.

27 *Cf.* Berkes and Farvar, 1989; Little Bear, 1998; Qitsualik, n.d.; Usher, 1983.

28 Nungak and Arima, 1988.

29 Gudeman, 2001.

30 Simmel, (1900) 1978, p. 353.

31 *Cf.* Kishigami, 2004. In other regions of the Canadian Arctic, this role is reserved for people who served different roles in a child's birth. In some areas, a child's first kill is reserved for the person who acted as the mother's midwife, or for the person who caught the child as it was being born, or for the person who cut the umbilical cord. This varies from region to region.

32 *Cf.* Berger, 1985; Dorais, 1997; Nuttall, 1992.

33 Saladin d'Anglure, 2000.

34 *Ibid.*

35 Saladin d'Anglure, 1984.

36 Fienup-Riordan, 1994.

37 *Cf.* Fienup-Riordan, 1994; Oosten and Laugrand, 2006; Saladin d'Anglure and Akuliaq, 1991.

38 Fienup-Riordan, 1994.

39 *Cf.* Hallowell, 1964.

40 Gombay, 1995, pp. 57-58.

41 *Cf.* Bennett and Rowley, 2004; Fienup-Riorden, 1994; Laugrand and Oosten, 2002; Nuttall, 1992. I use the word *inua* with reservation. People were told not to speak about the power of animals and places. Knowing this, I have generally avoided asking people about it directly. The people I asked about this word said they had not heard it. It may be that the word has fallen out of common use or that it is not used in the Puvirnituq region. However, the fact that people talk about animal spirits or the spirits in the land suggests that the concept continues to be meaningful to people.

42 *Cf.* Brody, 1976 and 1987; Hensel, 1996; Turner, 1990.

43 For a more detailed discussion on the role of polar bears in Inuit society, see Saladin d'Anglure, 1990a.

44 Ingold, 1996a.

45 Saladin d'Anglure, 1997 and 2000.

46 Ingold, 2000, p. 4.

47 Leads are naturally occurring cracks in sea ice. If travellers are not careful, they can fall into them.

48 Adamie in Gombay, 1995, p. 67.

49 *Cf.* Brody, 1976.

50 *Cf.* Fienup-Riordan, 1994.

51 *Cf.* Damas, 1972; Kishigami, 2004; Nuttall et al., 2005; Wenzel, 1991, 1995, 2005.

52 Nuttall et al., 2005.

53 Kishigami, 2004.

54 Balikci, 1964; Damas, 1972; Wenzel, 1995. Balikci describes how people would call one another by the cut of the seal meat that they received. So hunters "A" and "B" might address one another as *ukpatiga*, which literally means, "my but-tocks." Each hunter was obliged to give this portion of a seal to the other when they had a successful hunt. These partnerships were established by their mothers when boys were small. If, in a given camp, such relations were scarce, people would set up new sharing partnerships that might last only for the duration of the time that people were in the same camp. Damas makes similar observa-tions for the Copper (Kitlinermiut) and Nestilik (Netsilingmiut) Inuit. Wenzel stresses that such partnerships are regionally specific and are not found in all parts of the Canadian Arctic.

55 *Cf.* Ellanna and Sherrod, 1984; Langdon and Worl, 1981; Wenzel, 1995.

56 *Cf.* Briggs, 1998; Burch, 1988; Collings, Wenzel and Condon, 1998; Damas, 1972; Kishigami, 2000, 2004, and 2006; Nuttall et al., 2005; Stairs and Wenzel, 1992; Wenzel, 1981, 1991, 1995, 2000a, and 2005.

57 *Cf.* Kishigami, 2004.

58 Chabot, 2001 and 2003; Kishigami, 2004.

59 Kishigami, 2004.

60 Bodenhorn, 2000.

61 *Cf.* Bennett and Rowley, 2004.

62 Kishigami, 2004; Saladin d'Anglure, 1984.

63 Bodenhorn, 2000.

64 Kishigami, 2004.

65 Buijs, 1993; Mitchell, 1996.

66 For a discussion on the importance of midwives, see Saladin d'Anglure, 2000.

67 Polanyi, (1944) 1957a.

68 *Cf.* Brody, 2000; Dorais, 1997; Dybbroe, 1996; Hensel, 1996; Minor, 1992; Rasing, 1999.

69 Briggs, 1998; MacDonald, 2000.

70 Dorais, 1997.

71 See Dorais, 1997; Fienup-Riordan, 1994; Nuttall, 1992; and Saladin d'Anglure, 1997 for more in-depth discussions of Inuit ideas of souls and naming.

72 *Cf.* Saladin d'Anglure, 1986.

73 For a more detailed description of naming practices among the Inuit, see Bennett and Rowley, 2004; Guemple, 1971; and Trott, 2005.

74 Brody, 1976, p. 216.

75 *Cf.* Bodenhorn, 1990; Fienup-Riordan, 1994.

76 Quoted in Freeman, 1996, p. 66.

77 Sejersen, 1998.

78 Caulfield, 1997; Hensel, 1996; Rasing, 1999; Searles, 2002; Sejersen, 1998.

79 *Cf.* Balikci, 1964; Collignon, 2006a.

80 Mesher, 1995.

81 Mitchell, 1996.

82 Balikci, 1964, p. 39.

83 Nuttall, 1999.

84 This is the plural of *inuksuk*, a stone marker or cairn.

85 Nungak and Arima, 1988.

86 Brody, 1976; Saladin d'Anglure, 1984.

87 Qitsualik, n.d., n.p.

88 Moss, 1994, pp. 29-30.

89 *Cf.* Balikci, 1964; Brice-Bennett, 1977; Freeman, 1976; Makivik Corporation, 1997.

90 Cf. Aporta, 2004; Collignon, 2006a; MacDonald, 1998; McDonald, 1997; Wachowich, 1999.

91 Carpenter, 1973, p. 21.

92 Cf. Bjerregaard and Young, 1998; Blanchet et al., 2000; Jensen, 1997; Jensen, Adare, and Shearer, 1997; Lawn and Harvey, 2001; Willmott, 1959.

93 Cf. Ostertag et al., 2009.

94 Blanchet et al., 2000.

95 Makivik Corporation, n.d.

96 Cf. Adult Education Centre. 1989; Usher et al., 1995.

97 Steinmann, 1977.

98 Searles, 2002; Sejersen, 1998.

99 Usher et al., 1995.

100 Saladin d'Anglure, 1997.

101 Cf. Brody, 1976.

102 Cf. Adult Education Centre, 1989.

103 Usher et al., 1995.

104 Wachowich, 1999.

105 Briggs, 1970, does a wonderful job of explaining the ins and outs of how anger is not acceptable in Inuit society. As Adamie explained to me in simple terms, one doesn't want to be out on the land, where people are dependent on one another, with someone who is angry.

106 Gombay, 1995, pp. 57-58.

107 Nungak and Arima, 1988.

108 Cf. Wenzel, 1991.

109 Cf. Caulfield, 1997; Department of Fisheries and Oceans, 1994; George, 2002a, 2007a and 2007b; Tyrrell, 2008.

110 Nielsen, 1999.

111 Cf. Kemp, 1971.

112 Cf. Chabot, 2001; Duhaime, Chabot and Gaudreault, 2002; Usher, 1971; Wenzel, 1991.

113 Cf. Berkes et al., 1994; Myers, 2000a; Ross and Usher, 1986; Statistics Canada, 2006; Usher, 1971; Weihs, Higgins, and Boult, 1993; Wenzel, 1991.

114 Myers, 2000a.

115 Chabot, 2001.

116 Bernard, 2006.

117 Chabot, 2001.

118 *Ibid*. In fact, people now complain that they must prepare different meals for the different generations: country foods for adults and imported food for children.

119 Dahl, 1989,

120 Weihs, Higgins, and Boult, 1993.

121 Chabot, 2001.

122 Chabot, *ibid.* and 2003.

123 *Cf.* Stern, 2000.

Notes to Chapter 3

1   Seavoy, 2000.

2   Fort Richmond, the first Hudson's Bay Company trading post that served the region, was established in 1750 at Lac Guillaume-Delisle on the east coast of Hudson Bay. The post was transferred to Little Whale River in 1756.

3   *Cf.* Duffy, 1988.

4   *Cf.* Damas, 2002, Drummond, 1997; Duffy, 1988; Tester and Kulchyski, 1994.

5   Duffy, 1988, p. 147.

6   *Cf.* Saladin d'Anglure, 1984; Tester and Kulchyski, 1994.

7   Tester and Kulchyski, 1994.

8   *Ibid*.

9   Damas, 2002.

10   Tester and Kulchyski, 1994.

11   Duffy, 1988; *cf.* Tester and Kulchyski, 1994.

12   *Ibid.*; *cf.* Saladin d'Anglure, 1984.

13   Simard, 1979.

14   Tester and Kulchyski, 1994, p. 7.

15   *Cf.* Duffy, 1988; Tester and Kulchyski, 1994.

16 Damas, 2002, p. 45.

17 Mitchell, 1996.

18 *Cf.* Lotz, 1976.

19 Lotz, 1976; Mitchell, 1996.

20 Ross and Usher, 1986.

21 Max Budgell in Iglauer, (1962) 2000, p. 71.

22 Duhaime, 2007.

23 Panetta, 2002.

24 *Ibid.*

25 Bernard, 2006.

26 *Ibid.*

27 *Cf.* Hovelsrud-Broda, 1997; Myers, 2000a; Wenzel, 1991.

28 Hovelsrud-Broda, 1997.

29 Chabot, 2001.

30 Oakes and Riewe, 1997.

31 Chabot, 2001.

32 Makivik Corporation, 2007.

33 Chabot, 2001.

34 Kativik Regional Government, 2001.

35 *Cf.* D'Souza, 2003; George, 2001.

36 Chabot, 2001.

37 Makivik Corporation, 2007.

38 Chabot, 2001.

39 *Cf.* Condon et al., 1995.

40 Reimer, 1995.

41 Condon, Collings, and Wenzel, 1995.

42 *Cf.* Dragon, 1999 and 2002.

43 Canada, 1996, p. 780.

44 Goldring, 1986.

45   *Commission scolaire Kativik*, n.d.

46   *Cf.* Nasogaluak and Billingsley, 1981; Stager, 1984.

47   *Cf.* Graburn, 1969.

48   Weihs, Higgins, and Boult, 1993.

49   *Ibid.*; *cf.* Iglauer (1962) 2000.

50   Iglauer, (1962) 2000.

51   *Cf.* Iglauer, (1962) 2000; Graburn, 1969; Mitchell, 1996; Riches, 1977. Graburn also mentions the sale of country foods in Salluit, Payne Bay (Kangirsuk), and Ivujivik.

52   Bennett 1982; Government of Québec, 1998. An amendment to the JBNQA in 1998 allowed for the commercial harvest of caribou for export, but subject to a quota and only after domestic needs had been met.

53   George, 1998a and 1998b; Mitchell, 1996.

54   George, 1998b.

55   *Cf.* Chabot, 2001; George, 1998b and 1999; Weihs, Higgins, and Boult, 1993.

56   *Cf. Makivik Magazine*, 2001a and 2001b; George, 1998a, 1998b, and 1999.

57   George, 1999; *cf.* Lanari, 2002.

58   *Cf.* Cesa, 2002; Duhaime, 1990; Government of Quebec, 1982; Kativik Regional Government, 1998 and 2000; Kishigami, 2000 and 2006; Martin, 2000 and 2003.

59   Government of Quebec, 1982, p. 4.

60   Nelson, Matcher, and Hickey, 2005.

61   *Cf.* Feit, 1991; Government of Quebec, 1998; Scott and Feit, 1992.

62   Wenzel, 2000b.

63   Chabot, 2001 and 2003.

64   In 2001, the HSP had a budget of $405,492.29. Of that it allocated $65,000, or approximately 16 per cent, to buying country food. This included $60,000 for buying food locally and $5,000 for resale or exchange between communities.

Notes to Chapter 4

1   Balikci, 1959.

2   Balikci, 1964.

3   Simard, 1979.

4   *Cf.* Balikci, 1964; *Commission scolaire Kativik*, n.d.a; Vallee, 1967.

5   Balikci, 1964.

6   Vallee, 1967.

7   Vézinet, 1980.

8   Simard, 1979.

9   Tester and Kulchyski, 1994.

10 Balikci, 1959 and 1964.

11 Tulugak and Murdoch, 2007.

12 Vallee, 1967.

13 *Commission scolaire Kativik*, n.d.b.

14 Steinmann, 1977.

15 Qumaq, n.d.

16 Balikci, 1964.

17 Balikci, 1960 and 1964. Kublu confirmed Balikci's view. He told me in 2001 that most people in Puvirnituq had family to care and provide for them. Even in households where there was no one to provide country foods or there was no equipment for hunting or fishing received, most people still received country foods from other family members. He, for example, provided food for his wife's parents, who were too old to go out.

18 Mitchell, 1996.

19 Vallee, 1967.

20 *Ibid.*

21 Brody, (1975) 1983.

22 Martin, 2003.

23 Makivik Corporation, 2007.

24 *Cf.* Tester and Kulchysik, 1994.

25 Tulugak and Murdoch, 2007.

26 Simard, 1979.

27 Balikci, 1964.

28 *Cf. Commission scolaire Kativik*, n.d.a and n.d.c; Steinmann, 1977; Tulugak and Murdoch, 2007.

29 Mitchell, 1996.

30 Tester and Kulchyski, 1994.

31 *Cf.* Saladin d'Anglure, 1984.

32 Inuit Tungavingat Nunamini, n.d.

33 *Ibid.*

34 Saladin d'Anglure, 1984.

35 *Cf.* Arbess, 1967; Iglauer, (1962) 2000; Riches, 1977.

36 *Cf.* Simard, 1979; Steinmann, 1977; Tulugak and Murdoch, 2007.

37 Saladin d'Anglure. 1984.

38 Tulugak and Murdoch, 2007, p. 245.

39 Saladin d'Anglure, 1984; Inuit Tungavingat Nunamini, n.d.

40 Inuit Tungavingat Nunamini, n.d.

41 *Cf.* Saladin d'Anglure, 1984; Mitchell, 1996; Tulugak and Murdoch, 2007.

42 Salluit has since signed.

43 Nelson, 2002, n.p.

44 Mitchell, 1995.

45 Makivik Corporation, 2007; Inuit Tungavingat Nunamini, n.d. This excludes Kattiniq, the site of Raglan mine, the only fly-in fly-out mine site without official status as a settlement in Nunavik.

46 Statistics Canada, n.d.b.

47 *Ibid.*

48 Poppel et al., 2007.

49 Employment and Training Department, 1999.

50 Martin, 2003.

51 Polanyi, (1944) 1957a.

52 Bird-David, 1990; Godbout, 1998; Gregory, 1982; Gudeman, 2001; Mauss, (1925) 1990; Osteen, 2002; Parry, 1986; Sahlins, (1972) 1974.

53 *Cf.* Laidlaw, 2008.

54 *Cf.* Dahl, 2000; Hovelsrud-Broda, 2000; MacDonald, 2000.

55 *Cf.* Collings, Wenzel, and Condon, 1998.

56 Simmel, (1900) 1978.

57 Qitsualik, 1998.

58 Chabot, 2001. In 1995 Chabot found that 450 tonnes of country food were sold in Nunavik. Of these, 83.3 per cent were sold to the HSP, 4.5 per cent were sold to the Co-ops, and 12.3 per cent were sold to Nunavik Arctic Foods (Makivik's company). Because they are difficult to calculate, Chabot did not take informal sales of country foods into account, so sales of the kind made to the catering company did not figure in her calculations.

59 Dalton, 1967, p. 78.

60 *Cf.* Chabot, 2001; Kishigami, 2000.

61 Kishigami, 2000.

62 Kopytoff, 1986.

63 *Cf.* Caulfield, 1997; Happynook, n.d.; High North Alliance, 1995; MacDonald, 2000; Moeran, 1995; Sahlins, (1972) 1974; Wenzel, 1991.

64 Kopytoff, 1986.

65 *Ibid.*

66 Simmel, (1900) 1978.

67 Kopytoff, 1986, p. 82.

68 Nutaraluk Iyaituk in Mitchell, 1996, pp. 286-287.

69 *Cf.* Kishigami, 2004; Langdon and Worl, 1981; Searles, 2002; Wenzel, 1995.

70 Bodenhorn, 2000; Bourdieu, (1977) 1987; Dalton, 1967; Kishigami, 2004; Mauss, (1925) 1990.

71 Harhoff, 1991, p. 65.

72 *Cf.* Caulfield, 1997; Feit, 1991; Moeran, 1995.

73 Balikci, 1959, p. 131.

74 Vallee, 1967.

75 *Cf.* St-Pierre, 2001.

76 Because of regulations imposed by the federal government as a conservation measure, people from Puvirnituq must now travel some distance to the north to Hudson Strait in order to hunt beluga. Such travel entails great expense for things such as gas to supply the voyage.

Notes to Chapter 5

1 *Cf.* Murphy and Steward, 1955; Wenzel, 2001.

2 Sahlins, 1976, p. 72.

3 Polanyi, (1944) 1957a, p. 178.

4 *Cf.* Freese, 1997; Hansen, 2002.

5 *Cf.* Fafchamps, 1992.

6 Polanyi, (1944) 1957a, p. 164.

7 Simmel, (1900) 1978, p. 335.

8 Ingold, 2000.

9 Balikci, 1964; Buijs, 1993; Dahl, 2000; Graburn, 1969; Mitchell, 1996.

10 *Cf.* Cronon, 1995.

11 Chabot, 2001.

12 Chabot, 2003.

13 *Ibid.*

14 Sahlins, (1972) 1974, p. 216.

15 Chabot, 2001; St-Pierre, 2001.

16 Simmel, (1900) 1978.

17 Duffy, 1988; Mitchell, 1996; Searles, 2002.

18 Brody, 1987.

19 *Cf.* Condon, 1994.

20 Qitsualik, 2003a.

21 Otokiak, n.d., n.p.

22 Simmel, (1900) 1978.

23 Parry and Bloch, 1989.

24 *Cf.* Bohannan, 1967; Furnham and Argyle, 1998; Godelier, (1984) 1986; Gudeman, 2001; Parry and Bloch, 1989; Peterson, 1991a and 1991b.

25 Wachowich, 1999, p. 133.

26 Mesher, 1995, p. 94.

27 Chabot, 2001.

28 Basil Sansom in Peterson, 1991b.

29 Chabot, 2001.

30 Seavoy, 2000.

31 Kopytoff, 1986, p. 82.

32 Fafchamps, 1992; Martin, 2003.

33 Miller, 2000.

34 Graburn, 1969.

35 Bohannan,1967; Sahlins, (1972) 1974.

36 Parry and Bloch, 1989.

37 *Cf.* Tulugak and Murdoch, 2007.

38 Qitsualik, 2003a.

39 Kopytoff, 1986, p.73.

40 *Cf.* Austin-Broos, 1996.

41 Inuit Tungavingat Nunamini, n.d.

Bibliography

Adult Education Centre, Sanikiluaq. *Stories from Sanikiluaq*. Iqaluit: Arctic College, 1989.

Agnew, John A. and James S. Duncan. "Introduction," in *The Power of Place*. John A. Agnew and James S. Duncan (Eds.). Boston: Unwin Hyman, 1989, pp. 1-8.

Andrews, Elizabeth F. "Territoriality and Land Use Among the *Akulmiut* of Western Alaska," in *Key Issues in Hunter-gatherer Research*. E. S. Burch and L. J. Ellanna (Eds.), Providence, RI: Berg Publishers, 1994, pp. 65-93.

Aporta, Claudio. "Routes, Trails and Tracks: Trail breaking among the Inuit of Igloolik," in *Études/Inuit/Studies*, Vol. 28, No. 2, 2004, pp. 9-38.

Arbess, Saul E. "Values and Socio-economic Change: The George River Case." Unpublished doctoral dissertation, McGill University, 1967.

Austin-Broos, Diane. "Morality and the Culture of the Market," in *Economics and Ethics?* Peter Groenewegen (Ed.). London: Routledge, 1996, pp. 173-183.

Balikci, Asen. "Two Attempts at Community Organization among the Eastern Hudson Bay Eskimos," in *Anthropologica*, Vol. 1, No. 1-2, 1959, pp. 122-135.

_____. "Some Acculturative Trends Among the Eastern Canadian Eskimos," in *Anthropologica*, Vol. 2, No. 1, 1960, pp. 139-153.

_____. *Development of Basic Socio-economic Units in Two Eskimo Communities*. Ottawa: National Museum of Canada, 1964.

Bennett, David. "Subsistence versus Commercial Use: The Meaning of these Words in Relation to Hunting and Fishing by Canada's Native Peoples." CARC working Paper No. 3, Ottawa: Canadian Arctic Resources Committee, 1982.

Bennett, John and Susan D. M. Rowley. *Uqalurait: An Oral History of Nunavut*. Montreal: McGill-Queen's University Press, 2004.

Berger, Thomas. *Village Journey: The Report of the Alaska Native Review Commission*. New York: Hill and Wang, 1985.

Berkes, Fikret and M. Taghi Farvar. "Introduction and Overview," in *Common Property Resources: Ecology and Community-based Sustainable Development*. F. Berkes (Ed.). London: Belhaven Press, 1989, pp. 1-17.

Berkes, Fikret et al. "Wildlife Harvesting and Sustainable Regional Economy in Hudson and James Bay Lowland, Ontario," in *Arctic*, Vol. 47, No. 4, 1994, pp. 350-360.

Bernard, Nick. "Nunavik Comparative Price Index 2006." Quebec City: Université Laval, 2006.

Bird-David, Nurit. "The Giving Environment: Another Perspective on the Economic System of Gatherer-Hunters," in *Current Anthropology*, Vol. 31, No. 3, April 1990, pp. 189-196.

Bjerregaard, Peter and T. Kue Young. *The Circumpolar Inuit: Health of a Population in Transition*. Copenhagen: Munksgaard, 1998.

Blanchet, C. et al. "Contribution of Selected Traditional and Market Foods to the Diet of Nunavik Inuit Women," in *Canadian Journal of Dietetic Practice and Research*, Vol. 61, No. 2, 2000, pp. 50-59

Bodenhorn, Barbara. "'I'm Not the Great Hunter, My Wife Is': Iñupiat and Anthropological Models of Gender," in *Études/Inuit/Studies*, Vol. 14, No. 1-2, 1990, pp. 55-74.

_____. "It's Good to Know Who Your Relatives Are But We were Taught to Share with Everybody: Shares and Sharing among Inupiaq Households," in *The Social Economy of Sharing: Resource Allocation and Modern Hunter-Gatherers*, Senri Ethnological Studies, No. 53. George W. Wenzel, Grete Hovelsrud-Broda, and Nobuhiro Kishigami (Eds.). Osaka: National Museum of Ethnology, 2000, pp. 27-60.

Bohannan, Paul. "The Impact of Money on an African Subsistence Economy," in *Tribal and Peasant Economies*. G. Dalton (Ed.). USA: American Museum Sourcebooks in Anthropology, 1967, pp. 123-135.

Bourdieu, Pierre. *Outline of a Theory of Practice*. Cambridge: Cambridge University Press, 1987 (1977).

Brascoupé, Simon. "Strengthening Traditional Economies and Perspectives," in *Sharing the Harvest: The Road to Self-reliance: Report of the National Round Table on Aboriginal Economic Development and Resources*. Ottawa: Ministry of Supply and Services Canada, 1993, pp. 101-119.

Brice-Bennett, Carol. *Our Footprints are Everywhere*. Canada: Labrador Inuit Association, 1977.

Briggs, Jean L. *Never in Anger*. Cambridge: Harvard University Press, 1970.

_____. *Inuit Morality Play: the Emotional Education of a Three-Year-Old*. St. John's, Nfld.: Institute of Social and Economic Research, 1998.

Brody, Hugh. "Land Occupancy: Inuit Perceptions," in *Inuit Land Use and Occupancy Project* (Vol. 1). M. Freeman (Ed.), Ottawa: Indian and Northern Affairs Canada, 1976, pp. 185-142.

_____. *The People's Land*. Markham: Penguin Books Canada, 1983 (1975).

_____. *Living Arctic.* Vancouver: Douglas and McIntyre, 1987.

_____. *The Other Side of Eden: Hunters, Farmers and the Shaping of the World.* Vancouver: Douglas and McIntyre, 2000.

Buijs, Cunera C. "Disappearance of Traditional Meat-sharing Systems amongst the Tinitekilaamiut of East Greenland and the Arviligjuarmiut and Iglulingmiut of Canada," in *Continuity and Discontinuity in Arctic Cultures.* C. Buijs (Ed.). Leiden: National Museum of Ethnology, 1993, pp. 108-135.

Burch Jr., Ernest. "Modes of Exchange in North-West Alaska," in *Hunters and Gatherers: Property, Power and Ideology,* Vol. 2. Tim Ingold, David Riches, and James Woodburn (Eds.). Oxford: Berg Publishers, 1988, pp. 95-109.

Buttimer, Anne. "Home, Reach, and the Sense of Place," in *The Human Experience of Space and Place.* Anne Buttimer and David Seamon (Eds.). London: Crom Helm, 1980, pp. 166-187.

Canada. *Royal Commission on Aboriginal Peoples* (RCAP). "Economic Development," Ch. 5 of *The Report of the RCAP.* "Restructuring the Relationship," Vol. 2, Part 2. Ottawa: Ministry of Supply and Services Canada, 1996, pp. 775-996.

Carpenter, Edmund. *Eskimo Realities.* New York: Holt, Rinehart and Winston, 1973.

Carter, Erica, James Donald and Judith Squires "Introduction," in *Space and Place: Theories of Identity and Location.* Erica Carter, James Donald and Judith Squires (Eds.). London: Wishard, 1993, pp. vii-x.

Casey, Edward S. *Getting Back into Place: Toward and Renewed Understanding of the Place-world.* Bloomington: Indiana University Press, 1993.

_____. "How to get from Space to Place in a Fairly Short Stretch of Time: Phenomenological Prolegmena," in *Senses of Place.* Steven Feld and Keith H. Basso (Eds.). Santa Fe: School of American Research Advanced Seminar Series, 1996, pp. 13-51.

Caulfield, Richard A. *Greenlanders, Whales and Whaling: Sustainability and Self-determination in the Arctic.* Hanover, NH: University Press of New England, 1997.

Cesa, Y. «*Échange commercial et usages monétaires non-marchands dans le cadre du programme d'aide aux chasseurs du Nunavik* » in *Études/Inuit/Studies,* Vol. 26, No. 2, 2002, pp. 175-186.

Chabot, Marcelle. «*De la production domestique au marché: l'économie comtemporaine des familles Inuit du Nunavik.*» Unpublished doctoral dissertation, Department of Sociology, Université Laval, 2001.

_____. "Economic Changes, Household Strategies, and Social Relations of Contemporary Nunavik Inuit," in *Polar Record*, Vol. 39, No. 208, 2003, pp. 19-34.

Chipeta, C. *Indigenous Economics*. New York: Exosition Press, 1981.

Collignon, B. *Knowing Places: The Innuinnait, Landscapes, and the Environment*. Canada: Canadian Circumpolar Institute (CCI) Press, 2006a.

Collings, Peter, George Wenzel, and Richard G. Condon. "Modern Food Sharing Networks and Community Integration in the Central Canadian Arctic," in *Arctic*, Vol. 51, No. 4, 1998, pp. 301-314.

Commission scolaire Kativik. Unpublished notes from the *Programme des sciences humaines*, 4ᵗʰ year, français, n.d.a.

_____. *«Profiles des communautés nordiques du Québec.»* Unpublished notes, n.d.c.

Condon, Richard G. "East Meets West: Fort Collision, the Fur Trade, and the Economic Acculturation of the Northern Copper Inuit, 1928–1939," in *Études/Inuit/Studies*, Vol. 18, Nos. 1-2, 1994, pp. 109-135.

Condon, Richard G., Peter Collings, and George Wenzel. "The Best Part of Life: Subsistence Hunting, Ethnicity, and Economic Adaptation among Young Adult Inuit Males," in *Arctic*, Vol. 28, No. 1, March 1995, pp. 31-46.

Cresswell, Tim. *Place: A Short Introduction*. Malden: Blackwell Publishers, 2004.

Cronon, William. "The Trouble with Wilderness," in *Uncommon Ground: Rethinking the Human Place in Nature*. W. Cronon (Ed.). New York: W. W. Norton and Co., 1995, pp. 69-90.

Dahl, Jens. "The Integrative and Cultural Role of Hunting and Subsistence in Greenland," in *Études/Inuit/Studies*, Vol. 13, No. 1, 1989, pp. 23-42.

_____. *Saqqaq: An Inuit Hunting Community in the Modern World*. Toronto: University of Toronto Press, 2000.

Dalton, George. "Traditional Production in Primitive African Societies," in *Tribal and Peasant Economies*. G. Dalton (Ed.). USA: American Museum Sourcebooks in Anthropology, 1967, pp. 61-80.

Damas, David. "Central Eskimo Systems of Food Sharing," in *Ethnology* Vol. 11, No. 3, 1972, pp. 220-240.

_____. *Arctic Migrants/Arctic Villagers: The Transformation of Inuit Settlement in the Central Arctic*. Montreal: McGill-Queen's University Press, 2002.

Department of Fisheries and Oceans, Canada, Planning Committee for the Co-Management of Southeast Baffin Beluga. "Co-Management Plan for Southeast Baffin Beluga." Working Draft, April 22, 1994.

Denzin, Norman K. *Interpretive Ethnography: Ethnographic Practices for the 21ˢᵗ Century*. London: SAGE Publications, 1997.

Dorais, Louis-Jacques. *Quaqtaq: Modernity and Identity in an Inuit Community*. Toronto: University of Toronto Press, 1997.

Dorion-Robitaille, Yolande. *Captain J. E. Bernier's Contribution to Canadian Sovereignty in the Arctic*. Ottawa: Ministry of Indian and Northern Affairs, 1978.

Dragon, Joe. "Commercial Harvesting of Wild Ungulates in Northern Canada," in *Northern Eden: Community-based Wildlife Management in Canada*, Evaluating Eden Series, No. 2. Department of Renewable Resources, University of Alberta, and the International Institute for Environment and Development, 1999.

_____. "Commercial Use of Caribou (*Rangifer tarandus*) in the Canadian Arctic." Unpublished doctoral dissertation, Department of Renewable Resources, University of Alberta, 2002.

Drummond, Susan G. *Incorporating the Familiar: An Investigation into Legal Sensibilities in Nunavik*. Montreal: McGill-Queen's University Press, 1997.

D'Souza, Patricia. "Job description debate pits Inuit against Qallunaat," in *Nunatsiaq News*. June 6, 2003: www.nunatsiaq.com/archives/30606/news/nunavut/legislative.html.

Duffy, R. Quinn. *The Road to Nunavut*. Montreal: McGill-Queen's University Press, 1988.

Duhaime, Gérard. *«La chasse Inuit subventionnée: tradition et modernité,»* in *Recherches sociographiques*, Vol. 31, No. 1, 1990, pp. 45-62.

_____. Socio-economic Profile of Nunavik 2006. Quebec City: Université Laval, 2007.

Duhaime, Gérard, Marcelle Chabot, and Marco Gaudreault. "Food Consumption Patterns and Socio-economic Factors among the Inuit of Nunavik," in *Ecology of Food and Nutrition*, Vol. 41, No. 2, 2002, pp. 91-118.

Dybbroe, Susanne. "Questions of Identity and Issues of Self-determination," in *Études/Inuit/Studies*, Vol. 20, No. 2, 1996, pp. 39-53.

Egede, Ingmar. "A Third Option," in *Additional Essays on Whales and Man*. Address delivered to the IUCN General Assembly, Buenos Aires, Jan. 18, 1994: www.highnorth.no/Library/Culture/a-thi-op.htm.

Ellanna, Linda J. and George K. Sherrod. *The Role of Kinship Linkages in Subsistence Production: Some Implications for Community Organization*. Technical Paper Number 100, Alaska Department of Fish and Game, Division of Subsistence, Presented at the Annual Alaska Anthropological Association Meeting, Fairbanks, Alaska, March 16-17, 1984.

Employment and Training Department, Kativik Regional Government. Unpublished Labour Market Statistics. Kuujjuaq: Kativik Regional Government, 1999.

_____. *Annual Report 1999–2000*. Kuujjuaq: Kativik Regional Government, 2000.

_____. "Jobs in Nunavik in 2005: Results of a survey carried out with the Nunavik employers in 2005." Kuujjuaq: Kativik Regional Government, 2006.

Entrikin, J. Nicholas. *The Betweenness of Place*. Baltimore: Johns Hopkins University Press, 1991.

Eqilaq, L. Nuvalinga. "The 'People of the Islands' need Nunavut's help," in *Nunatsiaq News*. June 21, 2002: www.nunatsiaq.com/opinionEditorial/letters.html.

Eyles, John. *Senses of Place*. Warrington, UK: Silverbrook Press, 1985.

Fafchamps, M. "Solidarity Networks in Preindustrial Societies: Rational Peasants with a Moral Economy," in *Economic Development and Change*, Vol. 41, No. 1, 1992, pp. 147-174.

Fienup-Riordan, Ann. *Boundaries and Passages: Rule and Ritual in Yup'ik Eskimo Oral Tradition*. Norman: University of Oklahoma Press, 1994.

Feit, Harvey A. "Gifts of the Land: Hunting Territories, Guaranteed Incomes and the Construction of Social Relations in James Bay Cree Society," in *Cash, Commoditisation and Changing Forager*. Senri Ethnological Studies 30. Nicolas Peterson and Toshio Matsuyama (Eds.). Osaka: National Museum of Ethnology, 1991, pp. 223-268.

Feld, Steven and Keith H. Basso. "Introduction," in *Senses of Place*. Steven Feld and Keith H. Basso (Eds.). Santa Fe: School of American Research Advanced seminar series, 1996, pp. 1-11.

Freeman, Milton M. R. *Inuit Land Use and Occupancy Project*. Ottawa: Department of Indian and Northern Affairs, 1976.

_____. "Health and Social Order: Inuit Dietary Traditions in a Changing World," in *Human Ecology and Health: Adaptation to a Changing World*. Maj-Lis Follér and Lars O. Hansson (Eds.). Göteborg, Sweden: Department of Interdisciplinary Studies of the Human Condition, Göteborg University, 1996, pp. 57-71.

Freese, Curtis H. (Ed.). *Harvesting Wild Species: Implications for Biodiversity Conservation*. Baltimore: Johns Hopkins University Press, 1997.

Furnham, Adrian and Michael Argyle. *The Psychology of Money*. London: Routledge, 1998.

Geertz, Clifford. *The Interpretation of Cultures*. New York: HarperCollins Publishers, 1973.

George, Jane. "Caribou marketers pin hopes on portable abattoirs," in *Nunatsiaq News*, April 12, 1998a: www.nunatsiaq.com/archives/nunavut980930/nvt89011_06.html.

_____. "Commercial Char harvest sparks furor in Nunavik" in *Nunatsiaq News*, Sept. 10, 1998b: www.nunatsiaq.com/archives/nunavut980930/nvt89011_06.html.

_____. "Four fully-equipped slaughterhouses up for grabs in Nunavik," in *Nunatsiaq News*, April 15, 1999: www.nunatsiaq.com/archives/nunavut980930/nvt89011_06.html.

_____. "Raglan's rocky record of Inuit employment," in *Nunatsiaq News*, Oct. 5, 2001, p. 25.

_____. "Makivik: Nunavik hunters must kill fewer beluga," in *Nunatsiaq News*, April 19, 2002a: www.nunatsiaq.com/archives/nunavut020419/news/nunavut/20419_1.html.

_____. "Food mail project helps Kangiqsujuaq residents eat better for less," in *Nunatsiaq News*, Aug. 2, 2002b, p. 25.

_____. "Nunavik hunters plan to defy beluga quotas," in *Nunatsiaq News*, April 13, 2007a: www.nunatsiaq.com/news/nunavik/21_Nunavik_hunters_plan_to_defy_beluga_quotas.html.

_____. "Pay legal expenses for hunters, Senate panel urges," in *Nunatsiaq News*, April 13, 2007b: www.nunatsiaq.com/news/nunavik/21_Pay_legal_expenses_for_hunters_Senate_panel_urges.html.

Godbout, J. *The World of the Gift*. Montreal: McGill-Queen's University Press, 1998.

Godelier, Maurice. *The Mental and the Material*. London: Verso, 1986 (1984).

Goldring, Philip. "Inuit Economic Responses to Euro-American Contacts: Southeast Baffin Island, 1824–1940," in *Historical Papers/Communications historiques*, 1986, pp. 146–172.

Goldsmith, Edward. *The Way: An Ecological World-View*. Athens: University of Georgia Press, 1998 (1992).

Gombay, N. "Bowheads and Bureaucrats: Indigenous Ecological Knowledge and Natural Resource Management in Nunavut." Unpublished master's thesis in Environment and Resource Studies. Waterloo: University of Waterloo, 1995.

Government of Québec. *An Act respecting the support program for Inuit beneficiaries of the James Bay and Northern Québec Agreement for their hunting, fishing and trapping activities*. Bill 83 (Chapter 47) Passed by the National Assembly of Québec, 1982.

_____, *The James Bay and Northern Québec Agreement: Agreement between the Government of Québec, the Grand Council of the Crees (of Québec), the Northern Québec Inuit Association, and the Government of Canada.* Québec: *Editeur officiel du Québec*, 1998.

Graburn, Nelson H. H. *Eskimos without Igloos: Social and Economic Development in Sugluk.* Boston: Little, Brown and Co., 1969.

Gregory, C. A. *Gifts and Commodities.* London: Academic Press, 1982.

Gregory, C. A. and J. C. Altman. *Observing the Economy.* London: Routledge, 1989.

_____. *The Anthropology of Economy.* Oxford: Blackwell Publishers, 2001.

Guemple, Lee. "Kinship and Alliance in Belcher Island Eskimo Society," in *Alliance in Eskimo Society.* Lee Guemple (Ed.). Seattle: University of Washington Press, 1971, pp. 56-78.

Gupta, Akhil and James Ferguson. "Culture, Power, Place: Ethnography at the End of an Era," in *Culture, Power, Place: Explorations in Critical Anthropology.* Akhil Gupta and James Ferguson (Eds.). Durham, NC: Duke University Press, 1997a, pp. 1-29.

_____. "Beyond Culture: Space, Identity, and the Politics of Difference," in *Culture, Power, Place: Explorations in Critical Anthropology.* Akhil Gupta and James Ferguson (Eds.). Durham, NC: Duke University Press, 1997b, pp. 33-51.

Hall, Stuart. "New Cultures for Old," in *A Place in the World? Places, Cultures and Globalization.* Doreen Massey and Pat Jess (Eds.). Oxford: Oxford University Press, 1995, pp. 175-213.

Hallowell, A. I. "Ojibwa Ontology, Behaviour, and World View," in *Primitive Views of the World.* S. Diamond (Ed.). New York: Columbia University Press, 1964, pp. 49-82.

Hansen, Kjeld. *A Farewell to Greenland's Wildlife.* Denmark: BæreDygtighed, 2002.

Happynook, Tom Mexsis. "The Social, Cultural and Economic Importance of 'Subsistence' Whaling," n.d.: www.oregonstate.edu/dept/IIFET/2000/papers/happynook.pdf.

Harhoff, Frederik. "Indigenous Rights between Law and Sociology: Internationalising soft norms in a hard context," in *North Atlantic Studies*, Vol. 1, No. 2, 1991, pp. 64-70.

Harvey, David. *Justice, Nature and the Geography of Difference.* Cambridge, Mass.: Blackwell Publishers, 1996.

Hensel, Chase. *Telling Our Selves: Ethnicity and Discourse in Southwestern Alaska.* Oxford: Oxford University Press, 1996.

High North Alliance. "Editorial: The Right to be Commercial," in *The International Harpoon*, No. 4, 1995: www.highnorth.no/Library/Culture/th-ri-to.htm.

Hiss, Tony. *The Experience of Place.* New York: Vintage Books, 1991.

Hovelsrud-Broda, Grete. "Arctic Seal-hunting Households and the Anti-sealing Controversy," in *Research in Economic Anthropology*, Vol. 18, 1997, pp. 17-34.

_____. "'Sharing,' Transfers, Transactions and the Concept of Generalized Reciprocity," in *The Social Economy of Sharing: Resource Allocation and Modern Hunter-Gatherers*, Senri Ethnological Studies, No. 53. George W. Wenzel, Grete Hovelsrud-Broda, and Nobuhiro Kishigami (Eds.). Osaka: National Museum of Ethnology, 2000, pp. 193-214.

ICC (Inuit Circumpolar Conference). *Inuit Spirit for Global Partnership. ICC's Four-Year Mandate: 1998–2002.* Nuuk, 2000.

Iglauer, Edith. *Inuit Journey: The Co-operative Adventure in Canada's North.* Madeira Park, BC: Harbour Publishing, 2000 (1962).

Illich, Ivan. *Shadow Work.* London: Marion Boyars, 1981.

Ingold, Tim. *The Appropriation of Nature.* Manchester: Manchester University Press, 1986.

_____. "Hunting and Gathering Ways of Perceiving the Environment," in *Ecology, Culture and Domestication: Redefining Nature.* Roy Ellen and Katsuyoshi Fukui (Eds.). Oxford: Berg Publishers, 1996a, pp. 117-155.

_____. "The Optimal Forager and Economic Man," in *Nature and Society: Anthropological Perspectives.* Philippe Descola and Gísli Pálsson (Eds.). New York: Routledge, 1996b, pp. 25-44.

_____. *The Perception of the Environment: Essays on Livelihood, Dwelling and Skill.* London: Routledge, 2000.

International Whaling Commission. *The International Whaling Commission*, n.d.: www.iwcoffice.org/.

Inuit Tungavingat Nunamini. *Les Inuit dissident à l'entente de la Baie James.* Montreal: Les Publications La maîtresse d'école, n.d.

Jackson, Peter and Jan Penrose. "Introduction: Placing 'Race' and 'Nation'," in *Constructions of Race, Place and Nation.* Peter Jackson and Jan Penrose (Eds.). London: UCL Press, 1993, pp. 1-26.

Jensen, J. (Ed.). "Synopsis of Research Conducted under the 1995–1997 Northern Contaminants Program." *Environmental Studies* No. 74. Ottawa: Indian and Northern Affairs Canada, 1997.

Jensen J., K. Adare and R. Shearer (Eds.). *Canadian Arctic Contaminants Assessment Report.* Ottawa: Indian and Northern Affairs Canada, 1997.

Johnston, R. J. *A Question of Place: Exploring the Practice of Human Geography.* Oxford: Blackwell Publishers, 1991.

Jolles, C. Z. *Faith, Food, and Family in a Yupik Whaling Community.* Seattle: University of Washington Press, 2002.

Kalland, Arne. "Aboriginal Subsistence Whaling: A Concept in the Service of Imperialism," in *Essays on Whales and Man.* High North Alliance, 2nd edition, 26 Sep. 1994: www.highno/Library/Culture/a-con-in.htm.

Kativik Regional Government. *Annual Report 1998: Support Program for Inuit Beneficiaries for their Hunting, Fishing, and Trapping Activities.* Kuujjuaq: Kativik Regional Government, 1998.

_____. *Annual Report 2000.* Kuujjuaq: Kativik Regional Government, 2001.

Kemp, William B. "The Flow of Energy in a Hunting Society," in *Scientific American*, Vol. 225, No. 3, 1971, pp. 105-115.

Kishigami, Nobuhiro. "Contemporary Inuit Food Sharing and the Hunter Support Program of Nunavik, Canada," in *The Social Economy of Sharing: Resource Allocation and Modern Hunter-Gatherers*, Senri Ethnological Studies, No. 53. George W. Wenzel, Grete Hovelsrud-Broda, and Nobuhiro Kishigami (Eds.). Osaka: National Museum of Ethnology, 2000, pp. 171-192.

_____. "A New Typology of Sharing Practices among Hunter-Gatherers, with a Special Focus on Inuit Examples," in *Journal of Anthropological Research*, Vol. 60, No. 3, 2004, pp. 341-358.

_____ "Contemporary Inuit Food Sharing: a Case Study from Akulivik, PQ, Canada," in *Jinbun-Ronkyu (Journal of the Society of Liberal Arts)* No. 75, 2006, pp. 15-21.

_____.

Kopytoff, Igor. "The Cultural Biography of Things: Commoditization as Process," in *The Social Life of Things: Commodities in Cultural Perspective.* A. Appadurai (Ed.). Cambridge: Cambridge University Press, 1986, pp. 64-91.

Kunnuk, Simeonie. "Being Inuit," in *Inuktitut*, Vol. 73, 1991, pp. 50-51.

Laidlaw, James. "A Free Gift Makes no Friends," in *Journal of the Royal Anthropological Institute*, Vol. 15, No. 3, 2008, pp. 617-634.

Lanari, Robert. *Caribou Commercialization Project Environmental Impact Study: Phase 2*. Montreal: Makivik Corporation, Resource Development Department, 2002.

Langdon, Steve and Rosita Worl. *Distribution and Exchange of Subsistence Resources in Alaska*. U.S. Department of Fish and Game Technical Paper Number 55, Anchorage: University of Alaska Arctic Environmental Information and Data Center, 1981.

Laugrand, Frédéric and Jarich Oosten. "Canicide and Healing: The Position of the Dog in the Inuit Cultures of the Canadian Arctic," in *Anthropos*, Vol. 97, 2002, pp. 89-105.

Lawn, Judith and Dan Harvey (Dialogos Educational Consultants). *Change of Nutrition and Food Security in Two Inuit Communities, 1992 to 1997*. Prepared for the Department of Indian Affairs and Northern Development Canada, Ottawa: Minister of Public Works and Government Services Canada, 2001: www.ainc-inac.gc.ca/ps/nap/air/nutfoosec_e.pdf.

Lévesque, Carole and Dominique de Juriew. *«Dynamique et caractérisation des réseaux sociqux: Premiers resultats d'une enquête sur l'alimentation au Nunavik.»* Montreal: INRS Culture et Société, Université du Québec, 2000.

Lévesque, Carole et al. "Between Abundance and Scarcity: Food and the Institution of Sharing Among the Inuit of the Circumpolar Region during the Recent Historical Period," in *Sustainable Food Security in the Arctic: State of Knowledge*. Gérard Duhaime (Ed.). Canada: CCI Press, 2002, pp. 103-115.

Little Bear, Leroy. "Aboriginal Relationships to the Land and Resources," in *Sacred Lands*. Jill E. Oakes and R. R. Riewe (Eds.). Canada: Canadian Circumpolar Institute, 1998, pp. 15-20.

Lotz, Jim. "Area Economic Surveys: Critique and Assessment," in *Inuit Land Use and Occupancy Project: A Report*, Vol. 2. M. Freeman (Ed.). Ottawa: Dept. of Indian and Northern Affairs, 1976, pp. 23-29.

Lyall, William. "Retaining Wealth and Control in Remote Aboriginal Communities," in *Sharing the Harvest: The Road to Self-reliance: Report of the National Round Table on Aboriginal Economic Development and Resources*. Ottawa: Ministry of Supply and Services Canada, 1993, pp. 137-148.

Lynge, Finn. "Subsistence Values and Ethics," Speech delivered at the Inuit Circumpolar Conference's 8th General Assembly in Nuuk, Greenland, July 1998, n.p.

MacDonald, Gaynor. "Economies and Personhood: Demand Sharing among the Wiradjuri of New South Wales," in *The Social Economy of Sharing: Resource Allocation and Modern Hunter-Gatherers*, Senri Ethnological Studies, No. 53. George W. Wenzel, Grete Hovelsrud-Broda, and Nobuhiro Kishigami (Eds.). Osaka: National Museum of Ethnology, 2000, pp. 87-111.

MacDonald, John. *The Arctic Sky: Inuit astronomy, star lore, and legend*. Toronto: Royal Ontario Museum/Nunavut Research Institute, 1998

McDonald, Miriam, Lucassie Arragutainaq and Zack Novalinga. *Voices from the Bay: Traditional Ecological Knowledge of Inuit and Cree in the Hudson Bay Bioregion*. Ottawa: Canadian Arctic Resources Committee, 1997.

McDowell, Linda. *Gender, Identity and Place: Understanding Feminist Geographies*. Minneapolis: University of Minnesota Press, 1999.

Makivik Corporation. "Puvirnituq Land Use and Ecological Survey, 1997." Unpublished document, 1997.

_____. *Nunavik at a Glance: 2007*. Kuujjuaq: Makivik Corporation, Economic Development, 2007.

_____. *Community Profiles*: www.makivik.org/eng/communities/index.htm.

Makivik Magazine, "On the Hoof," unattributed article, Fall 2001a, p. 10.

_____, "Caught in the Trawl," unattributed article, Fall 2001b, p. 11.

Malpas, J. E. *Place and Experience: A Philosophical Topography*. Cambridge: Cambridge University Press, 1999.

Martin, Thibault. *Proceedings of the 6th National Student Conference on Northern Studies*, Université Laval, May 5-7, 2000, pp. 42-46.

_____. *De la banquise au congélateur: mondialisation et culture au Nunavik*. Quebec: Presses de l'Université Laval, 2003.

Massey, Doreen. *Space, Place, and Gender*. Minneapolis: University of Minnesota Press, 1994.

_____. "The Conceptualization of Place," in *A Place in the World? Places, Cultures and Globalization*. Doreen Massey and Pat Jess (Eds.). Oxford: Oxford University Press, 1995, pp. 45-85.

_____. *For Space*. London: SAGE Publications, 2005.

Mauss, Marcel. *The Gift: The Form and Reason for Exchange in Archaic Societies*. London: Routledge, 1990 (1925).

Mazzucato, Valentina. "Indigenous Economies: Bridging the Gap between Economics and Anthropology," in *Indigenous Knowledge and Development Monitor*, Vol. 5, No. 1, April 1997: www.nuffic.nl/ciran/ikdm/1-5/articles/mazzucato.htm.

Mesher, Dorothy. *Kuujjuaq: Memories and Musings*. Duncan: Unica Publishing, 1995.

Miller, Daniel. "The Birth of Value," in *Commercial Cultures: Economies, Practices, Spaces*. Peter Jackson, Michelle Lowe, Danier Miller, and Frank Mort (Eds.), Oxford: Berg, 2000, pp. 77-84.

Minor, Kit. *Issumatuq*. Halifax: Fenwood Publishing, 1992.

Mitchell, Marybelle. *From Talking Chiefs to a Native Corporate Elite: The Birth of Class and Nationalism among Canadian Inuit*. Montreal: McGill-Queen's University Press, 1996.

Moeran, Brian. "The Cultural Construction of Value: 'Subsistence,' 'Commercial' and Other Terms in the Debate about Whaling," in *MAST (Marine Anthropological Studies)*, Vol. 5, No. 2, 1995, pp. 1-15.

Moss, John. *Enduring Dreams: An Exploration of Arctic Landscape*. Concord: House of Anansi Press, 1994.

Murphy, R. F. and J. H. Steward. "Tappers and Trappers: Parallel Process in Acculturation," in *Economic Development and Change*, Vol. 4, 1955, pp. 335-355.

Myers, Heather. "Options for Appropriate Development in Nunavut Communities," in *Études/Inuit/Studies*, Vol. 24, No. 1, 2000a, pp. 25-40.

Narotzky, Susana. *New Directions in Economic Anthropology*. London: Pluto Press, 1997.

Nasogaluak, William and Douglas Billingsley. "The Reindeer Industry in the Western Canadian Arctic: Problems and Potential," in *Proceedings of the First International Symposium on Renewable Resources and the Economy of the North*. Milton M.R. Freeman (Ed.). Ottawa: ACUNS, 1981, pp. 86-95.

Nast, Heidi J. and Steve Pile. "Introduction: MakingPlacesBodies," in *Places Through the Body*. Heidi J. Nast and Steve Pile (Eds.). London: Routledge, 1998, pp. 1-20.

Nelson M., D. C. Natcher, and C. G. Hickey. "Social and Economic Barriers to Subsistence Harvesting in a Northern Alberta Aboriginal Community," in *Anthropologica*, Vol. 47, No. 2, 2005, pp. 289-301.

Nelson, Odile. "POV celebrates new Coop Superstore," in *Nunatsiaq News*, Dec. 13, 2002: www.nunatsiaq.com/archives/nunavut021213/news/nunavik/21213_01.html.

Nielsen, Søren Stach. "The Socio-cultural Importance of Seal Hunting," in *Dependency, Autonomy, Sustainability in the Arctic*. Hanne Petersen and Birger Poppel (Eds.). Brookfield: Ashgate Publishing, 1999, pp. 247-252.

Nungak, Zebedee and Eugene Arima. *Inuit Stories: Povungnituk*. Hull: National Museum of Canada, 1988.

Nuttall, Mark. *Arctic Homeland: Kinship, Community and Development in Northwest Greenland*. London: Belhaven Press, 1992.

_____. "Memoryscape: A Sense of Locality in North-West Greenland," in *North Atlantic Studies*, Vol. 1, No. 2, 1999, pp. 39-50.

Nuttall, M., F. Berkes, B. Forbes, G. Kofinas, T. Vlassova, and G. Wenzel. "Hunting, Herding, Fishing, and Gathering: Indigenous Peoples and Renewable Resource Use in the Arctic," in *Arctic Climate Impact Assessment* (ACIA). C. Symon, L. Arris, and B. Heal (Eds.). Cambridge: Cambridge University Press, 2005, pp. 649-690.

Oakes, Jill and Rick Riewe. *Culture, Economy and Ecology: Case Studies from the Circumpolar Region*. Millbrook: The Cider Press, 1997.

Oosten, J. and F. Laugrand. "The bringer of light: the raven in Inuit tradition," in *Polar Record*, Vol. 44, No. 222, 2006, pp. 187-204.

Ostertag, S. K., B. A. Tague, M. M. Humphries, S. A. Tittlemier, and H. M. Chan, "Estimated Dietary Exposure to Fluorinated Compounds from Traditional Foods among Inuit in Nunavut, Canada," in *Chemosphere*, Vol. 75, No. 9, 2009, pp. 1165-1172.

Osteen, M. *The Question of the Gift: Essays across disciplines*. London: Routledge, 2002.

Otokiak. "Inuit Culture: The Kitikmeot Region," in *Nunavut Handbook*, n.d.: www.arctic-travel.com/chapters/archeol2page.html.

Panetta, Alexandra. "New chapter for Inuit in Quebec," in *The Toronto Star*, April 20, 2002, p. H4.

Parry, Jonathan. "The gift, the Indian gift and the 'Indian gift'," *Man*, Vol. 21, No. 3, 1986, pp. 453-473.

Parry, Jonathan and Maurice Bloch. "Introduction: Money and the Morality of Exchange," in *Money and the Morality of Exchange*. M. Bloch and J. Parry (Eds.). Cambridge: Cambridge University Press, 1989, pp. 1-32.

Peterson, Nicholas. "Introduction," in *Cash, Commoditisation and Changing Foragers*. Senri Ethnological Studies, No. 30. N. Peterson and T. Matsuyama (Eds.). Osaka: National Museum of Ethnology, 1991a, pp. 1-16.

_____. "Cash, Commoditisation and Authenticity: When do Aborigianl People Stop being Hunter-Gatherers?" in *Cash, Commoditisation and Changing Foragers*. Senri Ethnological Studies, No. 30. N. Peterson and T. Matsuyama (Eds.). Osaka: National Museum of Ethnology, 1991b, pp. 67-90.

Polanyi, Karl. *The Great Transformation*. Boston: Beacon Paperback, 1957a (1944).

_____. "The Economy as Instituted Process," in *Trade and Market in the Early Empires: Economies in History and Theory*. Karl Polanyi, Conrad M. Arsenberg and Harry W. Pearson (Eds.). Glencoe, Ill.: The Free Press, 1957b, pp. 243-270.

Poppel, Birger, Jack Kruse, Gérard Duhaime, and Larissa Abryutina. *SLiCA Results*. Anchorage: Institute of Social and Economic Research, University of Alaska Anchorage, 2007: www.arcticlivingconditions.org.

Qitsualik, Rachel Attituq. "Ilira," in *Nunatsiaq News*. Nov. 26, 1998 www.nunatsiaq.com/archives/nunavut981130/nunani.html.

_____. "Want" (Parts I and II) in *Nunatsiaq News*, May 9 and 16, 2003a: www.nunatsiaq.com/archives/030530/news/editorial/columns.html #want1.

_____. "Esquimaux," in *Nunatsiaq News*. June 27, 2003b: www.nunatsiaq.com/opinionEditorial/columns.html.

_____. "Nunataaq: The Inuit Promised Land" n.d.: www.imdiversity.com/villages/native/Article_Detail.asp?Article_ID=628.

Qumaq, Taamusi. *«La toponymie inuit du Nunavik,»* in *Premières Nations/First Nations*. Incomplete photocopy from *Commission scolaire Kativik*: unpublished notes from the *Programme des sciences humaines*, 4th year, *français*, pp. 104-117

Rasing, Willem. "Hunting for Identity. Thoughts on the Practice of Hunting and its Significance for Iglulingmiut Identity," in *Arctic Identities: Continuity and Change in Inuit and Saami Societies*. Jarich Oosten and Cornelius Remie (Eds.). Leiden: Research School, CNWS, Leiden University, 1999, pp. 79-108.

Reimer, Gwen D. "Case Study of an Inuit Economy: Pangnirtung, NWT." Royal Commission on Aboriginal Peoples Report, 1995.

Relph, E. *Place and Placelessness*. London: Pion, 1976.

_____. "Geographical Experiences and Being-in-the-world: The Phenomenological Origins of Geography," in *Dwelling, Place and Environment: Toward a Phenomenology of Person and World*. David Seamon and Robert Mugerauer (Eds.). Dordrecht: Martinus Nijhoff Publishers, 1985, pp. 15-31.

Richardson, Miles. "Introduction" in *Place: Experience and Symbol*. Geoscience and Man Series, Vol. 24. Miles Richardson (Ed.). Baton Rouge: Louisiana State University, 1984, pp. 1-3.

Riches, David. "An Inuit Co-operative: The Contradiction," in *The White Arctic: Anthropological Essays on Tutelage and Ethnicity*. R. Paine (Ed.). St. John's: Memorial University of Newfoundland / University of Toronto Press, 1977, pp. 212-231.

Rosaldo, Renato. "Ideology, Place and People without Culture," in *Cultural Anthropology*, Vol. 3, No. 1, 1988, pp. 77-87.

Rose, Gillian. "Place and Identity: A Sense of Place," in *A Place in the World? Places, Cultures and Globalization*. Doreen Massey and Pat Jess (Eds.). Oxford: Oxford University Press, 1995, pp. 87-131.

Ross, David P. and Peter J. Usher. *From the Roots Up: Economic Development as if Community Mattered*. Ottawa: The Canadian Council on Social Development, 1986.

St-Pierre, Dominic. *«Hermès et Sila. Le fonctionnement de l'échange alimentaire sur la Côte nord du Labrador.»* Unpublished master's thesis, Department of Sociology, Université Laval, 2001.

Sack, Robert David. *Homo Geographicus*. Baltimore: Johns Hopkins University Press, 1997.

Sahlins, Marshall. *Stone Age Economics*. London: Tavistock Publications, 1974 (1972).

_____. *Culture and Practical Reason*. Chicago: University of Chicago Press, 1976.

Saladin d'Anglure, Bernard. "Inuit of Quebec," in *Handbook of North American Indians*: Vol. 5, *Arctic*. David Damas (Ed.). Washington: Smithsonian Institution, 1984, pp. 476-507.

_____ *«Du foetus au chamane: la construction d'un «troisième sexe» inuit,»* in *Études/Inuit/Studies*, Vol. 10, Nos. 1-2, 1986, pp. 25-113.

_____. "Nanook, super-male: the polar bear in the imaginary space and social time of the Inuit of the Canadian Arctic," in *Signifying Animals: Human Meaning in the Natural World*. Roy Willis (Ed.). London: Unwin Hyman, 1990a, pp. 178-195.

_____. *«Frère-lune (Taqqiq), soeur-soleil (Siqiniq) et l'intelligence du Monde (Sila): Cosmologie inuit, cosmgraphie arctique et espace-temps chamanique,»* in *Études/Inuit/Studies*, Vol. 14, Nos. 1-2, 1990b, pp. 75-139.

_____. *«Svend Frederiksen et le chamanisme inuit ou la circulation des noms (atiit), des âmes (tarniit), des dons (tunijjutit) et des esprits (tuurngait),»* in *Études/Inuit/Studies*, Vol. 21, Nos. 1-2, 1997, pp. 37-73.

_____.*«Pijariurniq. Performances et rituels inuit de la première fois,»* in *Études/Inuit/Studies*, Vol. 24, No. 2, 2000, pp. 89-113.

Saladin d'Anglure, Bernard and Akuliaq. "The Seagulls and the Whales," in *Tumivut*, Vol 2, Spring / Summer, 1991, p. 2.

Saladin d'Anglure, Bernard and Monique Vézinet. *«Chasses collectives au caribou dans le Québec arctique,»* in *Études/Inuit/Studies*, Vol. 1, No. 2, 1977, pp. 97-110.

Scott, Colin H. and Harvey A. Feit. *Income Security for Cree Hunters: Ecological, Social and Economic Effects.* Montreal: McGill Program in the Anthropology of Development Monograph Series, 1992.

Searles, Edmund. "Food and the Making of Modern Inuit Identities," in *Food and Foodways*, Vol. 10, 2002, pp. 55-78.

Seavoy, Ronald E. *Subsistence and Economic Development.* Westport, Conn.: Praeger Publishers, 2000.

Sejersen, Frank. "Strategies for Sustainability and Management of People: An Analysis of Hunting and Environmental Perceptions in Greenland with a Special Focus on Sisimiut." Unpublished doctoral dissertation, Department of Eskimology, University of Copenhagen, Denmark, 1998.

Silberbauer, George G. "A Sense of Place," in *Key Issues in Hunter-gatherer Research.* Ernest S. Burch, Jr. and Linda J. Ellanna (Eds.). Oxford: Berg Publishers, 1994, pp. 119-143.

Simard, Jean-Jacques. *«Terre et pouvoir au Nouveau-Québec,»* in *Études/Inuit/Studies*, Vol. 3, No. 1, 1979, pp. 101-129.

Simmel, Georg. *The Philosophy of Money.* London: Routledge and Kegan Paul, 1978 (1900).

Sioui, Georges E. *For an Amerindian Autohistory.* Montreal: McGill-Queen's University Press, 1992.

Stager, J. K. "Reindeer Herding as Private Enterprise in Canada," in *Polar Record*, Vol. 22, No. 137, 1984, pp. 127-136.

Stairs, Arlene and George Wenzel. "I am I and the Environment," in *Journal of Indigenous Studies*, Vol. 3, No. 1, 1992, pp. 1-12.

Statistics Canada. "Community Profiles," Census of 2001: www12.statcan.ca/english/profil01/Search/PlaceSearch1.cfm?SEARCH=BEGINSandLANG=EandProvince=24andPlaceName=Puvirnituq, n.d.a.

_____. "Community Profiles," Census of 2006: www12.statcan.ca/census-recensement/2006/dp-pd/prof/92-591/details/Page.cfm?Lang=EandGeo1=CSDandCode1=2499120andGeo2=PRandCode2=24andData=CountandSearchText=PuvirnituqandSearchType=BeginsandSearchPR=01andB1=AllandCustom=. n.d.b.

_____. "Total population by age (122) and sex (3) for Nunavik and for CSDs," 2001 Census. Unpublished data, n.d.c.

_____. "Harvesting and community well-being among Inuit in the Canadian Arctic: Preliminary findings from the 2001 Aboriginal Peoples Survey – Survey of Living Conditions in the Arctic," Statistics Canada, Ottawa, 2006.

Steinmann, André. *La Petite Barbe*. Bruxelles: *Les editions de l'homme, ltée*, 1977.

Stern, Pamela. "Subsistence: Work and Leisure" in *Études/Inuit/Studies*, Vol. 24, No. 1, 2000, pp. 9-24.

Tester, Frank J. and Peter Kulchyski. *Tammarniit (mistakes): Inuit Relocation in the Eastern Arctic*. Vancouver: University of British Columbia Press, 1994.

Trott, C. "Ilagiit and Tuqluraqtuq: Inuit understandings of kinship and social relatedness." Paper presented at First Nations, First Thoughts, Centre of Canadian Studies, University of Edinburgh, 2005: www.cst.ed.ac.uk/2005conference/papers/Trott_paper.pdf.

Tulugak, Aliva and Peter Murdoch. *A New Way of Sharing: A Personal History of the Cooperative Movement in Nunavik*. Baie-d'Urfé: *Fédération des coopératives du Nouveau-Québec*, 2007.

Turner, Edith, "The Whale Decides: Eskimos' and Ethnographer's Shared Consciousness in the Ice," in *Études/Inuit/Studies*, Vol. 14, No. 1-2, 1990, pp. 39-42.

Tuan, Yi-Fu. *Topophilia: A Study of Environmental Perception, Attitudes and Values*. Engelwood Cliffs: Prentice-Hall, 1974.

_____. *Space and Place: The Perspective of Experience*. Minneapolis: University of Minnesota Press, 1977.

_____. "In Place, Out of Place," in *Place: Experience and Symbol*, Geoscience and Man Series, Vol. 24. Miles Richardson (Ed.). Baton Rouge: Louisiana State University, 1984, pp. 3-10.

Tyrrell, Martina. "Nunavik Inuit Perspective on Beluga Whale Management in the Canadian Arctic," in *Human Organization*, Vol. 76, No. 3, 2008, pp. 322-334.

Usher, Peter J. *The Bankslanders: Economy and Ecology of a Frontier Trapping Community*. Ottawa: Department of Indian Affairs and Northern Development, 1971.

_____. "Property Rights: The Basis of Wildlife Management in National and Regional Interests in the North." Ottawa: Canadian Arctic Resources Committee, 1983, pp. 389-415.

Usher, Peter J. et al. *Communicating about Contaminants in Country Food: the experience in aboriginal communities*. Ottawa: Inuit Tapirisat of Canada, 1995.

Vallee, Frank G. *Povungnetuk and its Cooperative: A Case Study in Community Change*. Ottawa: Department of Indian Affairs and Northern Development, 1967.

Vézinet, M. *«Les Nunamiut, Inuit au coeur des terres.»* Québec: *Ministère des affaires culturelles*, 1980.

Wachowich, Nancy. *Saqiyuk*. Montreal: McGill-Queen's University Press, 1999.

Weihs, Frederick, Robert Higgins, and David Boult. "The Northern Economy: A Review and Assessment of the Economic Utilization and Potential of Country Foods in the Northern Economy." Research report for the Royal Commission on Aboriginal Peoples, 1993.

Wenzel, George W. *Clyde Inuit Adaptation and Ecology: The Organization of Subsistence*. Ottawa: National Museums of Canada, 1981.

_____. *Animal Rights, Human Rights: Ecology, Economy, and Ideology in the Canadian Arctic*. London: Belhaven, 1991.

_____. "Recent Change in Inuit Summer Residence Patterning at Clyde River, East Baffin Island," in *Key Issues in Hunter-Gartherer Research*. E. S. Burch and L. J. Ellanna (Eds.). Providence: Berg Publishers, 1994, pp. 289-308.

_____. "Ningiqtuq: Resource Sharing and Generalized Reciprocity in Clyde River, Nunavut," in *Arctic Anthropology*, Vol. 32, No. 2, 1995, pp. 43-60.

_____. "Sharing, Money, and Modern Inuit Subsistence: Obligation and Reciprocity at Clyde River, Nunavut," in *The Social Economy of Sharing: Resource Allocation and Modern Hunter-Gatherers*, Senri Ethnological Studies No. 53. George W. Wenzel, Grete Hovelsrud-Broda, and Nobuhiro Kishigami (Eds.). Osaka: National Museum of Ethnology, 2000a, pp. 61-85.

_____. "Inuit Subsistence and Hunter Support in Nunavut," in *Nunavut: Inuit Regain Control of their Lands*. J. Dahl, J. Hicks, and P. Jull (Eds.). Copenhagen: International Working Group for Indigenous Affairs, 2000b, pp. 180-195.

_____. "'Nunamiut' or 'Kablonamiut': Which 'Identity' best fits Inuit (and Does it Matter?)," in *Études/Inuit/Studies*, Vol. 25, Nos. 1-2, 2001, pp. 37-52.

_____. "Canadian Inuk subsistence and economy," in *Socio-economic Research on Management Systems of Living Resources: Strategies, Recommendations and Examples*. Proceedings of the Workshop on "Social and Economic Research related to the management of marine resources in West Greenland," 18-20 Nov. 2003. L. Müller-Wille, M. C. S. Kingsley, and S. S. Nielsen, (Eds.). Nuuk: Greenland Institute of Natural Resources, 2005, pp. 146-151.

Wenzel, George W., Grete Hovelsrud-Broda, and Nobuhiro Kishigami. "Introduction: Social Economy of Modern Hunter-Gatherers: Traditional Subsistence, New Resources," in *The Social Economy of Sharing: Resource Allocation and Modern Hunter-Gatherers*, Senri Ethnological Studies, No. 53. George W. Wenzel, Grete Hovelsrud-Broda and Nobuhiro Kishigami (Eds.). Osaka: National Museum of Ethnology, 2000: pp. 1-6.

Wilk, Richard R. *Economies and Cultures: Foundations of Economic Anthropology*. Boulder: Westview Press, 1996.

Willmott, William E. "An Eskimo Community." Unpublished master's thesis, Department of Sociology and Anthropology, McGill University, 1959.

Index

market economy; education and 67-68, 84-85; Inuit participation in 101, 103, 123, 132, 141, 154-55; self-regulating 11-12, 106, 160; and social relations 11-12; versus vernacular economy 10-14, 89, 120-22, 154-55, 161

Marxist economic analysis 13, 30, 106, 114-116, 151

memory 17, 20-21, 54, 58-62, 78

midwife 40, 49, 51

Mikikkatiit. *See* Hunter Support Program

misiraq (sauce made from the rendered whale or seal oil) 17, 125

missionaries 70, 81, 101, 102, 154

Mitchell, Marybelle 57-58

mixed economy 12

monetary value 67, 75, 78, 93, 151. *See also* exchange value; money: as storing value; social value; use value

money 145-53, 154-55, 157-62; as a medium of exchange 10-11, 94, 106, 113, 114-15, 139, 146-47, 150; as necessary to Inuit life 12-13, 15, 58, 76, 85-86, 89, 91, 92, 156163, 165-66; as storing value 76-77, 79, 110, 114, 120-21, 146-48, 152-53; western view of 24-25, 57-58, 148-49, 151-53

moral principles: Inuit 13, 25, 29, 42-46, 51-52, 109, 111, 113, 127, 160. *See also* sharing of food: moral imperative to

Moss, John 62

Myers, Heather 75

names 36, 47, 53-55

namesakes 47, 49, 54

nani nunaharpit? (Where are you from?) 61

nature: human dominance over 25-26, 35, 36-39, 73, 94

nikuk (dried caribou meat) 56

niqituinnaq (country food) 30

nirimatut (communal meal) 47

niujuattuq (sharing food with a hunting partner) 47

niujuqtissijuq (communal sharing of large game) 48

niujuliuqti (person responsible for distributing meat) 48

non-Inuit people 44, 72-73, 87, 100, 104, 142, 144, 148-49; food of: see imported food; hunters, 44; sale of country foods to 89, 90, 100, 107, 108-113, 126, 133, 157; wealth of, 100

Northern Quebec Inuit Association (NQIA) 102-03

nunamut ataqqinninneq (a sense of pride in knowing the land: Greenlandic) 29

Nungak, Zebedee 60, 72

Okpik, Peter 55

open access 36, 38

Otokiak 147

List of Speakers

Illustrations

JOY BISHOP

Educated in Canada, Nicole Gombay teaches Geography at the University of Canterbury in New Zealand. Her research has, in various ways, been linked to the experience of Indigenous people living in the context of a settler society, placing a particular emphasis on the impacts of the inclusion of Indigenous populations in the political and economic institutions associated with the state. The context for her research has been in the Arctic, with a particular emphasis on Inuit populations in Canada.

Nicole is currently involved in two research projects in Nunavik, in northern Quebec. The first project is related to poaching, and the second is related to Inuit entrepreneurs.